WINTER CLIMBS: BEN NEVIS

SNOW, ICE AND MIXED CLIMBS ON BEN NEVIS, MAMORES AND GREY CORRIES

by Mike Pescod

JUNIPER HOUSE, MURLEY MOSS,
OXENHOLME ROAD, KENDAL, CUMBRIA LA9 7RL
www.cicerone.co.uk

© Mike Pescod 2022
Eighth edition 2022
ISBN: 978 1 78631 101 6

Printed in China on responsibly sourced paper on behalf of Latitude Press Ltd
A catalogue record for this book is available from the British Library.
All photographs are by the author unless otherwise stated.

   © Crown copyright 2022 OS PU100012932

Updates to this Guide

While every effort is made by our authors to ensure the accuracy of guidebooks as they go to print, changes can occur during the lifetime of an edition. Any updates that we know of for this guide will be on the Cicerone website (www.cicerone.co.uk/1101/updates), so please check before planning your trip. We also advise that you check information about such things as transport, accommodation and shops locally. Even rights of way can be altered over time. We are always grateful for information about any discrepancies between a guidebook and the facts on the ground, sent by email to updates@cicerone.co.uk or by post to Cicerone, Juniper House, Murley Moss, Oxenholme Road, Kendal, LA9 7RL.

Register your book: To sign up to receive free updates, special offers and GPX files where available, register your book at www.cicerone.co.uk.

Front cover image by Rob Brown: The author climbing the Long Climb Finish of Orion Direct, sharing one of the best days ever with a good friend

CONTENTS

Topos key 5

INTRODUCTION 7
Using this guide 7

BEN NEVIS 13

Climbs from Coire Leis 24
Little Brenva Face 24

Climbs from Observatory Gully 31
North East Buttress First Platform 31
The Minus Face 34
The Orion Face 39
Point Five Gully area 46
Indicator Wall 55
Gardyloo Buttress 61
Tower Ridge East Side 64
Tower Ridge 69
Douglas Boulder 72

Climbs from Coire na Ciste 79
Tower Ridge West Side 79
Pinnacle Buttress 84
Goodeve's Buttress and the Cascades 88
The Comb 93
Number Three Gully Buttress 99
Creag Coire na Ciste 106
The Trident buttresses 113
Moonlight Gully Buttress 122
Càrn Dearg Buttress 125

Climbs from Castle Coire 132
Castle Coire 132
North Face of Castle Ridge 140

GLEN NEVIS		145
Mamores		146
Stob Bàn		146
Mullach nan Coirean		155
AONACH MÒR AND AONACH BEAG		159
Aonach Mòr East Face – Coire an Lochain		161
Aonach Mòr West Face		181
Aonach Beag North Face		187
Aonach Beag West Face		193
STOB COIRE AN LAOIGH		201
Stob Coire an Laoigh		202
Appendix A	Route summary table by area	211
Appendix B	Route summary table by style	235

Warning

Mountaineering is a dangerous activity carrying a risk of personal injury or death. It should be undertaken only by those with a full understanding of the risks and with the training and experience to evaluate them. Mountaineers should be appropriately equipped for the routes undertaken. Whilst every care and effort has been taken in the preparation of this guide, the user should be aware that conditions, especially in winter, can be highly variable and can change quickly. Holds may become loose or fall off, rockfall can affect the character of a route, snow and avalanche conditions must be carefully considered. These can materially affect the seriousness of a climb, tour or expedition.

Therefore, except for any liability which cannot be excluded by law, neither Cicerone nor the author accepts liability for damage of any nature (including damage to property, personal injury or death) arising directly or indirectly from the information in this guide.

Looking back at The Great Tower of Tower Ridge

Map and topo symbols

────────	route
─── ─── ───	intersecting route
────────	approach route (map)
··············	obscured route
▪ ▪ ▪ ▪ ▪ ▪ ▪ ▪	route (not described)
─ ─ ─ ─ ─	ascent and descent route
①	route number
❶	route number (route not described)
ER	escape route

Snow-ice on Point Five Gully, Ben Nevis

INTRODUCTION

Walking towards Number Five Gully

USING THIS GUIDE

Each area of climbs has an overview description, as well as an info box which provides the following: approach start point, route lengths, approach time, crag base altitude, route styles, and details of avalanche risk. There are also approach and descent directions provided for each set of climbs.

The climbs are then described individually under headings which include name, route length, overall and technical grade, star rating and climbing style category. First-ascent details are provided where available.

The route of each climb is shown on a photo topo unless otherwise indicated.

Style categories

Every route in this guide is assigned a category to indicate the overall style of that route. There are three basic categories: snow, ice and mixed.

Of course, almost all winter routes will have snow on them. However, only when snow is significant to the overall character of the route (mainly the easier gully lines) is the snow ◆ category used.

Climb style categories

- 🧗 snow ice
- 🧊 cascade ice
- ◪ rocky mixed
- ◆ snow
- ❄ snow patch cascade
- ◪ turfy mixed
- ⛏ mixed
- 💧 thin ice
- ◪ icy mixed

Ice climbs are categorised as: snow-ice, cascade, snow patch cascade and thin face.

Mixed climbs are categorised as: general mixed, rocky mixed, turfy mixed and icy mixed.

Mixed climbs have a combination of rock, ice and turf with varying amounts of each of these ingredients. For climbs that particularly rely on one or more of these ingredients, this book uses the subcategories of turfy mixed climb, icy mixed climb and rocky mixed climb to highlight that you want to have good conditions for these elements.

In some cases, two symbols are used. If a route has sections which have very different styles, both of which add something significant to the feel of the route, then two symbols are used. For example, Gemini on Ben Nevis has significant cascade ice pitches followed by mixed pitches. This route is classified as cascade ice 🧊 **and** mixed ⛏.

There are various routes in this guide where the whole character of the route can change depending on conditions. There are some routes that are usually climbed as mixed routes, but which sometimes form ice and feel much more akin to an ice route. For example, Number Two Gully on Ben Nevis starts out the winter with a couple of pitches of ice but banks out with snow later on. So, it's classified as ice 🧗 **or** snow ◆. Thompson's Route on Ben Nevis is usually an icy mixed ◪ climb but late in the season it can build so much ice that it's climbed entirely on ice and feels like an ice climb; this is classified as icy mixed ◪ **or** ice 🧗.

The dynamic and ever-changing nature of the environment is one of the appealing aspects of Scottish winter climbing. The same route can feel very different under different conditions. For this reason, it would be impossible to accurately describe all the possible conditions that could be found on a particular route. Therefore, this classification, a bit like winter grades, is meant only as a rough guide to indicate what's likely to be found most of the time.

Approach times

The times given in info boxes represent the time taken to walk from the most convenient parking place to the

Compression Crack, Ben Nevis – an ice climb with cascade ice at the start and snow-ice to finish

foot of the crag for average climbers on an average day. If it's very windy or there's deep snow cover, expect the walk in to take longer. Stops for rests, navigation or for gearing up will be in addition to the times given. Everyone walks at a different pace, of course, so don't see the time given as a challenge! Instead it will give you an idea of how much effort is required to reach the crags, which should help you choose the best place to climb.

Grades

The current two-tier grading system developed by the Scottish Mountaineering Club (SMC) is used throughout this guide. As in previous systems, the higher the number, the more difficult the climb. The grades of I and II can be considered as introductory; only experienced climbers should attempt grades higher than this.

The grades are for 'average' conditions, and it should be remembered that winter climbs can vary enormously, depending on snow or ice build-up and the weather. Early in the season, when conditions can be lean, certain routes – particularly on ice – will be harder than later on when a good plating covers blank stretches and improves the conditions. Mixed routes, by comparison with snow and ice climbs, can benefit from lean, cold conditions, with no ice in the cracks.

The two-tier system shows a Roman numeral first, indicating the

Walking up towards Creag Coire na Ciste in April

overall seriousness of the climb, while the accompanying Arabic numeral represents the technical difficulty of the hardest sections of climbing. The aim of this system is to distinguish between routes with high levels of technical difficulty but which are less serious overall, and longer, more serious routes that might be less technically demanding.

- Point Five Gully (V,5) in average conditions is the benchmark from which other routes are graded.
- The overall grade takes into account all factors affecting the difficulty of reaching the top of the climb, including its technical difficulty, seriousness (frequency of protection and reliability of belays) and how sustained it is (length of hard sections of climbing and number of hard pitches).
- The technical grade reflects the difficulty of the hardest section(s) of climbing, without reference to seriousness. It is not intended to be used as a technical pitch-by-pitch grading. A technical grade of 5 indicates relatively straightforward, steep ice climbing; a technical grade of 6 generally indicates more technical mixed climbing or sustained vertical ice; technical grades of 7 and 8 indicate much more intricate and harder snowed-up rock moves.
- The technical grade normally varies by not more than two below or two above the overall grade. Thus V,5 can be taken as an average grade V route. A higher technical grade than the overall grade would indicate greater technical difficulty, offset by better protection (as frequently found on mixed routes); a lower technical grade would indicate greater seriousness.

- The overall difficulty is reflected in the overall grade, and just as in rock climbing where an E1 5a can be a more serious proposition than an E1 5c, a V,4 is not necessarily easier overall than a V,6.
- Climbs of up to grade III rarely have a technical grade; the overall grade is usually sufficient.

Some degree of variability undoubtedly occurs according to the prevailing conditions. While some climbs will nearly always be possible at close to the given grade, others require special (or even extraordinary) ice build-up, and the grades apply to such favourable situations. At other times these climbs may simply be non-existent. The grades of climbs in this guidebook have been decided after extensive consultation, but further comment is always valuable.

OVERALL GRADES

The following list provides an approximate definition of the overall grades. It's assumed that a rope is always used.

- **Grade I:** Climbs for which only one axe and crampons are normally required; either snow gullies around 45 degrees or easy ridges. Cornices can present problems and the avalanche hazard is always greatest in grade I gullies.
- **Grade II:** A second tool should be carried because of steep snow, difficult cornices and the occasional short ice pitch. Difficulties are usually short. Ridges at this grade will normally be straightforward scrambles in the summer.
- **Grade III:** More sustained and often steeper than grade II. Sometimes short and technical, particularly for mixed ascents of moderate rock climbs.
- **Grade IV:** Steep ice, from short vertical steps to long sections of 60–70 degrees. The mixed climbs require more advanced techniques such as axe 'torquing' and 'hooking'.
- **Grade V:** Sustained steep ice at 70–80 degrees with short vertical steps. Mixed climbing requires linked hard moves.
- **Grade VI:** Long vertical sections or thin and tenuous ice. Mixed routes include all that has gone before but more of it.
- **Grade VII:** Multi-pitch routes with long sections linking thin vertical ice and hard mixed moves, requiring strength, skill and stamina of the highest order.

> - **Grade VIII:** By the time you tackle this grade and above you'll know exactly what's involved!
>
>   As a rough guideline to technical grades on ice, 3 = 60 degrees, 4 = 70 degrees, 5 = 80 degrees, 6 = vertical.
>
>   **Note:** A split grade such as II/III indicates the possibility of a wide variation in difficulties depending on condition, usually due to the possibility of great accumulations of snow over the course of the winter.

Length of climb

Lengths of climbs and, where possible, pitch lengths are given in metres. Route lengths are as accurate as possible and will hopefully give the climber at least a reasonable idea of the scale of the route.

Recommended routes

Where possible, a three-star system has been used to indicate quality under good conditions – the more stars, the better the route. However, many unstarred routes under good conditions would warrant special mention. The star system will hopefully allow strangers to the area to find some good climbing on their first visit. Difficulty is not a prerequisite for stars; many simple climbs get a mention on the basis of their character, continuity, structure and adventure at the grade. All very subjective!

Diagrams and route numbers

Nearly all cliffs have a corresponding diagram; for those without, the text is sufficient to locate a route. Lines marked on diagrams are as accurate as possible, but you should still use your judgement and the description to work out the best line to take in practice. Feedback is welcome. On some diagrams not all routes are shown, in order to avoid overcrowding. The routes shown offer good reference points for adjacent climbs that are not shown. On other diagrams, where there's space, routes are marked that are not described in the text. With an adventurous spirit, a line and a grade are all you need. A summary table of routes is included at the end of this guide.

Appendices

Summary tables of climbs by area (in the same order in which they appear in the guide) – Appendix A – and by style – Appendix B – are provided for easy reference.

BEN NEVIS

Climbing The Great Chimney, Tower Ridge East Side

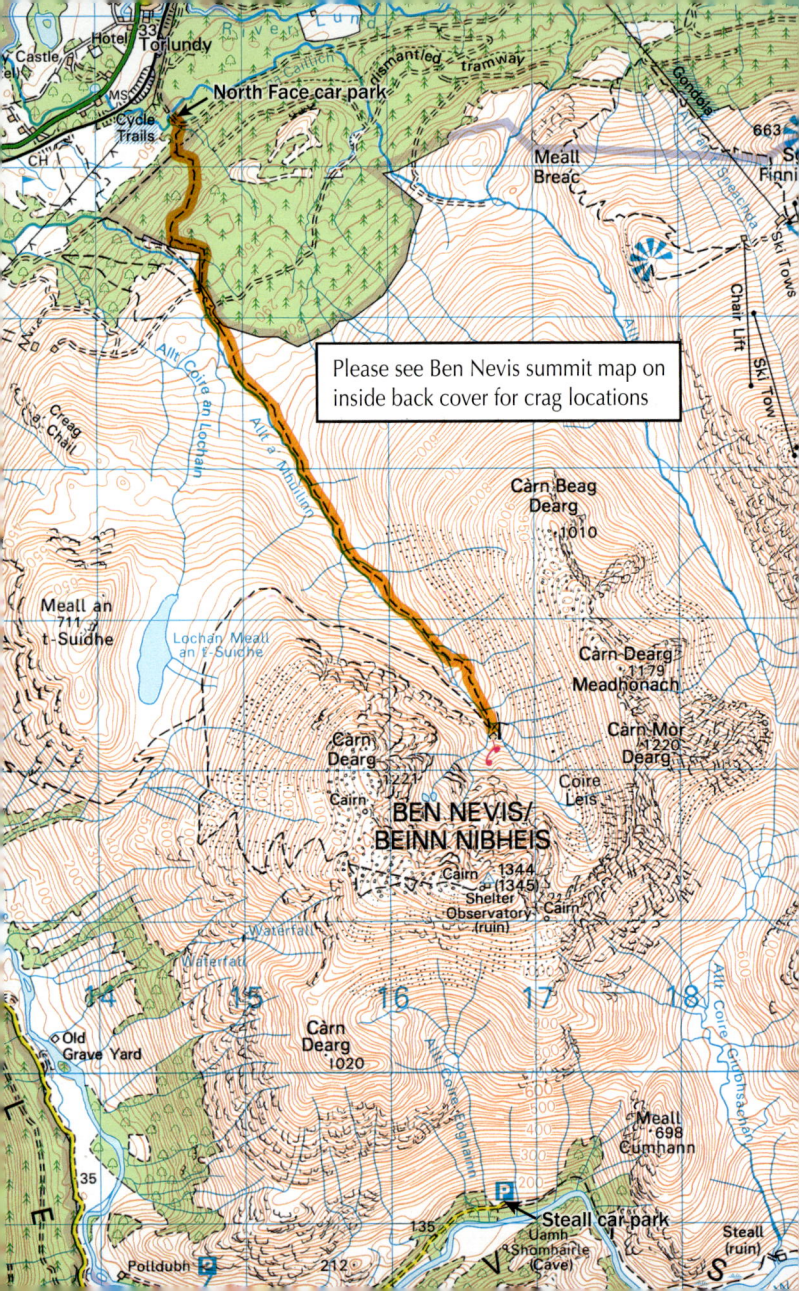

Ben Nevis is known around the world for its winter climbing. People travel from far and wide to enjoy the unique climbing here and to test themselves against the ever-changing and adventurous climbing conditions. There's a huge array of climbing here, of all styles.

The northerly faces of Ben Nevis and Càrn Dearg to its north-west form one continuous complex of cliffs which attain a maximum height of 500m and extend for 3.5km overlooking the upper part of Allt a' Mhuilinn. It is the most impressive mountain face in the British Isles. The incomparable classic ridges are flanked by formidable walls leading back into deeply recessed corries, which themselves contain numerous large buttresses and gullies. The scale is so vast that it's difficult to appreciate, particularly on first acquaintance. It's a mountain to keep coming back to again and again.

Ben Nevis from Allt a' Mhuilinn

APPROACHES FOR BEN NEVIS

Approaches for climbs on the northeast aspect of Ben Nevis all aim initially for the area of the CIC hut (NN 167 722; GPS NN 16739 72218). This hut is private and belongs to the Scottish Mountaineering Club. At the time of writing, bookings can be made through the Honorary Custodian Robin Clothier at cic@smc.org.uk. Do not expect to arrive and enter the hut without a booking.

Allt a' Mhuilinn – North Face approach

The North Face car park has been developed with help from the Forestry Commission and Mountaineering Scotland. Turn off the A82 at the sign in Torlundy, NN 143 771. Go over a hump-back railway bridge and turn right into the woods, then follow the rough vehicle track to the parking area at NN 145 765. Follow the signs which lead to a newly constructed path through the forest to Allt a' Mhuilinn. Allow 1hr 30min to the hut.

Glen Nevis approach

The approach from the west follows the zig-zag 'Mountain Track' to the summit as far as the broad saddle between Meall an t-Suidhe and the

The summit of Ben Nevis and the emergency shelter with good late-season snow cover

main massif of Càrn Dearg NW, Ben Nevis. This track can be started from the Ben Nevis Inn at Achintee (NN 125 729), the Youth Hostel in Glen Nevis (NN 127 717) or the Ben Nevis Visitor Centre (NN 123 731).

Above the saddle holding the large Lochan Meall an t-Suidhe (or 'Halfway Lochan', NN 14 72) the Mountain Track veers back to the right (south), crosses the Red Burn and zig-zags up the long slope to the summit plateau. However, instead of veering south on the Mountain Track, briefly follow a large path heading north to the far end of the lochan before taking a less obvious path contouring the lower slopes of Càrn Dearg for about 1km until it reaches the remains of an old fence on the lip of the Allt a' Mhuilinn glen.

From this point the path gradually descends for about 30m in a north-easterly direction and continues traversing south-east across the hillside until it reaches Allt a' Mhuilinn (500m below the CIC hut). A large boulder – the Lunching Stone – will be seen on the left of the path along this traverse.

The route now follows the right bank of Allt a' Mhuilinn until it's joined by another large stream coming in from the right (out of Coire na Ciste). This is crossed, and the hut, situated on the crest of a blunt spur between the streams, is about 100m above.

This approach is longer than from the North Face car park, and in bad visibility the route-finding is more difficult. After a big snowfall the traverse into and underneath the crags of Càrn Dearg can be prone to heavy drifting and possible avalanche below the Castle area. Allow 2hr to the hut.

DESCENTS FROM BEN NEVIS

The high summit plateau of Ben Nevis is surrounded on nearly all sides by steep and difficult ground. Many accidents have occurred in descent. Often, this part of the day will call for more concentration and judgement than any other time, especially in considering human factors that will influence decision-making.

The best descent will be determined not only by your point of arrival on the summit plateau but also by the weather and snow conditions. The shortest way will not necessarily be the easiest. The best and quickest descent is often by the Red Burn ('Mountain Track'). Careful use of map, compass, pacing, possibly GPS and details given in this guidebook will suffice to get you down, but local knowledge is invaluable.

When visibility is good, make a close study of the general topography of the mountain; if possible, visit the summit plateau with a view to memorising its details and recording important compass/GPS bearings. The ruined observatory, topped by a survival shelter, is an unmistakable landmark on the summit itself, even when the neighbouring triangulation point and numerous cairns are covered by snow. It's recommended to start all compass bearings and GPS waypoints from the shelter, even though the observatory ruins can intrude on the initial few metres of the 231° (grid) bearing if they're not covered with snow.

The best aids to descent from the summit of Ben Nevis are a 1:25,000 sheet map and a compass, together with the ability to use both in hostile weather conditions. These two items should form essential companions to this guidebook. The insert on the Harvey map (scale 1:12,500) is particularly useful. It shows the sharply indented plateau and the gullies, which must be avoided on compass bearings in poor visibility.

Anyone who visits the mountains in summer or winter without a map and a compass (and the ability to use them in 'white-out') is putting their life at risk.

Red Burn ('Mountain Track')

The easiest way down the mountain. Follow a grid bearing of 231° for 150 metres from the summit shelter (use a rope to measure it if you're not sure of your pacing), GPS NN 16558 71180. This will avoid the steep drop of Gardyloo Gully close on your right. There's a group of three purpose-built cairns at this point.

Now follow a grid bearing of 282°, GPS NN15721 71384 to the 1200m contour. In 2022, grid north is very close to magnetic north so you can set your compass to these bearings. In future years, magnetic north will move and you'll need to adjust these grid bearings accordingly.

On the second bearing you should reach a short steeper section after 300 metres – MacLean's 'Steep' – and continuously steeper ground after 900 metres of downhill travel. A line of well-built cairns now marks this route at 50-metre intervals to the point at which the 'Mountain Track' route meets the plateau; however, the cairns cannot be used alone in poor visibility without following a compass bearing.

Continue on down a steep but easy slope for another 1km on the same bearing or GPS NN 14756 71865, then turn north towards the 'Halfway Lochan' and follow the burn draining the lochan north towards Allt a' Mhuilinn.

Note: Along this route it's important not to stray left (south) in the first 2km, as this would lead to the steep and serious ground of Five Finger Gully. The steep lip of this gully is 800 metres (approx.) from the top of Gardyloo Gully. Accurate pacing and compass work are essential here and should be among the skills of anyone climbing on Ben Nevis. If after 800 metres on the recommended bearing you encounter steep ground and cliffs dead ahead, you're advised to try and avoid them by going right (north) until it's possible to continue on the bearing 282° (grid). This may require that you travel uphill for a short distance to skirt the top of Five Finger Gully.

If you finish up heading south, downhill, and skirting the top of steep cliffs to your right (west) after 800 metres from the top of Gardyloo Gully, it's highly likely you've made a navigation error and are very close to Five Finger Gully. Go back uphill until it's possible to continue on the original bearing 282° (grid).

The Red Burn is well known as a good 'bum slide'. Please be aware that there are large waterfalls at the bottom of the burn before it reaches the track, and many large rocks all the way up the burn; these will not only rip your expensive overtrousers but may put a hole in your head as well! This area has been the scene of fatal avalanche accidents after easterly winds and snowfall.

GPS towards the Mountain Track (Red Burn) descent as follows:
- Summit shelter NN16684 71256
- Gardyloo Gully NN16558 71180 (150m) 'dog-leg'
- MacLean's 'Steep' NN16262 71232 (310m)
- Red Burn track NN14756 71865 (1650m)

Number Four Gully

For climbers returning to the CIC hut or Allt a' Mhuilinn area, this descent is straightforward in good visibility. The top of the gully is marked by a hand-built cairn (NN 158 717; GPS NN 15837 71708). Sometimes the cornice can be impassable, but an abseil is often made from the cairn or a snow anchor. It's possible at times to move a few metres to the north along the rim and gain access to the gully down steeper ground. Avalanches often occur in this gully and the initial entry can be steep, but it soon eases. Take care.

Note: A compass bearing due west from the lip of this gully (270° grid) or GPS NN 14756 71865 is a descent to Glen Nevis via the Red Burn mentioned previously.

Coire Leis

This route can be used with care. It provides a method of descending quickly to a lower altitude, especially if the weather on the plateau is fierce. Many deaths have occurred on this descent over the years. Most of the fatalities have resulted from people straying too far left (north) from the summit on descent.

From the summit shelter, a bearing of 134° (grid) GPS NN 16897 71017 should be followed. Initially the ground will be flat. After 100 metres the gradient steepens abruptly and some short posts may be seen; follow these on a line curving south round to east.

From the steepening after approximately 200 metres of descent a slight col will be found to the left (east), 500 metres from the summit. At this point is a hand-built cairn (NN 171 710; GPS NN 17099 71005). The old abseil posts have been removed. With care, and passing a possible cornice, the descent is down grade I ground straight into

Winter climbs: Ben Nevis

Coire Leis. Often it's easier to traverse left (west) towards the Little Brenva Face before descending. However, snow build-up will dictate the easiest and most obvious route down.

The angle is steep at first, but eases after 150 metres. As with many snowy descents, be careful after strong winds during periods of heavy drifting to avoid being another avalanche victim on this slope.

EXTRA TIPS

For those climbers topping out on the following routes in poor visibility and not wishing to visit the summit, these bearings will help:
- Gardyloo Buttress 214° grid for 75 metres (GPS NN 16501 71181) then 282° grid to Red Burn or GPS NN 16262 71232 to GPS NN 14678 71590
- Tower Gully 214° grid for 50 metres (GPS NN 16426 71198) then 282° grid to Red Burn or GPS NN 16262 71232 to GPS NN 14678 71590
- Tower Ridge 214° grid for 130 metres (GPS NN 16378 71232) then 282° grid to Red Burn or GPS NN 16262 71232 to GPS NN 14678 71590
- Number Two Gully 282° grid to Red Burn or GPS NN 14678 71590
- Number Three Gully 282° grid to Red Burn or GPS NN 14756 71865
- Green/Comb Gully 220° grid for 150 metres (GPS NN 16082 71291) then 282° grid to Red Burn or GPS NN 14756 71865
- Ledge Route 270° grid for 200 metres (GPS NN 15675 72100) then 180° grid for 450 metres (GPS NN 15675 71655) then 270° grid to Red Burn (GPS NN 14756 71865)
- Castle Ridge 232° grid (GPS NN 15652 72374) for 200 metres then 308° grid. The descent to the 'Halfway Lochan' is over very rough, broken and rocky ground, with one or two small crags in places.

Note: The slope north of the Red Burn between the 1125m and 675m contour lines is not very pleasant for descent and contains a number of small crags.

For climbers finishing on routes to the east of the summit (North East Buttress and Little Brenva Face) it's advisable to try and find the summit shelter (GPS NN 16684 71256) as a definite reference point before descending if unsure about the descent. To do this, it should be possible to use the north-east edge of the plateau above Zero and Point Five gullies and Good Friday Climb as a 'handrail' to the summit trig point (15 metres north of the shelter). Cornice collapse has caused a few fatalities in this area; consider staying roped, with only one member of the party near the edge.

Rob Brown climbing Orion Direct

To extend your excursion

Given sufficient time and strength in the legs, a traverse of the Càrn Mòr Dearg (CMD) Arête is a great way to extend the day and gives the opportunity to see the crags of the north face of Ben Nevis from an excellent vantage point.

The crest of the arête is continuously narrow, exposed and rocky all the way to the summit of Càrn Mòr Dearg, from where an easy descent joins Allt a' Mhuilinn a few hundred metres above the forest.

BEN NEVIS – GENERAL TOPOGRAPHY

Walking up Allt a' Mhuilinn, the first feature you'll see on the right is Castle Ridge and its flanking North Wall. Beyond this and at a higher level is the recess of Castle Coire, which contains The Castle itself between North and South Castle Gullies and, to the left of these, the tapering pillar of Raeburn's Buttress.

The cliffs then jut out again. The left-hand side of Castle Coire is known as the North Wall of Càrn Dearg; this cliff connects with a 300m prow of compact rock, a truncated spur – Càrn Dearg Buttress. Waterfall Gully is the dividing line between these last two. Round the corner of Càrn Dearg Buttress is Number Five Gully, set at a reasonable angle but almost 500 metres in length. Ledge Route starts up Number Five Gully to gain the crest of the ridge at the top of Càrn Dearg Buttress and follows this to the summit of Càrn Dearg.

To the left (east) of Càrn Dearg Buttress, the cliffs fall back to form the great amphitheatre of Coire na Ciste, the floor of which, at over 900m, is a wild and magnificent place to visit. There are three relatively easy exits from the head of the corrie: Number Four Gully (hidden) on the right; Number Three Gully, appearing to be the lowest col in the centre; and Number Two Gully, which disappears to the left of the prominent triangular buttress of the Comb.

Tower Ridge is the next main feature and is one of the most important on the mountain. Narrow and very long, it projects for 750 metres from the summit plateau into the glen to terminate abruptly as the Douglas Boulder immediately above the hut.

The North Face of Ben Nevis

From the foot of the boulder (215m itself!) there's a vertical rise of over 550m before the junction with the plateau.

To the east of Tower Ridge is the long slope of Observatory Gully, which branches in its upper quarter to form Gardyloo and Tower gullies. Observatory Gully, broad in its lower part and tapering as it rises for 500m, is only an approach to other climbs and can be regarded almost as a deep corrie. Rising to the left of the gully are some of the most formidable climbs on the mountain: the Minus gullies and buttresses and the Orion Face (all on the flank of North East Buttress); Zero Gully which lies in the corner between Orion Face and the long spur of Observatory Ridge; and finally Point Five Gully and Observatory buttress.

The final great ridge is the skyline that dominates the view as you walk up Allt a' Mhuillin – this is North East Buttress. It is again a massive projection, almost 500m in vertical height, but is steeper and therefore not as long as Tower Ridge. Below it, the First Platform is the great rock nose not unlike the Douglas Boulder.

Allt a' Mhuilinn ends in Coire Leis below the col of the Càrn Mòr Dearg Arête. Overlooking this corrie is the east flank of the North East Buttress; now generally referred to as the Little Brenva Face.

The climbs are described from east to west (left to right), corrie by corrie.

CLIMBS FROM COIRE LEIS

Little Brenva Face

Start	North Face car park, Torlundy
Time	2hr 30min
Crag base altitude	1000–1100m
Route lengths	55–400m
Route styles	Snow-ice and cascade ice
Avalanches	The face catches early-morning sunshine which can trigger releases and deteriorate the condition of the ice.

Coire Leis is the basin at the head of Allt a' Mhuilinn: a huge bowl named for being sheltered on the 'lee' side of Ben Nevis, with CMD Arête running around its crest. Although all the routes on the Little Brenva Face follow fairly arbitrary lines, they are very nice and rarely busy. The climbs are generally wide-open ice lines that form quite readily. The face is alpine in character and receives the full benefit of any sun, which can cause icefall and cruddy conditions later in the season. Generally, the climbs are long (longer than they appear) and give some interesting route-finding; considerable difficulty may be experienced in misty conditions.

Approach
Follow the signed footpath, steeply at first, to the top of the forest, then the well-made path to the CIC hut (1hr 30min). From the hut, follow either bank of the burn until opposite the lowest rocks below the First Platform of North East Buttress, then traverse up the right-hand side of the corrie beneath the east face (about 1hr from the CIC hut). Walking up on the opposite side of the corrie allows a view of the face, which will be very useful to identify the climbs.

Descent
South then south-east back towards CMD Arête then down into Coire Leis, or over Ben Nevis summit.

Little Brenva Face

1. Final Buttress III
2. Bob Run II
3. Moonwalk IV,3**
4. Cresta III**
4a. Cresta Original Start
5. Slalom III**
6. Super G VI,6**
7. Isandhlwana V,5**
8. Route Major IV,3***

Final Buttress 55m III

At the extreme left side of the face is a short buttress. Climb an ice pitch in the centre.

Moonwalk 270m IV,3**
K. Hughes and J. Mothersele, March 1973

Start 10 metres left of Cresta below an ice pitch which can vary in difficulty depending on conditions. Climb the ice above and continue over a snow slope to the foot of an ice pitch formed by a rock corner (100m). Climb the ice above to another snow slope (45m). Move up to a steep ice wall (45m). Climb this for 15m and an ice groove to a snow-ice field (35m). Cross rightwards to belay below a rock wall (45m). Traverse horizontally right below the wall to a steep rock arête which is followed to the summit slopes.

Note: Many variations are possible in this area and escapes left (south) can be made with care towards Bob Run (see topo).

Cresta 275m III**
T.W. Patey, L.S. Lovat and A.G. Nicol, 16 February 1957

The main feature of this route is a 180m shallow couloir, which commences above and to the left of a rocky spur and finishes amongst the small cliffs at the exit from the highest part of the left-hand side of the face. The original start was from the right, but it is now more usual to commence to the left of the rocky spur. Some 30m of icy rocks (or ice) are climbed to gain a long broad snow shelf. A small gully leads up from the right-hand side of the shelf to reach the couloir proper, which is followed to its termination in an ice basin. Traverse up to the right to gain an easy snow slope which leads out to a finish about 50m from the top of North East Buttress.

Slalom 275m III**
D. Pipes, I. Clough, J.M. Alexander, R. Shaw and A. Flegg, 6 January 1959

The upper part of the right-hand side of the face is a steep rock wall, the Central Spur. Both Slalom and Frostbite start in the bay below this wall and to the right of a rocky spur. Slalom starts up a shallow tongue of snow from the left of the bay and zig-zags up through the rock bluffs towards the middle of the wall of the Central Spur. Below the Spur, a long rising leftwards traverse is made to gain an easy snow slope which leads to the foot of a rocky ridge overlooking the couloir of Cresta. The rocks usually give the crux of the climb and lead to the final easy exit slope which is shared with Cresta.

LITTLE BRENVA FACE

Super G 270m VI,6**
H. Burrows-Smith and D. McGimpsey, 20 March 2002
Every now and then an impressive icefall forms down the headwall of the face. It's approached in four pitches via the first pitches of Slalom, a rightwards traverse and easy-angled ice below and left of the icefall. Three pitches (40m, 50m and 20m) of very steep ice form the crux of the climb over iced steps and an icicle fringe, finishing slightly leftwards up an icy ramp.

Isandhlwana 280m V,5**
R. Clothier, G. Perroux, J-F Males and P. Touvet, 27 March 1999
Described by Perroux as one of his best moments on Ben Nevis! A varied icy mixed route left of Route Major. Climb icy slabs and mixed ground to start. At the top of the snow couloir, climb steep mixed ground for 30m to a snow bay. The icefall above and an icy ramp lead to a snow funnel that exits on NE Buttress.

Route Major 300m IV,3**
H. MacInnes and I. Clough, 16 February 1969
Not an easy route to find and follow, but for those who enjoy exploring middle-grade mixed ground it's excellent when in condition. A long mountaineering route with short harder sections. To get a good look at the route it's advisable to walk up the east side of Coire Leis above the hut until opposite the start of North East Buttress. A hanging ice field high on the face is a key feature towards which climbers should aim.

A start from the traverse line (left end) onto the First Platform of North East Buttress can be made. Follow ice ribs up the wall to gain a snow slope crossed by Isandhlwana; cross this and continue up the buttress by a chimney line going right (difficult route-finding). Where the route goes close to The Mantrap of North East Buttress, break out left on a horizontal traverse then up various small snowfields to the top.

Note: An alternative start to the climb can be made by walking up directly under North East Buttress and continuing until the ground levels out as it approaches upper Coire Leis. From here, turn up right and commence climbing.

North East Buttress 400m IV,5***
W.W. Naismith, W. Brunskill, A.B.W. Kennedy, W.W. King and F.C. Squance, 3 April 1896
One of the finest mountaineering objectives in the country. Interesting route-finding, shorter and steeper than Tower Ridge, with three very difficult pitches. Although it may be possible to climb this in early-season conditions of light snow on the rocks, it benefits from a good cover of snow transformed into snow-ice.

The normal winter route avoids the rocks below the First Platform by going up into Coire Leis until a broad easy shelf leads back up to the right to the First Platform. (Finding the start of this is difficult and it's well worth walking up the east side of Coire Leis to get a good look.) Getting onto the shelf can involve icy steps if there's little snow, and the shelf can be prone to avalanche.

Shortly above the First Platform the rocks on the crest become very steep. The easiest route is to climb two or three pitches up icy grooves on the left to where the ground opens up to easier snow. A rising traverse back right goes to the Second Platform – a slight flattening in the ridge.

Above the Second Platform the narrow ridge is followed, turning obstacles on the right, one of which is quite a tricky 7m pitch, until a smooth, blunt 4m rock step bars the way. This is the notorious Mantrap and it should be climbed directly – which can be extremely difficult in icy conditions when the cracks are full of ice. Above and sightly around to the right is The Forty Foot Corner; this too should be climbed, and can also be quite hard, delicate and not well protected.

The Man Trap can sometimes be avoided by a slight descent on the right and traverse to a scoop which leads up to the foot of The Forty Foot Corner. The Forty Foot Corner might be avoided down to the

Little Brenva Face and North-East Buttress, with the access to First Platform at the bottom right of the image

left, not far above the top of The Mantrap, by a shallow chimney leading up to the left of the ridge crest onto easier ground.

This upper part of the route is normally the crux of the climb, but the major difficulties are relatively short and it's not too far to the top; probably better to force the route than be faced with the long retreat.

A hard direct start is possible: from the Coire Leis approach traverse, approximately 50m before reaching the First Platform head up directly via steep icy walls to regain the route below the Second Platform (**Green Gaiters 120m IV,5** *R. Clothier and P. Pibarot, March 1994*).

CLIMBS FROM OBSERVATORY GULLY

This is the home of the biggest and best ice climbs in the country. Nearly all the climbs on this part of the mountain require good snow-ice and only form after snowfall and several thaw-freeze cycles. The rocks are generally not so good for mixed climbing, with blind cracks and sloping ledges. Lower buttresses (below the First Platform and the Minus Face) form snow-ice less often but the higher buttresses form good conditions every winter. Very large avalanches fall from the upper reaches of this gully, especially after a south-east wind has blown snow into the gullies. It would be wise to avoid the climbs from this gully during or after heavy snowfall, strong winds or during a thaw.

North East Buttress First Platform

Start	North Face car park, Torlundy
Time	2hr
Crag base altitude	850–950m
Route lengths	180–230m
Route styles	Snow-ice and icy mixed
Avalanches	Generally a very secure place to climb, but be wary of large avalanches out of Observatory Gully. The descent into Coire Leis can be particularly awkward and it's often better to abseil down Slingsby's Chimney.

Beneath the First Platform of North East Buttress are many good climbs, easily seen on the approach up Allt a' Mhuilinn, and when in condition provide good sport at a lower level. You may wish to consider an abseil descent of Slingsby's Chimney from these routes, as the traverse off into Coire Leis can be avalanche prone and is pretty exposed and steep.

Approach
Follow the signed footpath, steeply at first, to the top of the forest, then the well-made path to the CIC hut (1hr 30min). Carry on above the hut on the south-west side of the stream to the foot of NE Buttress, NN 170 717.

North East Buttress First Platform

> **Descent**
> Abseil down Slingsby's Chimney, or traverse off into Coire Leis as for the approach to NE Buttress if the snow is stable and there's not too much ice around.

Newbigging's Route – Far Right Variation 180m IV,4**
R. Campbell, R. Carrington and J.R. Marshall, February 1972
This route is on the triangular face that falls vertically into Coire Leis as seen from beneath the First Platform of North East Buttress. It starts 10 metres left of the rocky edge of the face (this edge forms the north and east facets of the buttress) and runs parallel to that edge. The route is a natural winter line and easily seen on the approach from the hut. Follow the big corner-groove and slabs, passing an overhang on the left. The main difficulties are in the lower 60m and will require good snow-ice, which rarely forms here.

Raeburn's Arête 230m IV,5***
D.F. Lang and C. Stead, 25 January 1986
Follows the arête formed by the north and east facets of the First Platform of North East Buttress. A good climb which is not often in condition because it requires a good coating of snow-ice. Go right below the first overhang to a deep groove, which is climbed to a belay (45m). Follow grooves up slightly right then go left beneath another overhang to a block belay on the edge (100m). Follow the arête more easily to the top of the First Platform (90m).

Green Hollow Route 200m IV,4**
J.R. Marshall and J. Moriarty, February 1965
Start at the lowest rocks on the left (often snow-covered) and trend diagonally up rightwards by iced slabs and grooves towards a large snow bay, high up in the middle of the face – the Green Hollow. From the highest point of the bay, climb an iced slab left onto the final arête. Follow this easily to the top of the First Platform.

Slingsby's Chimney 125m III
C. Donaldson and J. Russell, April 1950
A direct approach to the First Platform of North East Buttress, but never a quicker way to start North East Buttress. To the right of the slabby rocks of the nose leading to the First Platform is an obvious shallow gully fault; this gives the climb, with a difficult exit up and left that's much harder (grade IV) without a very good build-up of solid snow.

The Minus Face

Start	North Face car park, Torlundy
Time	2hr 15min
Crag base altitude	950–1000m
Route lengths	150–300m
Route styles	Snow-ice and thin face ice climbs, icy mixed climbs
Avalanches	The bowl under this face and Zero Gully is particularly suspect after south-easterly winds.

Home to some of the finest climbs on the mountain, the celebrated Minus gullies are much sought-after climbs and the buttresses in between are a very rare treat when they form good snow-ice. The Minus Face, between Slingsby's Chimney and Minus One Gully, often has less avalanche hazard, but the climbs finish on NE Buttress which will then need to be either climbed or descended (usually by abseil). Route lengths are given to the crest of North East Buttress.

The three Minus gullies are relatively shallow lines running diagonally left up the face with Minus Three Gully on the left and Minus Two and Minus One gullies starting at nearly the same point further right.

Approach
Follow the signed footpath, steeply at first, to the top of the forest, then the well-made path to the CIC hut (1hr 30min). Carry on above the hut on the south-west side of the stream to the bowl under the face, NN 169 716.

Descent
The Minus Face finishes on NE Buttress below The Mantrap and Forty Foot Corner. Either climb up to the summit in a couple of hours or abseil down NE Buttress to First Platform and down Slingsby's Chimney (or traverse off into Coire Leis). The Orion Face finishes near the summit, so either descend towards CMD Arête and into Coire Leis or go over Ben Nevis summit.

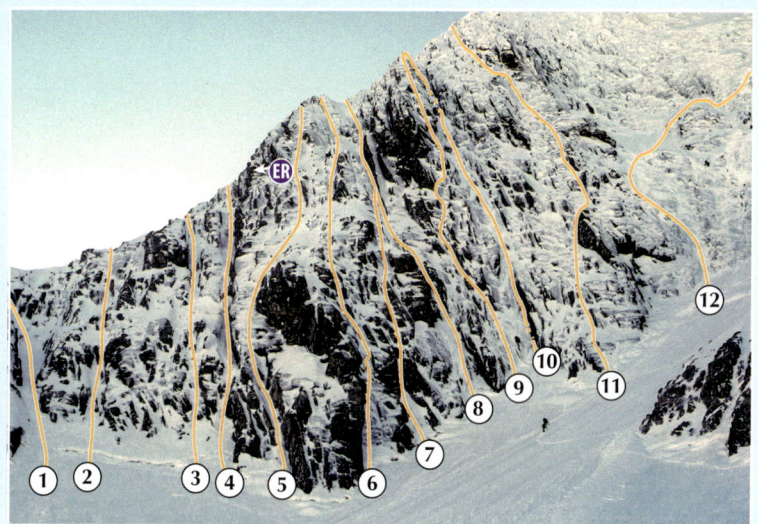

Minus Face

1. Slingsby's Chimney III
2. Right-hand Wall Route IV,5
3. Platforms Rib IV,4*
4. Minus Three Gully IV,5**
5. Left-Hand Route VI,6**
6. Right-Hand Route VI,6*
7. Subtraction VIII,8*
8. Minus Two Gully V,5***
9. Minus One Direct VIII,8***
10. Minus One Gully VI,6***
11. Astonomy VI,5***
12. Orion Direct V,5***

Right-Hand Wall Route 140m IV,5
R. Ferguson and J. Higham, March 1972
Just to the right of Slingsby's Chimney is a line of shallow chimneys: follow this line as closely as possible, the final slabby part below the First Platform giving the crux.

Platforms Rib 150m IV,4*
H. MacInnes, I. Clough, T. Sullivan and M. White, 8 March 1959
Follow the shallow chimney in the rib to the left of Minus Three Gully all the way to the First Platform of North East Buttress.

Climbing Minus Three Gully

Minus Three Gully 160m IV,5**
R. Smith and J.R. Marshall, 7 February 1960
When in condition, this is a classic. Climb steep snow to a cave belay, then climb steep ice on the left and continue by a groove to snow. Another steep pitch leads to easier climbing and North East Buttress.

Left-Hand Route 270m VI,6**
S. Docherty and N. Muir, 30 January 1972
A delicate climb on thinly iced slabs. Start immediately right of Minus Three Gully and ascend the huge groove/corner for 60m, passing an overhanging section.

The Minus Face

Steep ice leads to an easier section of slabby rocks (with a possible escape left to the First Platform) and eventually to the Second Platform.

Central Route 270m VI,7

A. Nisbet and B. Sprunt, 18 March 1979
(no photo topo)
The climb follows a line just to the right of the previous route, taking the raised crest on the front face to the overhangs. These are gained by a rightward traverse and turned on the right using aid to reach easier ground. The overhangs were climbed free, directly up a stepped corner, and called **Calculus VIII,8** *M. van Haeren and A. Inglis, 24 February 2020.*

Right-Hand Route 270m VI,6*

R. Carrington and A. Rouse, March 1972
To the right of the prominent ridge is a large slabby corner. Climb the large corner, then a short and more difficult corner to gain the easier-angled upper section of the buttress. Slabs and grooves lead to the North East Buttress.

Subtraction 270m VIII,8*

V. Scott and G. Robertson, 15 April 2008
Hard, varied and committing mixed climbing into Minus Two Gully. Start 10 metres right of Right-Hand Route and climb a well-defined groove to where it steepens and trends left (35m). From the rib on the right, climb the overhang (25m). Climb the arête above to a corner (40m) which leads into Minus Two Gully.

Minus Two Gully 270m V,5***

J.R. Marshall, J. Stenhouse and D. Haston, 11 February 1959
The best of the Nevis gullies when in condition. A long pitch of snow and ice leads to a belay below an overhang. Avoid the overhang by a detour to the left and regain the upper chimneys leading to the North East Buttress. The initial chimney pitch can be avoided by thinly iced slabs just to the left in a 55m pitch to a rock belay on the left.

Minus One Direct 290m VIII,8***

G. Robertson, P. Benson and N. Bullock, 10 March 2010
A direct and stunning line up the buttress – one of the best climbs in the country. Start up the first three pitches of Minus One Buttress then continue up and right to find a continuous crack line leading to the top of the buttress.

Minus Face and Orion Face

① Minus One Gully VI,6***
② The Black Hole VI,6**
③ Orion Direct V,5**
④ Astral Highway V,5***
⑤ Orion Direct Start V,5**
⑥ Slav Route V,5***
⑦ Zero Gully V,4**
⑧ Observatory Ridge V,4***

Minus One Gully 290m VI,6***
K.V. Crocket and C. Stead, 23 February 1974
The hardest of the Nevis gullies. Easy climbing leads to an ice wall giving access to a cave below the main overhang. Avoid the overhang on thin ice on the left before regaining the gully above. Continue past a snow bay to reach the crest of Minus One Buttress on the left and then North East Buttress.

The Orion Face

Start	North Face car park, Torlundy
Time	2hr 15min
Crag base altitude	1000–1050m
Route lengths	300–420m
Route styles	Snow-ice and thin face ice climbs, icy mixed climbs
Avalanches	The bowl under this face and Zero Gully is particularly suspect after south-easterly winds.

The biggest face on Ben Nevis forms a narrow fan shape between Minus One Gully and Zero Gully. The toe of the buttress takes the line of Astronomy and projects into the approach slopes leading to Orion Direct, which starts up a steep icefall with the Great Slab Rib to the left.

In the centre of the face lies The Basin, a large snow patch, at the top left side of which is a steep icy chimney known as Epsilon Chimney – the easiest escape from The Basin to NE Buttress in the event of poor snow conditions. Up right of The Basin is the Second Slab Rib, which is sometimes the only feature showing in the middle of the face when snow and ice obliterate all other detail. Higher up is another smaller snow patch, and left of this at a higher level is the exit chimney.

Approach
Follow the signed footpath, steeply at first, to the top of the forest, then the well-made path to the CIC hut (1hr 30min). Carry on above the hut on the south-west side of the stream to the bowl under the face, NN 161 715.

Descent
The Orion Face finishes at the top of North East Buttress near the summit, so either descend towards CMD Arête and into Coire Leis or go over Ben Nevis summit.

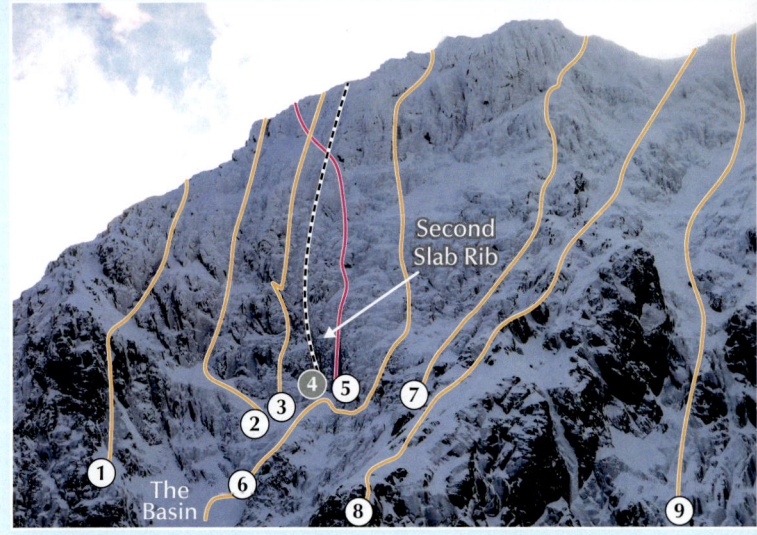

Orion Face Top Section

1. Urban Spaceman VII,6***
2. Astral Highway V,5***
3. Journey Into Space VII,6**
4. Spacewalk VII,6**
5. Long Climb Finish VI,5***
6. Orion Direct V,5***
7. Slav Route V,5***
8. Observatory Ridge V,4***
9. Hadrian's Wall Direct V,5***

Astronomy 300m VI,5*

H. MacInnes, A. Fyffe and K. Spence, March 1971

Less often in condition than other routes on the Orion Face. Start about 16 metres to the right of Minus One Gully and climb twin cracks to leftward-slanting snow patches. These snow patches lead to a groove. Climb the groove and go right to a large corner. Go up the corner then move right, then back left by walls and grooves. Here you can skirt left below the upper rocks and escape by descending into the top of Minus One Gully. To finish directly, trend slightly right to belay below the right-hand end of the steep upper rocks. Gain the crest of the buttress on the right and climb an iced slab, trending right to gain a fine ice groove near the crest of the buttress. Follow this steeply to easier ground.

THE ORION FACE

The Black Hole 350m VI,6**
A. Saunders and M. Fowler, 5 April 1986
Starts 15 metres left of Orion Direct. Climb an awkward right-facing corner to gain the left side of the Great Slab Rib (50m). Follow the corner on the left side of the rib for 30m, then move left to an obvious ice-choked overhanging crack, which is climbed to a snow patch (45m). Climb the overhanging fault line above to belay at the top left of another snow patch (35m). Move back right into the fault line, which is climbed to join Astronomy where it traverses left into Minus One Gully (45m). Climb another couple of pitches in the same line up thinly iced grooves (60m). Much of this route had been climbed previously.

Urban Spaceman 350m VII,6***
D. Hawthorn and A. Paul, 12 April 1983
An excellent route but very rarely in good condition. Start at the same point as for Orion Direct and move up left to below the Great Slab Rib (35m), which is followed on the crest to a stance (30m). Continue on a similar line to a belay (40m). Reach a set of open grooves up right (30m) and follow them to beneath the steep upper section (50m). Move over slabs up right to a stance (30m). Follow a steep ice-filled chimney which overlooks The Basin, then go up steep mixed ground (45m). A further 90m leads to North East Buttress.

Orion Direct 420m V,5***
R. Smith and J.R. Marshall, 13 February 1960
An absolutely wonderful route. The technical difficulty is often low, but in such conditions belays might be poor with consecutive belays on ice. Climb the steep slopes to the start, just to the left of Zero Gully. An open scoop leads up and right to a snow shelf (40m). Take a steep chimney line above which opens out and leads left to a rock belay at the bottom left side of The Basin (60m). It's possible to climb straight up into The Basin from the chimney, but harder.

Move up rightwards and climb diagonally right across The Basin (60m). Ice at the top of The Basin leads to a snow crest on the right which is crossed, then a few metres of downclimbing to an obvious rock rib, Second Slab Rib (40m). Step down then traverse delicately right across the wall, before going up and right in a sensational position and straight up easier snow and ice (50m). Trend up leftwards to find the steep icy exit chimneys (60m) and climb the one on the left (50m). Simple snow leads to the top of North East Buttress (60m).

A direct start in two pitches of steep sustained ice is possible in good conditions to reach the right side of The Basin. Starts just left of Slav Route and stays right of the lower pitches of Orion Direct original route (**V,5***, *S. Docherty and N. Muir, March 1971*).

Winter climbs: Ben Nevis

The Basin has an ice-filled chimney on its left side – Epsilon Chimney. This and a traverse left can provide an escape onto North East Buttress.

> The following routes are described from The Basin, with lengths of climb given from here to the top.

Astral Highway 240m V,5***
C. Higgins and A. Kimber, 28 December 1976
A direct finish starting at the top of The Basin, left of centre at the groove right of and above Epsilon Chimney. Gain the groove and climb it and successive grooves to reach the North East Buttress straight into or above and right of the Forty Foot Corner.

Climbing the second pitch of Orion Direct

The author climbing the Long Climb Finish of Orion Direct (photo: Rob Brown)

Journey into Space 240m VII,6**

A. Kimber and C. Higgins, 8 March 1980

Start midway between Astral Highway and Second Slab Rib. Climb directly to the right of a short corner, where a delicate traverse right leads to a short ice wall, which is climbed to a belay ledge. Climb diagonally leftwards by an obvious iced slab until a break right can be made onto the upper section of the wall. Climb another slab, move right beneath an overhang then follow a groove direct, climbing the occasional bulge until the right end of a prominent snowfield is reached. Move diagonally left up the snowfield to an obvious corner finish (it's possible to finish direct by Spacewalk).

Long Climb Finish 240m VI,5***

A. Cain and R. Clothier, March 1983

A steep alternative finish to Orion Direct which follows the steep and icy tapering groove that forms the right side Second Slab Rib. Above Second Slab Rib, climb steeply up left by grooves and a slab, and eventually follow the same snow ledge left as Journey into Space or find and follow a steep line of fat ice in a groove, the last section of Spacewalk.

> The following routes are described from the foot of the face.

Slav Route 420m V,5***
D. Lang and N. Quinn, 23 March 1974
Takes a line just to the left of Zero Gully but is completely independent. An obvious icefall at 50m is climbed directly, or possibly avoided a long way to the left. Near the top an exit can be made into Zero Gully, but a better line slightly leftwards is taken to an obvious open corner up left of the gully.

Zero Gully 300m V,4**
H. MacInnes, A. Nicol and T.W. Patey, 18 February 1957
The easiest but most serious of the big three classics (Point Five Gully, Orion Direct and Zero Gully). The lack of rock belays gives it the V grade. Climb the gully to a stance below a left-facing chimney to the left of the main gully. Ascend the chimney then traverse right to an amphitheatre in the gully. Take the narrow gully above to easy ground by a long pitch.

A start can also be made by climbing the steep ice on the right, thus avoiding the rightward traverse higher up. This option varies with conditions and is often more sustained. Above are seemingly endless pitches of calf-burning easier ground.

As with all steep gully lines, Zero Gully is not a nice place to be when the wind blows vast quantities of powder snow down the climb! Beware of debris from other parties.

OBSERVATORY RIDGE
> The ridge itself is the narrow buttress to the right of Zero Gully, but as an area it's taken to stretch from Zero Gully to Point Five Gully.

East Face 170m to Observatory Ridge IV,5*
B. Dunn and C. Higgins, 3 March 1974
(no photo topo)
Below and to the right of Zero Gully, the left side of Observatory Ridge is split by a line of grooves which give the route, until they merge into the ridge itself.

Climbing the upper sections of Observatory Ridge

Observatory Ridge 500m V,4***
H. Raeburn, F.S. Goggs and W.A. Mounsey, April 1920

The finest and most difficult of the classic ridges, the line of the route generally follows the crest of the ridge. It's a long and serious climb. Without snow-ice, and especially under powder snow, this will be a long and arduous climb. With good snow-ice and dry rocks in between (like you might find in the spring) this climb is at its best and simply stunning.

The first third of the ridge normally gives the most serious problems and can be climbed in five pitches. At the start, a simple left-trending line leads to a terrace/ledge (60m). Delicate climbing in grooves goes to another ledge (40m). Climb a left-facing corner with a mantle-shelf move which often gives the crux of the whole climb (30m). Above this corner, on a good ledge, go right blindly around the crest to find grooves leading up the right side to the first shoulder in the ridge (40m, 40m). Above this, a much easier section (60m) leads to another hard short pitch (30m), climbed on the right side. The upper part of the ridge is then less steep and you can easily move into the top part of Zero Gully. About 12–14 pitches in total.

Point Five Gully area

Start	North Face car park, Torlundy
Time	2hr 15min
Crag base altitude	1050–1100m
Route lengths	100–360m
Route styles	Snow-ice and thin face ice climbs, icy mixed climbs
Avalanches	The bowl under these faces and Point Five Gully is particularly suspect after south-easterly winds.

The area between Observatory Ridge and Observatory Buttress holds some of the best and most reliable snow-ice climbs on the mountain. Point Five Gully is the ultimate classic and there are many comparable climbs here to consider when other teams are already established on the most popular climbs.

Approach
Follow the signed footpath, steeply at first, to the top of the forest, then the well-made path to the CIC hut (1hr 30min). Carry on above the hut on the south-west side of the stream to Observatory Gully. Walk up the gully to 1050m and traverse across to the face.

Descent
Descend towards CMD Arête and into Coire Leis, or go over Ben Nevis summit.

Abacus 110m (to Observatory Ridge) IV,4*
N. Muir and A. Paul, 27 November 1977
(no photo topo)
The route climbs the obvious bow-shaped chimney groove in the middle of the face between Observatory Ridge and Hadrian's Wall to reach the ridge.

Antonine Wall 150m (to Observatory Ridge) V,5*
N. Muir and A. Paul, 3 December 1977
(no photo topo)
Just right of Abacus is a steep ice-filled groove leading to a slab capped by a huge roof. Climb the groove to below the roof and move right over slabs to a snow groove leading to the crest.

Hadrian's Wall

1. Vade Mecum V,5***
2. Hadrian's Wall Direct V,5***
3. Sickle V,5***
4. Galactic Hitchhiker VI,5***
5. Nemesis VI,5*
6. Interstellar Overdrive VI,5*
7. Matchpoint VI,5*
8. Observatory Buttress V,5

Point Five Gully V,5***

Vade Mecum 180m (to Observatory Ridge) V,5***

D. Knowles, D. Wilson and party, 1974

Start just left of the ice-smear of Hadrian's Wall Direct and climb over slabby mixed ground to an obvious pointed block. Move left and finish by a very steep ice pillar to Observatory Ridge.

Hadrian's Wall Direct 320m V,5***

M.G. Geddes and G. Little, April 1971

Between Observatory Ridge and Point Five Gully is a very obvious ice-smear. It forms readily due to a spring very high on the face that dribbles water into the snow on the face. It's nowhere very steep, but this popular climb is rather poorly protected lower down (poor belay stance after first pitch unless a 60m pitch is taken). Climb the smear in one or two pitches then go slightly right to a chimney with good belay. Take the chimney to a snow patch and climb this in two or three long pitches. Follow excellent ice bulges directly to the top, just to the right of Observatory Ridge.

Sickle 300m V,5***

B. Hall and M.G. Geddes, December 1977

Start to the right of Hadrian's Wall Direct and move up to climb a groove parallel with, and close to, Hadrian's Wall Direct; then go back right to find a steep ice corner leading to the snow patch on Hadrian's Wall Direct, just above its

Observatory Ridge and climbers on Hadrian's Wall Direct

Climbers enjoying excellent ice on Hadrian's Wall Direct and Sickle

chimney. Continue to the plateau by following an open groove system, staying right of Hadrian's Wall Direct.

Galactic Hitchhiker 300m VI,5★★★
M.G. Geddes and C. Higgins, 14 April 1978
One of the first grade VIs climbed on Ben Nevis. Right of Hadrian's Wall Direct, the main feature is the rightward stepped corner system above the great slab left of Point Five Gully. Climb just left of the centre of the slab to a small nose (50m). Move up right into the main groove system beneath the corner. Traverse right above the slab in an exposed position via a pointed block to belay on the right. Continue above by very steep and difficult walls and ledges right of the main corner system to easier ground which is followed to the top.

   Note: An easier start (V,5) can sometimes be made on the left and nearer to Sickle, followed by a traverse right to a pointed block.

Nemesis 290m VI,5*

M. Nunwick and S. Reid, 14 March 2002

The great slab between Galactic Hitchhiker and Pointless is rarely in condition but is particularly compelling when it is. Climb a short pitch to the foot of the slab. The slab itself is taken just left of the corner at its top before a 10m traverse leftwards is made to the pointed block of Galactic Hitchhiker. Two further pitches climb grooves to the right of Galactic Hitchhiker before continuing directly to the plateau.

Pointless 300m VII,6*

N. Banks and G. Smith, 19 February 1978
(no photo topo)

A difficult climb, especially on the second pitch. Start on the obvious slab close to the left side of Point Five Gully. Follow the right edge of the slab towards a rock barrier which is level with the normal first belay of Point Five Gully (bottom of the chimney). Trend up left at the rock barrier to a spike belay beneath a steep, obvious corner (50m). Climb the corner with difficulty (possible peg on left wall) and trend right at the top. Continue directly for two interesting (III) pitches. Easier climbing leads in three pitches to the plateau rim.

A variation start (**50m VI,5** *M. Fowler and A.V. Saunders, 29 March 1986*) can be made by climbing a short corner from the foot of Point Five Gully (8m) followed by a traverse left above the prominent steep slab to the foot of the difficult second pitch.

Note: As with many climbs, the first pitch of this route may be longer if the build-up of snow at the base of the cliff is lacking.

Interstellar Overdrive 300m VI,5*

I. Kennedy and R. Anderson, March 1980

Climb the left-hand rib of Point Five Gully to belay below a wall (30m). Go right across the wall until immediately above Point Five Gully. Follow a groove running left to a chimney, which is the right side of an enormous perched block. Climb the chimney to a belay on top of the block (40m). Climb a corner and ice wall (crux) rightwards above to a ledge in a snow bay (40m), followed by a groove on the right, which trends back left to meet Pointless above the difficult section (40m).

Point Five Gully 325m V,5***

I.S. Clough, D. Pipes, R. Shaw and J.M. Alexander, 12–16 January 1959

A justifiably popular route, often in condition, and the benchmark grade V,5 from which all other steep snow-ice gully climbs are graded. It is a large natural funnel, so it collects snow and dribbles water down the chimneys to form ice quickly.

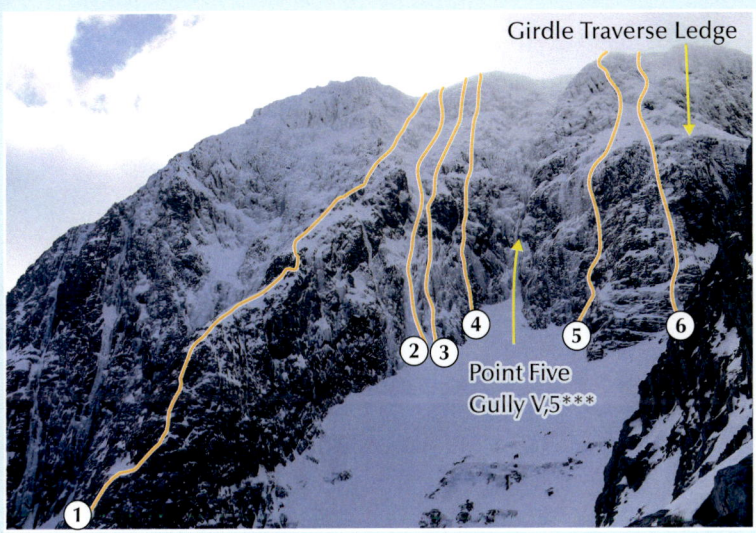

Point Five Gully

1. Observatory Ridge V,4***
2. Hadrian's Wall Direct V,5***
3. Sickle V,5***
4. Galactic Hitchhiker VI,5***
5. Rubicon Wall VI,5**
6. Observatory Buttress V,5**

It still requires a few thaw-freeze cycles, but it's one of the first big ice climbs to form. It also collects terrifying amounts of spindrift when there's wind on the summit.

Approach from high up Observatory Gully by a traverse under Observatory Buttress. The first three long pitches give sustained steep climbing, either of which might present the crux. The first is to a belay on the left, then the chimney pitch to a belay on the right in a deep recess followed by the Rogue Pitch to easier ground. Above, there's one steeper section (II/III) before trending right to pass the cornice. Beware of spindrift avalanches and falling debris from other parties.

Note: Climbers on top form and requiring more excitement could take to the left wall of the gully after the third hard pitch. Find your own way to the top at about grade IV,4 depending on the line chosen. An escape rightwards is possible (III) onto the Girdle Traverse ledge running towards Good Friday Climb. Move out right from beneath the Rogue Pitch (pitch 3).

Climbers on the second pitch of Point Five Gully

OBSERVATORY BUTTRESS

The buttress stretching rightwards from Point Five Gully to Good Friday Climb.

Point Blank 340m VII,6***

M. Duff and J. Tinker, 4 March 1984; direct version second ascent, as described: M. Duff and R. Nowack, 24 February 1988

This route climbs the buttress immediately right of Point Five Gully. Start below the foot of Point Five Gully and climb a small steep groove left of Left Edge Route to the snow patch of that route and move up right to a corner and belay. Climb the right-hand groove/crack on rocky mixed ground and thin icy slabs to a corner and capping roof, then enter a short groove leading to a narrow chimney-crack to a belay below a roof.

Traverse diagonally left until overlooking Point Five Gully and go directly up on ice in a steep groovy ramp and wall to a snow bay and ledge system. Belay on a rounded spike (43m). Right of the belay, climb a sloping groove and more easily above to a series of steps (40m). Follow a series of indistinct corners and steps in the crest on the right of Point Five Gully.

The upper section of this climb and small parts of the lower pitches had previously been climbed by Dave Wilkinson on a variant ascent of Left Edge Route.

Left Edge Route 360m V,5**
D. Lang and N. Quinn, 9 March 1974
Quite serious, and 60m ropes are useful. Start at the foot of Point Five Gully and climb a rib to a snow patch. From the right end of the snow patch climb the left-hand groove above, then move up right to the left of two icefalls which is followed to the terrace. Either move right along the terrace and finish by Observatory

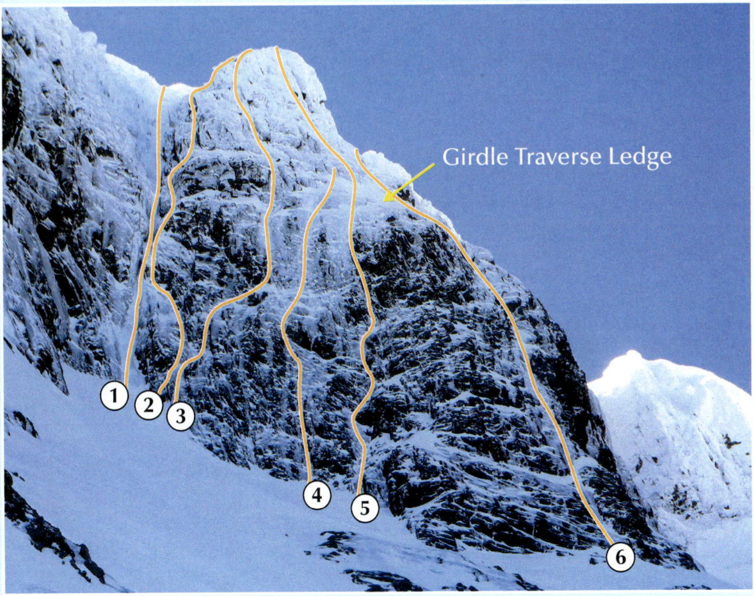

Observatory Buttress

① Point Five Gully V,5***
② Point Blank VII,6***
③ Left Edge Route V,5**
④ Matchpoint VI,5***
⑤ Rubicon Wall VI,5**
⑥ Observatory Buttress V,5***

Buttress (see below), or follow the Direct Finish (**V,5** *D. Wilkinson and M. Burt, 8 March 1980*). Climb straight up icy grooves right of the crest overlooking Point Five Gully.

Matchpoint 360m VI,5*
S. Richardson and E. Hart, 29 March 1986
Between Left Edge and Rubicon Wall are two left-facing corner systems. Climb the right-hand one (50m). Climb a short, steep snow slope to an overhanging inverted triangular wall. Traverse left and climb an icicle fringe to a snowfield. Climb the right-hand icefall above to the terrace (the left-hand one being on Left Edge Route) and continue up the buttress as for Left Edge Route's Direct Finish.

Rubicon Wall 360m VI,5**
N. Muir and A. Paul, 14 April 1977
A prominent icefall forming in a left-facing corner gives the line of this good route, taking three pitches to the Girdle Traverse ledge. Start about 20m right of Left Edge Route and take a zig-zag line more or less directly up to the terrace. Finish up grooves in the upper buttress to the final snow crest.

Observatory Buttress 360m V,5***
J.R. Marshall and R. Smith, 9 February 1960
In good conditions an obvious narrow icefall forms on the right side of the buttress. Start well to the right of Rubicon Wall below a chimney some way up the buttress. Climb the buttress by a shallow depression to reach the chimney, which usually gives the crux. There are no obvious places to belay or definite pitches. From the terrace above the chimney go up leftwards to gain the final easy crest.

North-West Face 100m (to the Girdle Traverse ledge) IV,4*
K. Crocket and C. Stead, 21 March 1975
(no photo topo)
Start halfway up the right-hand side of the buttress at a bay and follow a chimney line leading to the foot of Indicator Wall, for which this route provides a good start.

Two more lines can be made to the right of North-West Face climb. The first is 25m right (100m V,6), and the second easier climb (100m, III) takes a corner-groove at the right end of the buttress opposite and level with Tower Scoop.

Indicator Wall

Start	North Face car park, Torlundy
Time	2hr 30min
Crag base altitude	1200m
Route lengths	120–170m
Route styles	Snow-ice and thin face ice climbs, icy mixed climbs
Avalanches	The bowl under this face and Gardyloo Gully is particularly suspect after south-easterly winds.

The home of the best thin face ice climbs in the country is located above the terrace cutting the upper part of Observatory Buttress, bounded on the left by Good Friday Climb and on the right by Gardyloo Gully. Ice climbs here are the highest in the British Isles, starting at 1200m. They are fine routes when in condition, and well worth the long walk. Be prepared for poorly protected leads on steep ground!

Approach
Follow the signed footpath, steeply at first, to the top of the forest, then the well-made path to the CIC hut (1hr 30min). Carry on above the hut on the south-west side of the stream to Observatory Gully. Walk up the gully, through the narrows at 1150m, and go left to Indicator Wall.

Descent
This face finishes very close to the summit, so descend by either the Red Burn, Coire Leis or Number Four Gully.

Good Friday Climb 150m III**
G.G. MacPhee, R.W. Lovel, H.R. Shepherd and D. Edwards, 7 April 1939
Start below Gardyloo Gully and traverse left along the snow shelf until a deep wide gully can be followed for 60m to where it's blocked by a wall. Go right on ice then up to a snowfield. Go left up another gully to the plateau. A possible left-hand finish (90m, III,4) can be made from the top of the initial gully by climbing the rock wall directly and trending left above.

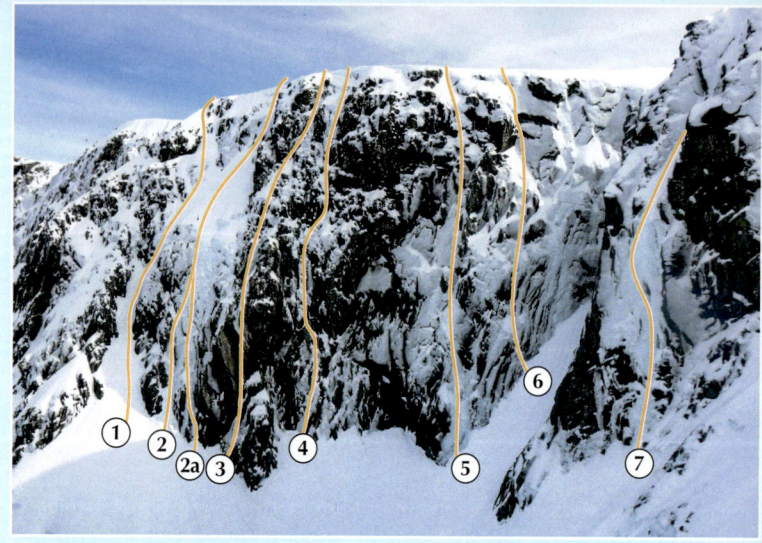

Indicator Wall

① Good Friday Climb III**
② Indicator Wall V,4***
②a Indicator Wall Right-Hand Variant V,5**
③ Riders on the Storm VI,5***
④ Albatross VI,5***
⑤ Psychedelic Wall VI,5***
⑥ Satanic Verses V,5***
⑦ Smith's Route V,5***

Indicator Wall 160m V,4*

G. Smith and T. King, February 1975

About 50 metres right of the gully of Good Friday Climb is an obvious icefall on the left side of the buttress that can be climbed by various lines. This is the first climb to form on the crag, since water dribbles down from the final gully underneath the summit of Ben Nevis, allowing ice to build here relatively easily. Start at an iced-chimney groove and climb to a ledge beneath a wall (35m). Step right and climb sustained ice to snow slopes topped by a gully (50m). Climb the gully to finish at the summit. Belay on the trig point.

A Right-Hand Variant (**160m V,5**** *D.F. Lang and N.W. Quinn, February 1975*) is steeper and more direct. Start 15 metres right of the original route.

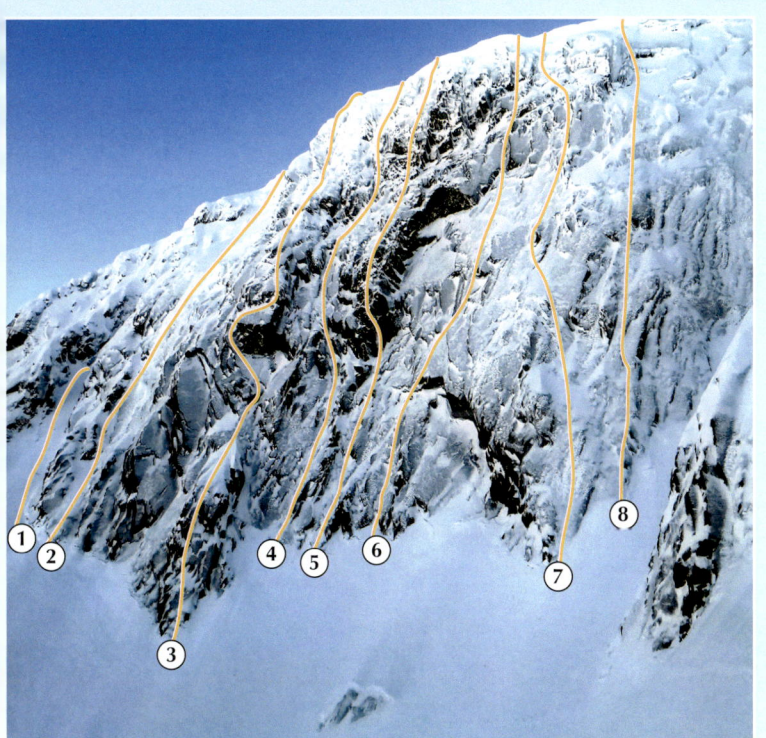

Indicator Wall

1. Good Friday Climb III**
2. Indicator Wall V,4***
3. Ship of Fools VIII,7**
4. Albatross VI,5***
5. Rime of the Ancient Mariner VII,7**
6. Stormy Petrel VII,6***
7. Psychedelic Wall VI,5***
8. Satanic Verses V,5***

Riders on the Storm 165m VI,5*

D. Hawthorn and E. Todd, April 1986
Climb the obvious buttress to the right of Indicator Wall by a series of corners and stepped icy grooves. Start just to the left of the lowest point of the buttress.

Ship of Fools 170m VIII,7**
S. Richardson and I. Small, 1 April 2007
A brilliant route. Start from the base of the pillar right of Riders on the Storm and climb the discontinuous groove up the broad rib to below the steep pillar (30m). Move up the hanging slab right of Riders on the Storm on thin ice over an overlap and second slab to a small ledge.

Continue until a 3m traverse right can be made over the overhang to the foot of the upper pillar (30m). Climb a steep break in the wall above and then right to overlook Albatross. Move left 2m along a crack before more thinly iced slabs and roofs lead to easier ground below the final icefall (60m). Climb an icy fault left of the icefall for 10m then step left onto the sharp arête. Sensational climbing up this leads to the top (30m).

Albatross 160m VI,5***
C. Higgins and M. Geddes, 21 January 1978
A very open corner descends the face of the buttress about midway between Indicator Wall and Psychedelic Wall. Climb a groove for a pitch to below twin icy grooves leading up and left. Climb these, then go up the main corner line to a ledge. A groove on the right leads to another ledge, which is followed leftwards to a groove that leads to the summit.

An alternative start on the left is possible by climbing a groove above the top left-hand corner of the snowy bay at the foot of the route. Climb the groove to a belay at a slab below an overhang (25m). Move up right into a narrow groove above the overlap on the second pitch of Albatross (30m) (**Fascist Groove 55m VI,6*** *C. Rice and R. Webb, 12 February 1983*).

Rime of the Ancient Mariner 160m VII,7**
B. Fyffe and E. Tressider, 19 March 2002
This route climbs to the obvious large hanging corner between Albatross and Stormy Petrel, breaking out left onto the arête, and taking a series of icy groves parallel to Albatross. The first two pitches are very similar to the right-hand start of Albatross, but the last two are separate.

The Direct Start (*I. Parnell and V. Scott, 24 March 2007*) is the line originally attempted by B. Fyffe and now the line usually taken. After 30m, break out left, up an obvious corner groove (protected by a crack just above). From the top of the groove step left onto a hanging slab and traverse left to belay below a hanging icicle (50m). Steep mixed moves up an overhanging groove gain the icicle and lead to the original route.

Stormy Petrel 160m VII,6***
D. Cuthbertson and R. Kane, 1982
A serious route with poor protection and one of the last climbs to form on this crag. Climb slabs right of the big open corner right of Albatross. Climb rightwards up a shallow ramp, then direct to a rock spike beneath an overlap (30m). Cross the overlap then go right horizontally over ribs to belay at the roof of an impressive corner (20m).

Climb the left wall of the corner to a large slab above. Ascend steeply right in two pitches over slabs, corners and grooves (crux), turning a roof on the right. Belay at the foot of another corner. Climb the corner then go left, weaving through bulges, and right to a shallow chimney and on to the final slopes, just left of Psychedelic Wall.

Psychedelic Wall 165m VI,5***
N. Muir and A. Paul, January 1978
A direct line starting from the rocks opposite the foot of the left edge of Gardyloo Buttress. Climb iced rocks to a snow bay. Continue up steeply to gain a left-trending snow ramp, and from near its top take a groove leading to the left edge of a large plinth (50m). Continue up slabs and an open corner to beneath thin slabs, which are followed up to a corner, high on the right (40m). Climb the corner and a chimney to a steep wall. Go left and ascend the right-hand of three corners to easier ground (45m). Climb up left to pass the cornice (30m).

Note: On the second pitch it's possible to climb directly until 5m below an icicle fringe (belay). Climb to the icicle fringe, step left and follow ice to the top.

Satanic Verses 130m V,5***
C. Cartwright and R. Clothier, 7 April 1989
Start immediately right of Psychedelic Wall and climb the left-hand of four parallel ramps that rise up right across the slabby wall. Climb to a second snow patch at 50m. Ascend grooves directly to a large snow bay (35m), belay. Climb the steep left wall and grooves above to the cornice, which may be overcome to the left if it's too large at the approach point.

Shot in the Dark 120m V,5***
M. Geddes and A. Rouse, 11 February 1978
(no photo topo)
On the left wall of Gardyloo Gully, 30m up from the toe of the buttress and right of Psychedelic Wall route. Aim initially for the oblong roof high on the wall above. Cross several rightward-slanting overlapping grooves to a short corner. Climb this, then traverse right across another groove and steep slab to finish some distance right of the oblong roof.

Gardyloo Buttress

① Gardyloo Gully II/III**
② Kellett's Route VI,6***
③ Smith's Route V,5***
④ Tower Gully I
⑤ Tower Scoop III***
⑥ Upper Tower Cascade Left III

Gardyloo Gully 170m II/III* ◆ or 🏃
G. Hastings and W.P. Haskett-Smith, 26 April 1896
The obvious direct continuation to Observatory Gully. Normally, a snow slope leads to a great chockstone about 40m below the cornice. With very little snow build-up it's easy to walk underneath the chockstone, and you might find a nice grade IV pitch of ice. With more snow there's sometimes a tunnel beneath the chockstone, which leads to a short, steep ice pitch. But in exceptional winters the whole route banks out. The cornice can be difficult.

Gardyloo Buttress

Start	North Face car park, Torlundy
Time	2hr 30min
Crag base altitude	1200m
Route lengths	120–130m
Route styles	Snow-ice
Avalanches	The slope under this buttress and Gardyloo Gully is particularly suspect after south-easterly winds.

This buttress is in a very exposed position at the top of Observatory Gully between Gardyloo Gully on the left and Tower Gully on the right. Tower Scoop can be climbed on the way to break the endless climb up Observatory Gully. The cornices can be very considerable above this buttress and may be impossible to breach.

Approach
Follow the signed footpath, steeply at first, to the top of the forest, then the well-made path to the CIC hut (1hr 30min). Carry on above the hut on the south-west side of the stream to Observatory Gully. Walk up the gully, through the narrows at 1150m, and go right to Gardyloo Buttress.

Descent
This face finishes very close to the summit, so descend either by the Red Burn, Coire Leis or Number Four Gully.

Kellett's Route 120m VI,6***
A. Paul and K. Leinster, 1980
The most obvious line up the buttress is the leftward-slanting icefall of Smith's Route leading to a snow chute in the upper part. Kellett's Route starts to the left of this and climbs directly to join Smith's Route (original) just below the chute. Finish up the left-hand ridge (**Augean Alley V,5**).

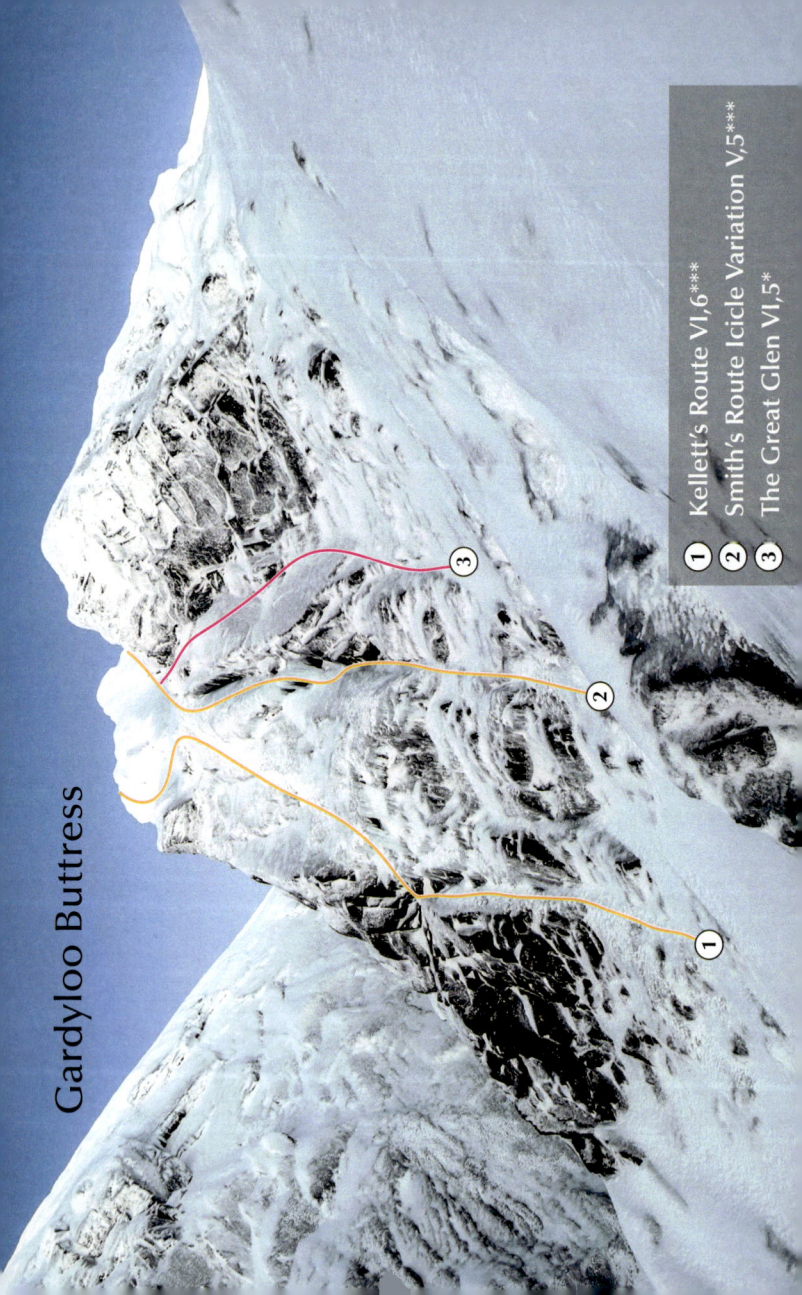

Smith's Route, Ben Nevis

Smith's Route 130m V,5***
R. Smith and J.R .Marshall, 8 February 1960
Climb leftwards up the obvious slanting ice grooves and slabs to a belay in an icy bay with an icicle fringe (45m). Move diagonally leftwards to steeper ground then back up and right to the right-hand groove. Go up this to the snow chute (40m) and an easier finish.

A variation is to climb an icicle direct from the icy bay to gain the right-hand groove, which is followed to the snow chute (**V,5*** *K.V. Crocket and C. Gilmore, February 1975*).

If the cornice is very large it may be possible to avoid it to the left by a steep wall and narrow ridge finish.

The Great Glen 130m VI,5*
P. Braithwaite and P. Moores, 12 February 1978
A serious climb – 60m ropes advised. The route follows the steep shallow groove right of Smith's Route to exit left across a gangway to belay right of Smith's Route (50m). Re-enter the groove and follow a steep arête on the right to snow.

Tower Gully above Tower Scoop

Tower Gully 120m I
G. Hastings, E.L.W. and W.P. Haskett-Smith, 25 April 1897
Follow a broad snow terrace rightwards from the foot of Gardyloo Gully, below the buttress and above Tower Scoop, to gain the gully proper. This is easy but the cornice is often large.

To the right of Tower Gully, three cascades form, starting at the foot of the gully and reaching the top close to Tower Ridge in 100m – **The Upper Tower Cascades**. The left-hand line is III, the central line IV,5 and 100m, and the right-hand line is III.

Tower Ridge East Side

Start	North Face car park, Torlundy
Time	2hr 15min
Crag base altitude	850–1150m
Route lengths	65–200m
Route styles	Snow-ice and mixed rock and ice
Avalanches	Observatory Gully is particularly suspect after south-easterly winds.

On the opposite side of Observatory Gully to Orion Face and Point Five Gully, the East Side of Tower Ridge has a selection of excellent climbs. Many are awkward to get to and more avalanche-prone than other areas, but in stable conditions you'll find good climbing and few other people here.

Tower Ridge with a good covering of snow

Approach
Follow the signed footpath, steeply at first, to the top of the forest, then the well-made path to the CIC hut (1hr 30min). Carry on above the hut on the south-west side of the stream to Observatory Gully. Walk up the gully to the face on the right.

Descent
These climbs finish at various points on Tower Ridge. If you finish above The Little Tower (Clefthanger to The Edge of Beyond) it's best to climb up Tower Ridge. If you finish below The Little Tower it's best to descend Tower Ridge. To do the latter, follow the crest down to a steep section above the first horizontal section of Tower Ridge, about level with Douglas Boulder. Make one abseil here, descend the ridge to 20m above Douglas Gap, then follow a near-horizontal shelf on the right (Observatory Gully side) which leads very easily to easy slopes heading down into Observatory Gully.

Winter climbs: Ben Nevis

Tower Scoop 75m III***
I. Clough and G. Grandison, 4 January 1961
Below the snow terrace that runs from the foot of Gardyloo Gully, beneath Gardyloo Buttress to Tower Gully, is a band of icy cliffs which almost block off Observatory Gully at 1150m. Ice forms easily here due to snow and water pouring down from above. The route follows a central ice-smear in two or three pitches. Various exits are possible from the top.

Note: To the left of this ice-smear, various short lines are possible; they're a little harder than Tower Scoop.

Tower Cleft 75m III*
G. Pratt and J. Francis, 19 February 1949
(no photo topo)
To the right of Tower Scoop is a deep cave-like cleft formed in the angle with the east flank of Tower Ridge, into which pours a lot of snow from Tower Gully. It can be very entertaining, or impossible! (Move out left to escape from the cleft and beware of trolls and pterodactyls.)

Clefthanger 90m VI,6**
D. Hawthorn and A. Paul, January 1985
(no photo topo)
Start at the foot of Tower Cleft and climb a corner system on the right wall. Climb 20m to a large ledge below a corner. Traverse right round an arête into a clean corner, which is climbed passing a large dubious flake halfway on the left. Move up left by slabs, chimney and grooves to reach the large snow ledge of The Eastern Traverse of Tower Ridge. Traverse off left, or right to finish up Tower Ridge.

> The next four climbs finish in Tower Ridge, which can be climbed or descended. Lengths of climbs are given to Tower Ridge.

Faith Healer 170m VIII,7*
I. Small and I. Parnell, 28 January 2010
An absorbing and delicate icy mixed climb with a superb but savage sting in the tail. Ice on the ledges and slabs was found very useful on the first ascent, but the final corner (avoidable) will always be hard and serious.

Climb Echo Traverse for a few metres before a delicate traverse left gains a prominent ramp, which is followed leftwards for 30m. Move up to belay at the base of the big leftward-slanting corner (50m). Climb the corner to a large snow

Tower Ridge East Side
1. Left III
2. Tower Gully I
3. Central VI,5
4. Right III
5. Tower Ridge IV,3 ***
6. Faith Healer VIII,7 *

ledge (50m). Follow the snow ledge diagonally up left until below a steep corner on the left of a rock prow.

Climb the first section of the corner for 10m on helpful turf to reach a ledge on the left. Follow this leftwards and step down a short corner to belay on in situ threads (50m). Step back right and climb the steep corner to reach the large snow ledge of The Eastern Traverse of Tower Ridge (20m). Follow Tower Ridge to the summit.

The Edge of Beyond 200m VI,6 **
D.F. Lang and C. Stead, 26 March 1994
Left of The Great Chimney (see below) is the impressively steep Echo Wall. This route starts 15m up left of the projecting left edge of Echo Wall. Gain a ledge

system and go rightwards, passing an obvious flake at 10m. Keep going right until it's possible to move up left to a ledge (40m). Go right for 6m then up an icy corner and grooves to gain a ledge on the left, then right to an icefall which ascends to easy ground (45m). A further 25m leads to the traverse ledge of East Wall Route, from which Tower Ridge can be gained to the right or by continuing straight up to the top of the Little Tower.

The Brass Monkey 135m VII,8**
T. Marsh and P. Davies, 5 December 2008
A superb mixed climb following the corner right of Echo Wall. Climb directly up slabs towards the corner (40m). Climb the short wall on the left on thin ice and follow the icy upper slab to the base of the main corner (20m). Climb the corner for 3m before strenuous moves right (crux) to reach more cracks leading to a belay (10m). The sustained offwidth crack, exiting right, leads to a good ledge (40m). Continue up the corner-crack and back-and-foot the top chimney in a superb position (25m).

The Great Chimney 65m V,6***
J.R. Marshall and R. Smith, 6 February 1960
Climbs the obvious deep chimney that arrives on the ridge 50m below the Little Tower. Ascend the chimney past a belay under a vertical block, then take the left crack and walls to the ridge.

Tower Ridge

Start	North Face car park, Torlundy
Time	2hr
Crag base altitude	850m
Route lengths	500m ascent; 1000m of climbing
Route styles	Mixed rock and ice
Avalanches	Very secure once out of Observatory Gully and East Gully of Douglas Gap

This, the most famous of the great Nevis ridges, is a magnificent expedition. Although technically easier than North East Buttress and Observatory Ridge, it should not be underestimated. The main difficulties are concentrated high up, and the whole route is exceptionally long and arduous, fully justifying its grade of IV.

Tower Ridge

① Gutless IV,5*
② 1934 Route II/III**
③ Vanishing Gully V,5***
④ Tower Ridge IV,3***
⑤ Garadh Gully II/III

Approach
Follow the signed footpath, steeply at first, to the top of the forest, then the well-made path to the CIC hut (1hr 30min). Carry on above the hut to the foot of Observatory Gully. Access can be made at 850m to the East Gully of Douglas Gap.

Descent
Red Burn, Coire Leis or Number Four Gully.

Tower Ridge

Tower Ridge 500m ascent, 1000m of climbing IV,3***
J.N. Collie, G.A. Solly and J. Collier, 30 March 1894

The normal winter route avoids Douglas Boulder by entering the foot of Observatory Gully to the left and then cutting back right to climb the East Gully to Douglas Gap (I). From the gap, an awkward 20m groove/chimney leads to the crest of the ridge, which rises gently and becomes very narrow. It's possible to reach this section and avoid the moves out of Douglas Gap by traversing in rightwards from higher up Observatory Gully along a gently rising snow ledge (II).

From the very narrow horizontal section of ridge, go out right on a gently rising steep snow ramp, past an icy groove above, until overlooking the west flank above Vanishing Gully. Cut back up left and up easier ground onto the crest. Follow the crest past The Great Chimney on the left with its obvious chockstone, to beneath the Little Tower. This usually requires three pitches of climbing, the first past a huge spike into a left-facing corner, then a step right to stay on the crest to a terrace; the second slightly left to find a groove going back right leading up to a huge flat boulder; and the third to the right of the flat boulder, moving back left on the crest to the flat top of the Little Tower.

An easier section leads to the foot of the Great Tower, an impossibly steep rock step. On the left side of the tower a very exposed and steeply banked snow

Climbing the awkward chimney out of Douglas Gap

ledge (The Eastern Traverse) is followed horizontally left, down slightly and round an edge to beneath a huge fallen-block chimney. A common mistake is to go left too early trying to find the Eastern Traverse; keep going up until you can't go straight up any further and you'll find the Eastern Traverse.

Pass the block at the top of the chimney, then follow grooves in steep walls and ledges to the top of the Great Tower with some difficulty. Follow the very narrow and exposed crest towards Tower Gap, descending slightly. Climb down into the gap by a small groove on the left (Tower Gully side). Climb straight out of the gap on the other side. The main difficulties are over once Tower Gap has been negotiated. Climb the final section of the ridge to the plateau, moving right beneath a steep wall at the top.

Note: It's possible to continue the Eastern Traverse by an exposed delicate step further left from the foot of the fallen block chimney. This leads to a very exposed and steeply banked snowfield traverse to Tower Gully and avoids the difficulties higher up. This may be a good plan if it's late in the day and the team members are tired and want to avoid a night out.

On reaching Tower Gully it's also possible to descend with care to the hut by a traverse beneath Gardyloo Buttress and on down Observatory Gully. However, neither of these options is a good idea when the avalanche hazard is considerable or high.

The first ascensionist overcame the Great Tower by taking the cliff on the west side (**Western Traverse 70m IV,4****). For fast parties on top form and blighted by queues on the Eastern Traverse, this more difficult way may offer a chance to get in front (or to avoid losing your place in the line). Not for the faint-hearted!

Douglas Boulder

Start	North Face car park, Torlundy
Time	2hr
Crag base altitude	850–950m
Route lengths	70–250m
Route styles	Mixed rock, turf and ice
Avalanches	Often a safer place to climb in a westerly wind, but cross-loading is always a problem.

DOUGLAS BOULDER

This large area of rock is the lower termination of Tower Ridge and lies immediately above the hut. It's triangular in shape and may provide good mixed climbing when higher routes are out of condition due to strong winds and avalanche potential.

Approach
Follow the signed footpath, steeply at first, to the top of the forest, then the well-made path to the CIC hut (1hr 30min). Carry on above the hut and curve right above a band of rocks to the foot of the face.

Descent
Make one short abseil into Douglas Gap then a 60m abseil down East Gully (or two abseils down West Gully if the snow is more secure).

Douglas Gap East Gully 70m I**

A straightforward ascent on steep snow. Most commonly used as a start to Tower Ridge or a descent from Douglas Boulder. Many avalanches occur in this gully

Tower Ridge below The Little Tower in early-season lean conditions

Winter climbs: Ben Nevis

Douglas Boulder

1. Turf War V,6**
2. Left-Hand Chimney V,6
3. North-West Face Route V,5
4. Gutless IV,5*
5. Cutlass VI,7**
6. SW Ridge III,4*

Douglas Boulder

since it catches snow blown from many different wind directions, especially the normal westerly. The top of the gully is at 960m.

Direct Route 215m IV,4*
J.R. Marshall and party, 1958
(no photo topo)
Start at the lowest rocks left of an obvious smooth slab. Follow a shallow groove (45m) to an open chimney. Follow this (60m) to a good ledge. Traverse right and climb steeply to the top of the Boulder. **Note:** Could be very difficult in lean conditions with no snow-ice on the ledges.

Turf War 250m V,6**
G. Hughes and J. Edwards, 21 January 2003
Based on the chimney left of Left-Hand Chimney, starting in the middle of the lower tier directly below the chimney. Climb up into a bay in the middle of the lower tier and head for a short V-groove in the second band. Climb the groove and slant right to overhangs (60m). Avoid the knobbly wall by going right then left, heading for the chimney. Climb this to a thread on a ledge (40m).

Climbing Turf War on Douglas Boulder

Continue up, then traverse delicately right across slabs to climb a right-facing corner on turf to a large block (50m). Climb a short overhanging chimney to a slab. Climb a corner to reach a ledge on the right, then back left to climb the poorly protected arête. Step right to belay (60m). Move up easy ground to the top (20m).

Left-Hand Chimney 215m V,6
R. Carrington and J.R. Marshall, February 1972
This route climbs the left-hand chimney (see next route). Start from the left and traverse over snow from the lowest rocks. Gain the chimney by a short vertical wall and follow it with sustained difficulties to the top. An alternative start in two pitches takes a left-trending line heading for a black overhanging wall, avoided on the right.

North-West Face Route 215m V,5
A. Slater and G. Grassam, February 1980
Seen from the CIC hut, three chimneys form an inverted 'N' on the Douglas Boulder. This route follows the central, diagonal chimney. Gain the chimney, which is followed until 6m below a chockstone. Traverse slabs to a rib on the right and climb up to regain the top of the chimney. Follow snow ramps and grooves to the South West Ridge which is followed to the top. Ice is required in the chimney.

Right-Hand Chimney 215m VI,7
O. Metherell and G. Hughes, 19 December 2004
(no photo topo)
Starting directly under the chimney in a bay, climb to the foot of the chimney (45m). Bridge up the first overhang and belay on the left (15m). Follow the chimney, turning an overhang on the right to a recess. Exit left up slabs to above a second recess (50m). Traverse right to SW Ridge which is followed to the top.

Gutless 150m (to South West Ridge) IV,5*
P. McKenna and D. Sanderson, March 1979
Left of Cutlass is a prominent deep chimney. Climb a pitch to the chimney that can form ice at its base, then climb the chimney itself, exiting right into a turfy groove to a rightward-sloping ledge (90m). Climb this ledge rightwards to South West Ridge and follow this to the top of Douglas Boulder.

Cutlass 145m to South West Ridge VI,7** or
A. Clarke and J. Main, 24 March 1989
The clean-cut corner 30 metres left of the South West Ridge. Climb a pitch to the corner, the corner to a ledge, then a chimney and a cracked wall to reach the

Douglas Boulder

South West Ridge which is followed to the top. This is positive and well protected in rocky mixed conditions, but the corner sometimes forms good ice which makes the climbing easier and protection harder to find.

Jacknife 90m to South West Ridge IV,6
J. Baird and A. Turner, 26 November 2003
(no photo topo)
The first right-facing corner groove left of the South West Ridge. Starting to the left, climb slabs to the groove (50m). Climb the groove and the right crack to a ledge (25m). Climb a crack and loose flake then go right to the South West Ridge (15m) which is followed to the top.

South West Ridge 180m III,4*
J.Y. McDonald and H.W. Turnbull, March 1934
Start up Douglas Gap West Gully and step left onto the crest of the ridge bounding the left side of the gully. Steep steps up short walls lead to an easier section. Pass a tower on the left and find grooves and ledges to the top. A harder start climbs a groove on the left at the base of the ridge (IV,5).

Douglas Gap West Gully 180m I**
A straightforward ascent on steep snow with better scenery than the East Gully. A good low-level outing is the combination of Douglas Gap West Gully followed by the descent of the Douglas Gap East Gully.

South West Ridge of Douglas Boulder

CLIMBS FROM COIRE NA CISTE

Generally, the climbs in Coire na Ciste are shorter and less committing than those in Observatory Gully. However, it also holds some of the hardest winter climbs in the world.

From the CIC hut there are several approach routes into Coire na Ciste, and the time taken to reach the higher routes can be as much as an hour. About 200 metres south-west of the CIC hut is a steep rocky bluff with deep gorges on its left- and right-hand sides. The most straightforward approach into Coire na Ciste is by the slopes right (north-west) of the right-hand gorge. This approach can be reached from a crossing of the stream a few hundred metres below the hut and passes underneath Number Five Gully – which is a notorious avalanche trap, with the runout zone occasionally reaching the lower corrie at 750m.

The left-hand gorge has been the scene of some fatal avalanche accidents over the years. When approaching routes on the left (south) side of the corrie, it's best to skirt this gorge on the right, where it looks easiest, and traverse in high above the gorge beneath Garadh Buttress. Vanishing Gully area can be approached by moving in from close beneath the Douglas Boulder, well above the gorge on its left.

The major features of Coire na Ciste when seen from the hut are, from left to right: Tower Ridge and Secondary Tower Ridge, Garadh Gully and Buttress (Garadh na Ciste), the thin gullies of Number Two Gully and Comb Gully (exits unseen), the triangle of Comb Buttress, the obvious gap of Number Three Gully (lowest point on the skyline), Creag Coire na Ciste, the Trident Buttress area, and Number Five Gully on the right with Moonlight Gully Buttress at its base on the left.

Tower Ridge West Side

Start	North Face car park, Torlundy
Time	2hr 15min
Crag base altitude	900–950m
Route lengths	95–230m
Route styles	Snow-ice and icy mixed
Avalanches	The Left-Hand Gulch is an obvious terrain trap that lies beneath all of these climbs. The slopes above have caused very bad accidents and avalanches.

Being clearly visible from the walk in and having a shorter approach than many other areas, these are popular climbs when in condition. The icy mixed climbs on Pinnacle Buttress to the left of Glover's Chimney offer long routes in an excellent position and deserve greater popularity. All these climbs finish at various places on Tower Ridge, which then needs to be climbed or descended. Route lengths are to Tower Ridge.

Approach
Follow the signed footpath, steeply at first, to the top of the forest, then the well-made path to the CIC hut (1hr 30min). For access to the climbs Fawlty Towers to 1931 Route, carry on above the hut and curve right above a band of rocks, then cross snow slopes above the Left-Hand Gulch. For access to Italian Climb and Garadh Gully, go into Coire na Ciste and traverse across from the lochans.

Descent
These climbs finish at various points on Tower Ridge. Below the Little Tower, it's best to descend Tower Ridge by following the crest down to a steep section above the first horizontal section of Tower Ridge, about level with Douglas Boulder. Make one abseil here, descend the ridge to 20m above Douglas Gap, then follow a near-horizontal shelf on the right (Observatory Gully side) which leads very easily to easy slopes heading down into Observatory Gully.

The Chute finishes above the Little Tower, from where it's best to climb up Tower Ridge.

Fawlty Towers 155m II/III
T. McAulay and N. Muir, 2 April 1980
Take the first icefall right of Douglas Gap West Gully and follow slightly rightwards to the first narrow crest of Tower Ridge. At the start, the right-hand option offers a harder pitch of ice climbing (IV), and further variation above is possible.

1934 Route 200m II/III**
J.Y. MacDonald and H.W. Turnbull, March 1934
Start 45m right of Douglas Gap West Gully, further right again than Fawlty Towers. Climb via grooves and snow bays until a shallow gully can be gained via icy slabs

Tower Ridge West Side

① Gutless VI,5*
② Fawlty Towers II/III
③ 1934 Route II/III**
④ Vanishing Gully V,5***
⑤ Fish Eye Chimney V,5
⑥ 1931 Route IV,4
⑦ Italian Right-Hand IV,4***
⑧ The Chute V,4**
⑨ Garadh Gully II/III
⑩ Broad Gully II
⑪ Glover's Chimney III,4**
⑫ The White Line IV,3**
⑬ Raeburn's Easy Route II/III*
⑭ The Cascade IV,5**

on the right (50m). This gully leads to the snow shelf above the hard pitches of Vanishing Gully, which in turn leads with one short icy section to Tower Ridge below the Little Tower.

Vanishing Gully 200m V,5***
R. Marshall and G. Tiso, 15 January 1961
Start at an icefall about 100m right of Douglas Gap West Gully and climb to a cave with good belays. The cave is 5m to the right of a collection of pegs and 3m lower down. The entrance sometimes ices over but it's worth finding because it

Tower Ridge below the Little Tower with a good cover of snow

makes one of the most comfortable belays on Ben Nevis. Climb out of the cave on very steep ice and continue to easier snow slopes. These lead right, past one short icy section, to Tower Ridge below the Little Tower. It's quicker to descend the ridge from this point than to carry on up.

At the top of the second long pitch, a shallow gully over a snow crest on the left (1934 Route) can be abseiled leftwards in two pitches. This is a good alternative if short on time or good weather.

Pirate 200m IV,4

M. Duff and A. Nisbet, 3 January 1986
(no photo topo)
This is 20m right of Vanishing Gully. Move easily up left on a snow ramp, over a wall and into a small left-facing corner (45m). Climb slabs left of the corner to a steep wall bounded on the right by a large corner. Go right beneath the corner and ascend the rib right of the second corner, then slant left into a vertical corner (45m). Follow this corner, then go right into a shallow chimney (30m) and grooves to the crest of Secondary Tower Ridge (45m). Snow then leads to Tower Ridge below the Little Tower.

Fish Eye Chimney 150m V,5

N. Holmes and D. Lampard, January 1987

Start just left of 1931 Route and traverse on mixed ground awkwardly up left to the base of the chimney. Climb the chimney (50m) and a large groove to the crest of Secondary Tower Ridge. Snow leads to Tower Ridge below the Little Tower.

1931 Route 125m IV,4

G. Wallace and R. Shaw, 21 January 1961

Start in a bay 150m right of Douglas Gap West Gully, formed by a steep buttress from which two chimneys lead to the crest of Secondary Tower Ridge. Climb the right-hand chimney for three short pitches past various chockstones to the large snowfield of 1934 Route, which is followed to Tower Ridge below the Little Tower. The left-hand chimney is **Fat Boy Slim VI,6***.

The Italian Climb 180m III*

J. Marshall, A. MacCorquodale and G. Ritchie, January 1958
(no photo topo)

Continuing along beneath the west side of Tower Ridge you come to a deep gully bounded on the left by a prominent two-tier rib. Climb the gully; after a starting pitch, easy snow leads to another pitch giving access to a huge recess. Traverse right and ascend an easy snow slope (frequent avalanche danger) to Tower Ridge. The true finish through the huge overhang above the recess is **The Italian Job VIII,9***.

Italian Climb – Right-Hand 180m IV,4***

S. Belk and I. Fulton, February 1973

A popular variation which takes the obvious icefall parallel to and right of the main gully. Climb the first pitch as for Italian Climb, then the icefall is followed in one long pitch to a good belay. Many parties abseil from the end of the difficult pitch in order to save a long ascent of Tower Ridge. In this way it's possible to do another route, such as Vanishing Gully, plus another abseil descent.

The Chute 230m V,4**

J.R. Marshall, R.N. Campbell and R. Holt, February 1965

About 40m right of Italian Climb, this route does not often come into condition, but when it does an excellent route is the result. Climb by an extremely steep entry pitch, and go left then right into a groove which is followed to a ledge (45m) that leads across a steep wall into a small gully (35m). Traverse up right to beneath a steep ice wall (35m). Climb the ice (25m) and the gully beyond (65m) to the base of a steep buttress. Move easily right into Broad Gully, which can be descended to the corrie or ascended to Tower Ridge.

Garadh Gully 95m II/III 🧗 or ◈
I. Clough and M. Burke, 16 February 1958
Starts just right of Italian Climb and separates the steep little buttress of Garadh na Ciste from Tower Ridge. Early in the season, before much snowfall, cascade ice can form here giving lovely grade IV climbing. Later on the gully fills with snow, leaving short ice steps (easily seen from the CIC hut). The flat top of The Garadh leads very nicely to the foot of Broad Gully, Glover's Chimney and other climbs in that area.

Pinnacle Buttress

Start	North Face car park, Torlundy
Time	2hr 30min
Crag base altitude	1100–1150m
Route lengths	200–240m
Route styles	Snow-ice and icy mixed
Avalanches	The slopes running up to all of the routes in this area of Ben Nevis are prone to serious avalanche risk after periods of strong winds and/or heavy snowfall.

A long, steep snow slope tapers up from Coire na Ciste between The Garadh and the prominent triangular buttress of The Comb, with The Cascade and Number Two Gully at its top. Pinnacle Buttress is found directly above The Garadh and goes up to the Great Tower of Tower Ridge. It is a spectacular place to climb and is home to some fantastic long climbs.

Approach
Follow the signed footpath, steeply at first, to the top of the forest, then the well-made path towards the CIC hut (1hr 30min). Cross the stream 150m below the hut and walk up into Coire na Ciste. Go through a band of rocks under Number Five Gully then diagonally left to the lochans. Head up towards Number Two Gully and left to the foot of the face.

PINNACLE BUTTRESS

Descent
Pinnacle Buttress finishes on the Great Tower of Tower Ridge and route lengths are given to this point. From here, either climb Tower Ridge past Tower Gap to the top (IV,3***) or keep traversing from the Eastern Traverse to the foot of Tower Gully and return down Observatory Gully.

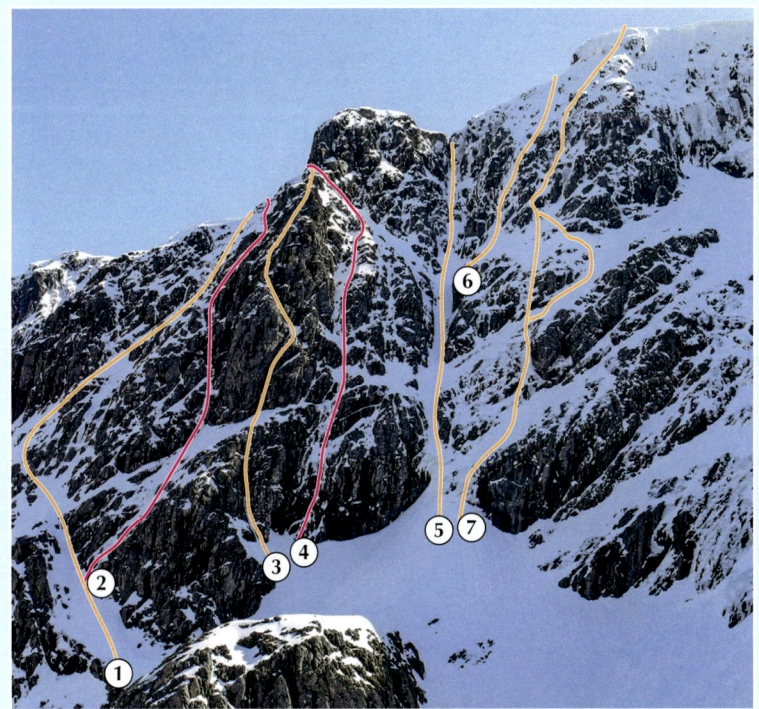

Pinnacle Buttress of The Tower

1. Broad Gully II
2. Fatal Error IV,4**
3. Stringfellow VI,6**
4. Pinnacle Buttress Direct V,5**
5. Glover's Chimney III,4**
6. The Gutter IV,4**
7. The White Line IV,3***

Broad Gully 230m II
I.S. Clough and M. Burke, 16 February 1958
From the top of Garadh Gully, follow the line of least resistance up leftwards, skirting the large buttress above (Pinnacle Buttress) to the crest of Tower Ridge below the Great Tower. A nice adventure.

Fatal Error 230m IV,4**
G. Dudley and S. Richardson, 24 March 1996
Starts 50m up Broad Gully. Climb up over flakes and a short wall to the snow terrace (60m). Climb an icy slab to enter the prominent gully line on the left flank of the buttress above. Go up the gully to a steepening (35m), then left to the end of a ramp and block belay (5m). Go right along an upper ramp to regain the gully, which is climbed to its end, followed by an ascending leftward traverse to the left edge of the buttress (45m). Ascend the edge of the buttress to a snowy ledge (35m). Go left onto Tower Ridge 30m below the Great Tower (50m).

Stringfellow 240m VI,6**
C. Cartwright and S. Richardson, 11 March 1996
Start 30 metres left of Pinnacle Buttress Direct below a shallow gully. Climb the gully to the terrace, which is crossed to below a rake slanting left to right up the lower section of the buttress (50m). Climb the rake to its right end over a steep wall to a cave belay (50m). Climb up left via a shallow gully to a platform just left of the crest (25m).

A short icy wall cut by a crack is climbed from the right of the platform, followed by the rightmost of twin grooves above. Climb up to a block, which is climbed by a wide crack on its left, then on up to a belay on the crest of the buttress – a hard pitch (40m). A step down is taken into a short gully on the right, which is climbed to the crest (25m). Carry on up the crest to the foot of the Great Tower on Tower Ridge.

Pinnacle Buttress Direct 200m V,5**
R. Clothier and G. Armstrong, March 1989
Start midway between Glover's Chimney and Broad Gully in a snow bay, below an icefall and an obvious groove in the upper buttress. Follow a break up on the right side. Climb a ramp, then an icy wall followed by the main groove-line to the Great Tower.

Climbing Glover's Chimney

Glover's Chimney 200m III,4**
G.G. MacPhee, G.C. Williams and D. Henderson, 17 March 1935
Starts above Garadh na Ciste and follows a long couloir leading to a chimney below the Tower Gap. The entry is made by an icefall, often over 35m high and very steep, usually climbed from left to right. The final chimney is the crux. The climb finishes in Tower Gap. It's possible to descend from here into Observatory Gully and climb another route if time allows.

Goodeve's Buttress and the Cascades

Start	North Face car park, Torlundy
Time	2hr 30min
Crag base altitude	1100–1150m
Route lengths	50–275m
Route styles	Snow-ice and snow patch cascade ice
Avalanches	The slopes running up to all of the routes in this area of Ben Nevis are prone to serious avalanche risk after periods of strong winds and/or heavy snowfall.

The area from Glover's Chimney to the Upper Cascades is called Goodeve's Buttress. All but the initial icefall of The White Line was originally descended then climbed by T.E. Goodeve, C. Inglis-Clark and J.H.A. McIntyre on 28 December 1907 on an epic escape from Tower Ridge.

Approach
Follow the signed footpath, steeply at first, to the top of the forest, then the well-made path towards the CIC hut (1hr 30min). Cross the stream 150m below the hut and walk up into Coire na Ciste. Go through a band of rocks under Number Five Gully then diagonally left to the lochans. Head up towards Number Two Gully and left to the foot of the face.

Descent
Goodeve's Buttress finishes close to the top of Tower Ridge. Descend by the Red Burn or Number Four Gully.

The Gutter 275m IV,4**
Climb halfway up Glover's Chimney until an icefall (obvious from below) can be gained by a steep snow ramp on the right. Climb the icefall (50m) to easier ground and finish by the final section of Tower Ridge.

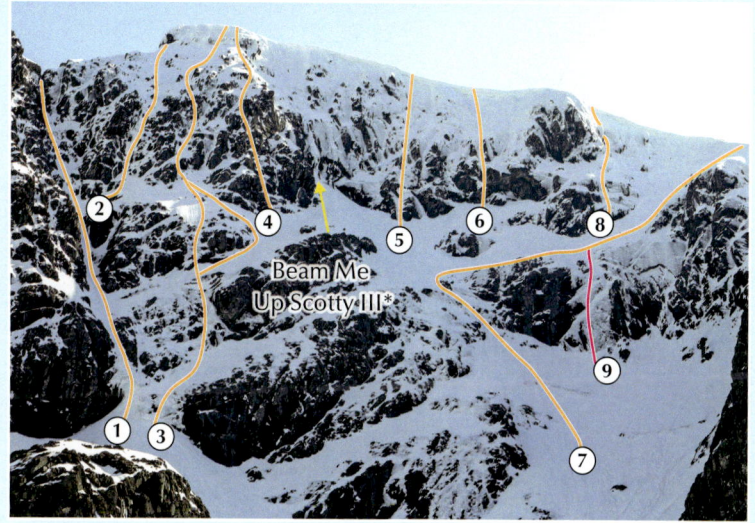

Goodeve's Buttress

① Glover's Chimney III,4**
② The Gutter IV,4**
③ The White Line IV,3***
④ Goodytwoshoes V,6*
⑤ Upper Cascades V,6**
⑥ La Panthere Rose VI,6*
⑦ Raeburn's Easy Route II/III*
⑧ Experts Choice III,4*
⑨ The Cascade IV,5**

The White Line 275m IV,3***
M. Geddes and H. Gillespie, 18 March 1971
An excellent, long climb of seven or eight pitches. Climb the icefall to the right of Glover's Chimney and continue to the right of the Chimney on sustained ice to a rightward-slanting snow ledge. Climb an icefall to a snowfield (or right up snow and back left). Traverse the snowfield leftwards to climb a gully. Climb a chimney leading left out of the gully then finish up snow slopes to the right of Tower Ridge.

Goodytwoshoes 140m V,6*
S. Richardson and C. Cartwright, 6 April 2002
Start below a gully in the centre of the face. Climb the gully to an alcove at 40m, then pull right over an overhang to a gully leading to a steep wall (50m). Climb

the right-hand of two cracks in the wall for 10m before stepping to the left-hand crack which leads to easier ground. Move up and right up a couloir to a huge spike (40m). The icy groove of Hale Bopp Groove leads to the top (50m).

Beam Me Up Scotty 155m III*
R.G. Reid and I. Crofton, March 1987
Start in a narrow snow bay above the beginning of the rightward traverse of Raeburn's Easy Route and left of Upper Cascade. Follow a ramp-line right before climbing icy grooves straight up. This route may coincide with an earlier line by R. Harvey and A. Meekin, 1986 (see Raeburn's Easy Route).

Upper Cascades 125m V,6**
G. Perroux and J-P. Destercke, April 1991
About 100m above The Cascade (see below), several steep ice lines form. About six separate lines can be found, all at about the same grade and all in the same style. Take your pick and follow your nose.

Adieu and Farewell 100m V,5
S. Richardson and C. Cartwright, 6 April 2002
(no photo topo)
Named in memory of Godefroy Perroux. Starting in the cave stance of Le Panthere Rose, this climb starts with steep mixed moves to reach the icefall (rarely formed) to the left of that route. Finish up icy grooves through mixed ground.

Le Panthere Rose 50m VI,6*
R. Clothier, B. Goodlad, G. Perroux and F. Bossier, 11 April 1993
Above The Cascade at the top of the snowfield is a large overhung rocky bay. Climb the icefall that forms a detached vertical column of ice on its left side, followed by easier ground in the headwall. The cornice may be a problem.

Expert's Choice 150m III,4*
G. Perroux and party, 1990s
The most popular route to the plateau after climbing The Cascade. Go up and slightly right from the top of The Cascade to climb icy mixed ground and the icefall running down the right side of the steep upper buttress.

Raeburn's Easy Route 250m II/III*
SMC party, April 1920
The most obvious feature to the right of Glover's Chimney is the deep slit of Number Two Gully with The Comb to its right. To the left of Number Two Gully

Goodeve's Buttress and the Cascades

is Number Two Gully Buttress, and to the left again an indefinite wall up which this route winds. Make a long traverse leftwards out of Number Two Gully across a snow slope beneath The Cascade and aiming for a point where the crags peter out. Climb a low-angled ice pitch then follow a snow shelf back right for a long way until a shallow gully gives access to the plateau 50 metres left of Number Two Gully Buttress.

The Cascade 50m V,5**

The obvious steep, broad icefall below the right traverse of Raeburn's Easy Route. This route gives a sustained pitch and makes a good start to the harder climbs on the Upper Cascade area. It's clearly seen from low down in the corrie and forms quickly. It was graded IV previously due to its short length, but it's a serious pitch and feels considerably harder than Green Gully, for example.

Five-Finger Discount 135m IV,4**

M.G. Geddes and C. Higgins, 4 February 1978

In the corner between the slabby face of Raeburn's Easy Route and Number Two Gully Buttress is a deep groove, defining the left edge of the buttress. Climb the groove till it bends left and steepens. Move left up an edge to a small gully and the finish.

Burrito's Groove 135m IV,5**

M.G. Geddes and C. Higgins, 8 April 1978

Between Five-Finger Discount and Number Two Gully Buttress is a distinct groove leading directly up the buttress, well seen from below Comb Buttress. Climb the groove, passing an overhang on the left (45m).

JP is Back 120m III,4

Twenty metres to the right of Burrito's Groove. Start up a steep iced slab, which is bounded on its right by a steep rock wall leading to a snow ledge. Follow another similar pitch, then trend right from time to time to avoid overlaps.

> The slopes running up to all of the routes in this area of Ben Nevis are prone to serious avalanche risk after periods of strong winds and/or heavy snowfall.

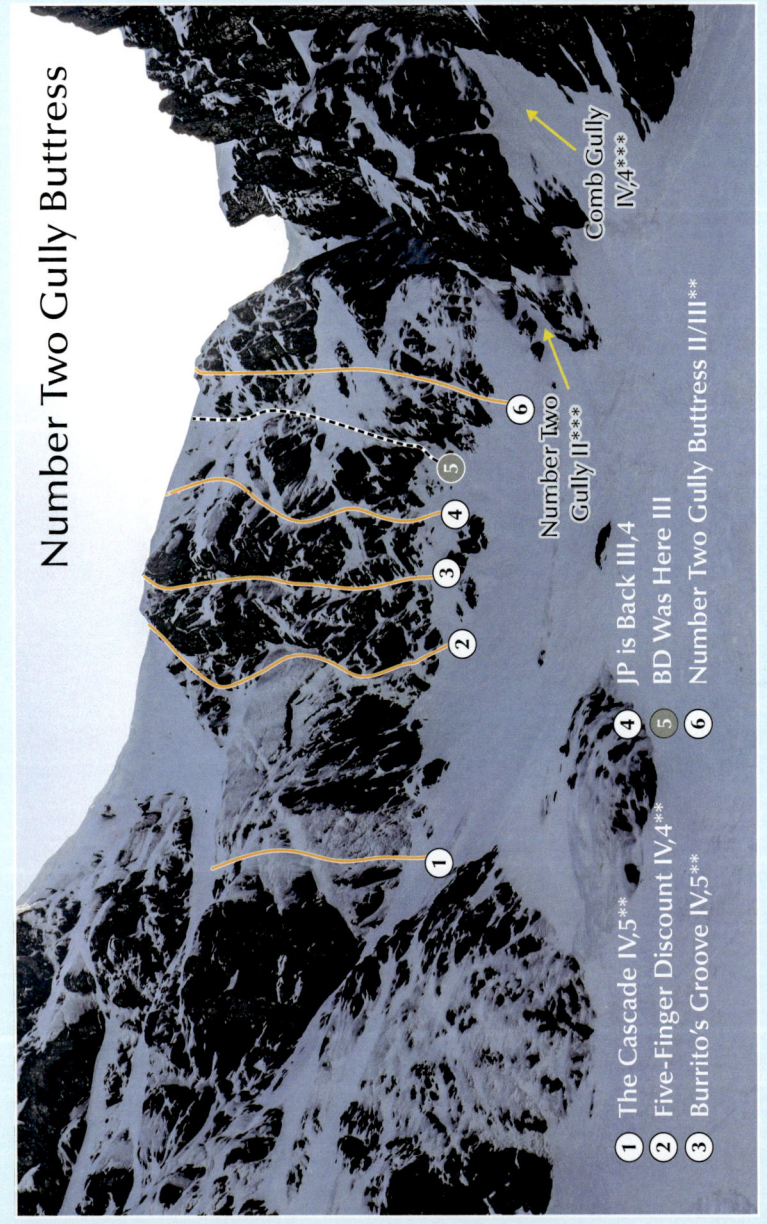

Number Two Gully Buttress 120m II/III**

J.R. Marshall, L.S. Lovat and A.H. Hendry, 23 March 1958
Immediately to the left of Number Two Gully. Steep snow and occasionally iced rocks lead to a shelf below a vertical upper wall. A short but difficult ice pitch on the left leads to easier ground.

Number Two Gully 120m II*** or

J. Collier, G. Hastings and W.C. Slingsby, Easter 1896
The hardest and possibly the most interesting of the easier gullies on Ben Nevis, this is found to the left of The Comb, often with a steep ice column at its base on the right. Above the introductory slopes it becomes a deep slot, generally a straightforward but steadily steepening slope. It can offer an ice pitch early in the season before there's much snow. The cornice is often quite difficult and usually turned on the left.

The Comb

Start	North Face car park, Torlundy
Time	2hr 15min
Crag base altitude	1050–1100m
Route lengths	100–250m
Route styles	Snow-ice and mixed rock and ice
Avalanches	Number Two and Number Three gullies often avalanche and large cornices grow above these faces.

This obvious triangular buttress is named after the narrow crenellated ridge at its top. The classic snow-ice lines of Comb Gully and Green Gully are reliable and popular. In between, the overhanging buttress is the playground of a very few elite climbers.

Approach
Follow the signed footpath, steeply at first, to the top of the forest, then the well-made path towards the CIC hut (1hr 30min). Cross the stream 150m below the hut and walk up into Coire na Ciste. Go through a band of rocks

> under Number Five Gully then diagonally left to the lochans. Walk above the west side of the lochans then curve left at 970m to a good gearing-up spot. The Comb is directly above (south).
>
> **Descent**
> Descend by the Red Burn or Number Four Gully.

Comb Gully Buttress 150m IV,4**
I. Fulton and D. Gardner, 3 January 1971
Immediately right of Number Two Gully is Comb Gully Buttress, with Comb Gully on its right side. Climb ice from just below the entrance to Number Two Gully to gain the central snowfield. At the top left of the snowfield, climb ice-filled grooves, left and then right, in two or three pitches to the top.

Clough's Chimney 150m VI,6*
I.S. Clough and J.M. Alexander, 8 January 1960
The central snowfield leads up to the foot of a prominent chimney containing a large downward-pointing spike. Follow this chimney and the left-slanting chimney above. Climbs well as a mixed route with no ice.

Roaring Forties 150m V,5**
D. Lang and C. Stead, 28 February 1988
Gain a belay right of Clough's Chimney. Follow the deep groove 15m right of the chimney to a ledge on the left (40m). Traverse left to the obvious V-groove, which is climbed to the top (50m), ideally on snow-ice.

Comb Gully 160m IV,4**
F.G. Stangle, R. Morsley and P.A. Small, 12 April 1938
The obvious gully running up the left side of The Comb, just about as quick to form and as reliable as Green Gully. Easy snow leads to the narrows, from where a chimney leads to a bay. Above is a short, steep wall which often gives the crux. Easy ground then leads to the top. It's best to climb a short initial pitch in the narrows to good belays on the right wall, followed by a long second pitch to good belays above all major difficulties, and a final snow pitch.

The Comb – Left Flank 160m IV,4*
G.E. Little and R. Richardson, 21 February 1981
Starts 20m above Hesperides Ledge in Comb Gully, just above the first narrows. Step steeply out right and climb the steep icefall to a belay in a shallow gully

Classic snow-ice climbing in Comb Gully

(50m) and then on to the top. The steep ice pitch may be split with a belay on the right wall.

Hesperides Ledge 200m III*
J.R. Marshall, J. Stenhouse and D. Haston, 12 February 1959
Follows the lower 75m of Comb Gully and then a relatively easy but highly spectacular steep curving shelf, which leads rightwards across the wall to the crest of The Comb. This very narrow blocky crest is climbed to the top.

The Good Groove 200m VII,7**
S.M. Richardson and R.D. Everett, 27 March 1993
A tiered ramp cuts the wall above Hesperides Ledge. Gain the start of the ramp and move left along the second narrow ramp to a corner, which is followed to a belay at the end of a curving groove just right of The Comb – Left Flank (40m). Climb slabs right of the groove to a small stance below a steep tapering corner (25m). Climb the corner with difficulty, eventually arriving at a platform (25m). Climb the wall above to an arête (50m).

Tower Face of The Comb

1. Comb Gully Buttress IV,4**
2. Clough's Chimney VI,6*
3. Roaring Forties V,5**
4. The Comb Left Flank IV,4*
5. The Good Groove VII,7**
6. Hesperides Ledge III*
7. Quisling Wall IV,6*
8. Tower Face of The Comb VI,6***
9. Bell's Chimney: Variation V,

Tower Face of The Comb 250m VI,6*
R. Smith and R. Holt, 1 January 1959
A difficult and sustained mixed climb, which is open to much variation/mystery, and benefits from plenty of snow-ice on the face. A large ledge splits the buttress diagonally at one-third height from left to right. From the bottom left end of this ledge, move up to another ledge running parallel to the lower ledge, and go right to the foot of an obvious groove (30m).

Traverse a little further right before climbing a steep, slabby groove back left to broken blocks and the base of a steep wall (25m). Step left and ascend the groove and cracked wall above (30m) crux. From this point, Bell's Chimney Variation works up right (see below). Climb the snow patch above to a steep wall, which is passed on the left (30m). Steep broken ground now leads up and right to a snow ledge beneath steep walls (20m). Traverse right to the buttress crest and up to easier ground above.

Bell's Chimney: Variation 250m V,5
R. Everett and S. Richardson, 31 March 1996
From the belay of Tower Face of The Comb after the 30m hard pitch, work up and right via short, steep walls and grooves to the base of an obvious chimney (25m). Climb the chimney to exit right onto an awkward rib. Follow the awkward crest to where it eases and joins the original line coming in from the left (45m).

Don't Die of Ignorance 200m XI,11
D. MacLeod and J. French, 16 March 2008
A free ascent based on the 1987 aid route, taking a more direct line at the crux. Climbed ground up, onsight, at the sixth attempt. Follow the easy snow and ice ramps to a belay before the ledge runs out (30m). Step down into the wide undercut crack and tin-opener tenuously to the arete (cams, bulldog). A foot-off tin-opener move gains access to the rib on the right (peg). The aid route continues along the crack.

Quit the crack and climb leftwards on the tenuous wall above to gain a ledge. Go right beneath a steep groove and move round its base to gain a thin crack in an open slab. Climb this to below a chimney (30m). Step up and right to gain the huge open groove and follow this with sustained interest to a hanging belay on the right at a large block (55m). Step left and follow the crest, moving left again across a fault to a ledge and good belay at a flake (25m).

Mantel the flake and step right to regain the crest, which is followed to the snow crest on the apex of the buttress (good spike belay, 20m). Climb the easy snow crest to a steepening (60m). Climb snow grooves in the buttress crest to a flat knife-edge (40m). The knife-edge leads easily to the plateau (15m).

Anubis 200m XII
D. MacLeod, 26 February 2010
(no photo topo)
Takes a 40m cracked prow in the centre of the face and ice grooves above, following the line of the summer E8. The hardest route on the mountain and one of the hardest naturally protected climbs in the world.

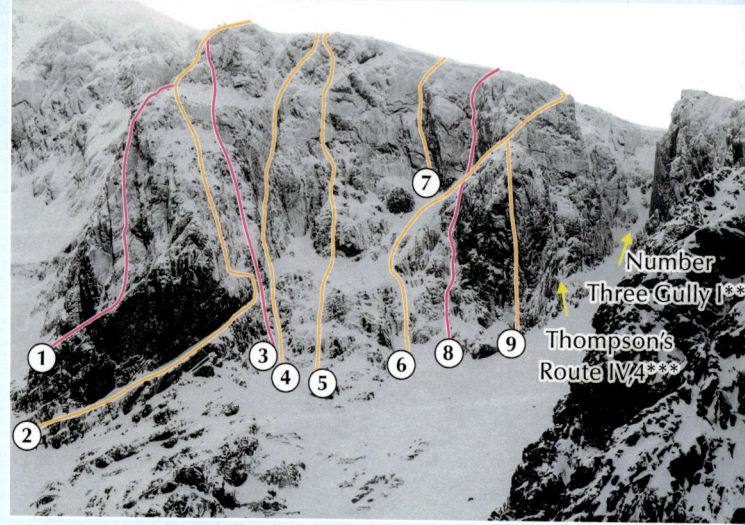

The Comb and Number Three Gully Buttress

① Don't Die of Ignorance XI,11
② Pigott's Route V,6*
③ Mercury V,5**
④ Green Gully IV,4***
⑤ Diana V,5*
⑥ Number Three Gully Buttress III***
⑦ Quickstep V,5**
⑧ Two-Step corner V,5**
⑨ The Knuckleduster VIII,9***

Pigott's Route 245m V,6*
J. Marshall and R. Smith, 12 February 1960
From the CIC hut an obvious large ramp/ledge can be seen cutting up from left to right across the bottom section of the triangle of Comb Buttress. Follow this ramp up right till beneath a flake chimney with a large boulder just down from its base (35m left of Green Gully). Climb the chimney (hard) and traverse left into steep ice-filled grooves which are followed to the buttress crest.

Mercury 180m V,5**

M. Hind and J. Christie, 26 January 1985

Ascends the rightmost of four parallel grooves just left of Green Gully. Climb Green Gully for 10m and move left around a rib to belay beneath a chimney with a chockstone (20m, might be possible to climb direct). Climb up and traverse left (loose) past a small overhang to the main groove-line on the left (30m, crux). Continue up more easily to the crest of the buttress.

Green Gully 180m IV,4***

H. Raeburn and E. Phildius, April 1906

A classic climb on snow-ice that forms readily and is one of the most reliable and first-to-form ice climbs on Ben Nevis. It takes the obvious gully running up the right side of Comb Buttress. The first pitch changes in character from steep ice to a grade III snow slope, depending on build-up. Above, there are normally three good ice pitches with belays on the right side of the gully wall. When the gully opens out to a steep snow slope near the top, three exits present themselves: easy snow to the right; a fine direct ice pitch; or a traverse left to the ridge. If the cornice presents a problem, one of these finishes should fix it!

Number Three Gully Buttress

Start	North Face car park, Torlundy
Time	2hr 15min
Crag base altitude	1050–1100m
Route lengths	60–200m
Route styles	Snow-ice and mixed rock and ice
Avalanches	Number Three Gully often avalanches and large cornices grow above these faces, especially above Quickstep and Two-Step Corner.

Number Three Gully Buttress is the name given to the steep cliffs extending right from Green Gully to Number Three Gully. The very steep rocks at the left-hand side of the mouth of Number Three Gully are the home of some of the best mixed routes on the mountain. Being high up, this area provides reliable climbing, and the nature of the rock is relatively helpful for rocky mixed climbing once the routes are frozen and rimed up.

> **Approach**
> Follow the signed footpath, steeply at first, to the top of the forest, then the well-made path towards the CIC hut (1hr 30min). Cross the stream 150m below the hut and walk up into Coire na Ciste. Go through a band of rocks under Number Five Gully then diagonally left to the lochans. Walk above the west side of the lochans, then curve left at 970m to a good gearing-up spot. The Comb is directly above (south) and Number Three Gully Buttress is on its right side, left of Number Three Gully.
>
> **Descent**
> Descend by the Red Burn or Number Four Gully.

Tramp 180m IV,4*

R. Clothier and C. Cartwright, January 1987
(no photo topo)
Start diagonally right up the icefall right of Green Gully. Cross the snow ledge above to beneath a left-facing chimney which is hidden from below. Ascend the chimney and the huge pedestal above and then a corner-crack which leads to the groove beside a rib right of Green Gully. Climb the groove and then the arête beside Green Gully, moving right at the top to a cornice which can be huge.

Diana 195m V,5*

M. Duff and J. Tinker, 16 February 1985
Start further right than Tramp. Climb the icefall direct past a horizontal snow band to belay beneath a steep rock wall (55m). On the left, climb a groove/chimney past a roof/chockstone to another snow bank and huge block stance (45m). Follow corners to beneath a huge right-facing corner (30m). Go up to the overlap and pull onto the right wall of the corner, then go straight up on steep thin ice to easier ground (45m). Follow snow to a possible large cornice finish.

Vulture 180m V,5**

M. Edwards, D. McGimpsey and A. Nisbet, 2 April 2002
(no photo topo)
Another route requiring a good build-up of ice. Start up Number Three Gully Buttress to the slabby wall below the line of overhangs at the foot of the big slab left of Quickstep (50m). Go right around the overhangs to find a groove 10m left of Quickstep. This leads to the slab, which is climbed slightly leftwards to a rock outcrop (60m). Climb more easily to another area of rock (30m). Continue to the cornice, which can be big and possibly avoided on the left on Diana.

Sioux Wall

1. Quickstep V,5**
2. Two-Step Corner V,5***
3. The Survivor VII,8
4. The Knuckleduster VIII,9***
5. The Banshee V,5
6. Sioux Wall VII,8***

Quickstep 180m V,5**
R. Townshend and T. Bray, 26 March 1983
The huge leftward-facing corner with steep slabs on its left, directly above the start of Number Three Gully Buttress. Climb this to the traverse ledge, then continue up to the foot of the corner. Climb steep ice on the left of the corner to belay at 45m. The final pitch leads to a conical basin above, which is often overhung by massive cornices – these may be passable to the right by exposed and steep climbing.

Number Three Gully Buttress 200m III***
L.S. Lovat and D.J. Bennet, 18 February 1957
(See The Comb and Number Three Gully Buttress topo)

This is one of the first patches of ice to form each winter. Climb ice up into the large snow bay below the prow of the buttress. From the top of the bay, traverse delicately right across a rock wall to a platform. Follow grooves rightwards to a small platform. Make an awkward step right and take a long, exposed traverse up rightwards. The upper part of the route is magnificently exposed. Much variation is possible with more direct lines to the platform and from here to the top.

Two-Step Corner 180m V,5***
D. Kirtley and D. Montgomery, March 1975
Starts 20 metres to the right of Number Three Gully Buttress and follows a corner to the traverse ledge of that route. Go straight up across the traverse line of Number Three Gully Buttress and climb directly up the steep corner above, step right into a bay and make a difficult cornice exit on the right.

Chinook 65m IV,5 or
M. Edwards, D. McGimpsey and A. Nisbet, 3 April 2002
(no photo topo)
Starting from the platform of Number Three Gully Buttress 10 metres right of Two-Step Corner, climbed on ice. Follow the obvious left-facing corner groove, trending left at about 25m, then move back right to climb a crack to a large ledge (35m). The left-slanting chimney leads to the top past an entertaining chockstone (30m). Without ice, this is climbed as a snowed-up rock route at V,6.

The Survivor 180m VII,8
S. Richardson and I. Small. 9 March 2008
The prominent triangular corner on the left side of the front face of Number Three Gully Buttress provides a difficult mixed climb. Start directly below the niche and climb snow and ice, trending left across a shallow depression to a short wall. Climb this and a second wall on the right to the niche (40m). Climb the corner to a small triangular ledge and traverse left along a hidden horizontal break to a good stance (20m). Climb a steep bulge and continue up the diagonal fault line to a narrow ledge at 20m. The steep icy groove above leads to the platform on Number Three Gully Buttress (30m) which is followed to the top.

The Knuckleduster 180m VIII,9***
B. Fyffe and S. Ashworth, 12 February 2007
A winter ascent based on the summer route, initially following the great groove in the buttress. Climb the groove to belay under an overhang (40m). Turn the

overhang by a wall on the right and belay on the outer edge (15m). Climb small grooves in the arête to the right of the main groove to a ledge on the right (35m). The wall on the right leads to the large platform (30m). Climb Number Three Gully Buttress to the top.

Sioux Wall 150m VII,8***
O. Metherell and I. Parnell, 1 January 2006
The groove line just left of centre of the smooth wall to the right of the arête. Start directly into the groove to an obvious belay niche. Climb up the steep wall (strenuous but well protected) into a ledge at the base of the obvious corner groove. Climb the groove with surprisingly good protection. A rightward line was chosen to finish on the first ascent. The first ascent of the complete line up the continuation crack was by A. Turner and D. Hodgson on 29 January 2006.

The Banshee 150m V,5
C. Cartwright and S. Richardson, 1 January 1999
Start at the base of Number Three Gully Buttress and follow a line of right-trending grooves and chimneys past an obvious flake to a steep wall. Climb the wall by a crack on the left (40m). Step right into Thompson's Route and up to a belay on the right (10m). Go left into a right-angled corner which is climbed to the easy ledges on Number Three Gully Buttress (40m). Follow No.3 Gully Buttress to the plateau.

Thompson's Route 130m IV,4*** or
R. Marshall, J.R. Marshall and J. Stenhouse, December 1963
Immediately on the right of the very steep front face of the buttress at the bottom left of Number Three Gully is an ice-filled chimney. Follow this steeply and with interest for 60m to a good spike belay. Climb easier slopes up and left to join Number Three Gully Buttress at the platform and follow this or a more direct finish. The first pitch is difficult and poorly protected with little ice. The large right-facing corner above the right end of the Number Three Gully Buttress platform can be climbed in snowed-up rock conditions at VII,7, and occasionally climbed on ice.

Gremlins 120m VI,6*
G. Perroux, C. Merlin, C. Biard and S. Hophster, March 1989
Climb the groove to the right of and parallel with Thompson's Route to a steep icicle, which is climbed to the spike belay (60m). Climb ice on a steep wall through overhangs then follow grooves to a ledge. The crack above goes directly to the plateau.

Gargoyle Wall

1. Sioux Wall VII, 8***
2. The Banshee V,5
3. Thompson's Route IV, 4***
4. Gremlins VI,6*
5. Gargoyle Wall VI,6**
6. Hobgoblin VI,7***

Gargoyle Wall 120m VI,6** or

S. Richardson and C. Cartwright, 22 February 1998

A great rocky mixed route that's also very good with some ice on the face. Starting 10m up and right of Thompson's Route, climb a small right-facing corner to a ledge. Enter a chimney on the left, which is followed to a bay with the Gargoyle visible on the right – a prominent head-shaped feature. Traverse onto the Gargoyle, climb the ridge above to a ledge, then traverse right into a corner. Climb the corner and a steep crack in the wall above to a platform. Go left to a chimney-crack, which is climbed with a step left to a belay (30m) and then to the top (15m).

Hobgoblin 120m VI,7***

S. Richardson and C. Cartwright, 5 December 1998

Start as for Gargoyle Wall to the first ledge, then go straight up for 15m, up cracks and a short right-angled corner slightly to the right to a belay level with and right of the Gargoyle (30m). Move up and right to reach a stepped ledge, which is climbed to beneath a cracked wall as for Gargoyle Wall (30m). Climb the wall to a ledge (10m) then go left to a chimney-crack, which is climbed, followed by an off-width to a ledge (30m). Continue straight up to the top (10m).

Babylon 115m VII,7**

S. Richardson and C. Cartwright, 8 April 2001
(no photo topo)

Steep and sustained mixed climbing that gets harder the higher you go, taking the right edge of the buttress and finishing up the hanging chimney overlooking Winter Chimney. Start just left of Winter Chimney and climb the buttress on its left by a flake crack and open groove to a rectangular rib, leading to the platform below the corner and crack of Gargoyle Wall (40m). Climb the corner and Gargoyle Cracks to another platform (25m). Step up and right to make a tenuous traverse right to a small ledge below a roof, then pull over the roof and climb the off-width above to the chimney and follow this to the top (50m).

Winter Chimney 60m IV,5*

D. Haston and D. Gray, March 1963
(no photo topo)

Lies in the back of the bay that defines the right side of Gargoyle Wall well up Number Three Gully, and is much harder and mixed before the ice builds up. The ice-smear that forms on the right wall at the start of the chimney provides two pitches (III,4**). This can be reached by abseiling into Number Three Gully from its south-east rim off rock belays, if approaching from above and not wishing to confront the large cornices. Two 60m ropes are useful.

Number Three Gully 150m I***
J.N. Collie and M.W. Travers, April 1895
The lowest point in the skyline looking into Coire na Ciste from the CIC hut. The angle of the approach slope gradually increases as it rises from the basin of Coire na Ciste, and by the time it narrows to a gully proper it's quite steep. No pitches, but the final section is divided by a pinnacle rib. The exit will be dictated by the cornice.

Creag Coire na Ciste

Start	North Face car park, Torlundy
Time	2hr 15min
Crag base altitude	1100m
Route lengths	70–150m
Route styles	Snow-ice and mixed rock and ice
Avalanches	Number Three and Number Four gullies often avalanche and large cornices grow above these faces, especially above South, Central and North Gullies.

The left end of this crag has well-featured rock that lends itself to mixed climbing, although it's all very steep. This is the home of The Secret – a climb that was popularised by the internet even before the first ascensionists were back down off the mountain! It also has a selection of very nice mid-grade ice climbs in the gullies.

Approach
Follow the signed footpath, steeply at first, to the top of the forest, then the well-made path towards the CIC hut (1hr 30min). Cross the stream 150m below the hut and walk up into Coire na Ciste. Go through a band of rocks under Number Five Gully then diagonally left to the lochans. Walk above the west side of the lochans, then curve left at 970m to a good gearing-up spot. Climb the slope towards Number Three Gully and step right to the face.

Descent
Descend by the Red Burn or Number Four Gully.

Number Three Gully I***

Creag Coire na Ciste

1. The Secret VIII,8***
2. Darth Vader VII,7***
3. Avenging Angel Direct VIII,8***
4. Cold Play VIII,8
5. South Gully III*
6. Lost the Place V,5**

The Secret 70m VIII,8***
A. Turner, S. Ashworth and V. Scott, 10 December 2007
The obvious and much sought-after crack in the right wall of Number Three Gully gives a sustained 35m crack pitch ranging from fist to finger width. The route was led onsight and in perfect style on the first ascent.

Cornucopia 100m VII,8*
C. Cartwright and S. Richardson, 14 April 1996
(no photo topo)
The smooth steep corner at the left end of Creag Coire na Ciste overlooking Number Three Gully. Needs a good freeze, otherwise it's horribly loose. Ascend left of large blocks, then go up a slabby corner to below the corner (20m). Climb a crack-line right of the corner for 5m, then move into the corner (a thread aid/

rest point was used on the first ascent). Climb the difficult corner to an alcove.

Go right on a narrow ledge, then up to a small stance on the buttress edge (25m). Ascend the booming flake above (3m) then go left into the corner/chimney, which is climbed over two chockstones with difficulty to a large platform (20m). Leave the platform from the top right corner, then go up an overhanging wall left of an arête with a large spike and on to the top (35m).

Darth Vader 100m VII,7***

S. Richardson and C. Cartwright, 30 March 1997

Climbs the chimney-crack that cuts through the vertical wall at the left end of Creag Coire na Ciste just right of Number Three Gully. Start directly below the chimney and climb up then right to a block belay just right of the chimney-crack (25m). Climb an awkward 3m wall, then go up the chimney to a hidden cave (20m). Climb the roof of the cave into a hanging groove (crux) and continue to the large platform. Climb the chimney at the back of the platform, then go up and right to finish (30m). A bit of snow-ice will help on the crux moves, and the last pitch is just as hard as the rest of the climb.

Avenging Angel Direct 110m VIII,8***

J. Higgins and N. Adams, 2 February 2013

A complete ascent of the main line of overhanging corners to the right of Darth Vader. All the sections of this climb had been done previously, but Higgins and Adams were the first to link them all together into this very impressive climb. The

Ali Rose enjoying steep rocky mixed climbing on Darth Vader

four steps in the corners are all climbed, with ledges for belays in between. Other routes come in from the left and exit to the right.

Cold Play 110m VIII,8
I. Small and S. Richardson, 6 April 2008
Start as for South Gully and climb to the foot of a deep groove that cuts up and left just right of the crest of the obvious rib (20m). Climb the groove past a tower-flake on the left to where it steepens and turns into an offwidth. Climb this to a steepening split by a Y-shaped crack and belay on the left at a good block (30m). The Y-shaped crack (crux) is climbed, then move up a shallow slot on the left to a good ledge across the crest of the rib (20m). Climb the left-trending fault line on the right to an exposed position on the left edge of the rib. The overhanging wall on the right leads to the crest again and a finish up the impending crack in the wall above (20m). Continue up easy snow to the cornice (20m).

South Sea Bubble 110m VII,7
S. Richardson and C. Cartwright, 8 March 1997
On the steep wall left of South Gully, this route links two right-to-left ice ramps and a hanging icicle. Go up the lower ramp of South Gully to below the hanging icicle (30m). Climb up left to the first ice ramp, which is climbed for 5m, after which a vertical wall is climbed to gain the start of the second ramp. Climb this ramp and traverse right to a hanging stance right of the icicle (40m). Climb the icicle then continue on to the top (40m).

South Gully 125m III*
G.G. MacPhee, 10 April 1936
Starts high up on the left-hand side of Creag Coire na Ciste and just below Number Three Gully proper. Use an obvious ramp slanting diagonally to the right. This leads to an ice pitch which gives entry to a final steep funnel. The cornice is often difficult but might be passed on the left.

The Sorcerer 140m VII,8
S. Ashworth and N. Nielsen, 1 March 2007
(no photo topo)
Much like White Magic in the Cairngorms but longer and harder! Start below a steep corner left of Lost the Place. Climb over ledges to gain the corner, which is climbed with an exit on its right wall. Trend left over ledges to belay directly below the crack splitting the wall above (40m) – the magic crack pitch! Easy ground leads to a belay on Lost the Place (50m). Pull round the corner as for Lost

Creag Coire na Ciste

1. Number Three Gully I
2. South Sea Bubble VII,7
3. South Gully III*
4. Lost the Place V,5***
5. Une Journée Ordinaire VI,6**
6. Central Gully III,4**
7. Central Gully Right-Hand IV,4***
8. Wendigo IV,4**
9. North Gully II*

the Place and immediately take a right-trending ramp-line on a diagonal across the steep upper buttress (50m).

Lost the Place 140m V,5** or
C. Cartwright and R. Clothier, 17 December 1988
An excellent climb that's good in rocky mixed conditions but also benefits from some ice in the chimney. Follow a groove starting just left of Central Gully until it overlooks South Gully, then a tricky pitch (either right then left, or left then right) to reach a chossy chimney. Climb this to the cornice. A direct start (60m, V,6) takes the left-facing groove through the lower face of the buttress 30m right of South Gully through a prominent chimney slot.

Une Journée Ordinaire dans un Enfer Quotidien 105m VI,6**
G. Perroux, F. Bossier and J. Douay, 15 April 1993
Ascend Central Gully for 10m then go left to a small cave at the foot of another icefall which forms slowly. This is climbed with an exit left and continuation to belay on the left (45m). Continue up snow and more ice to the cornice, which can be huge and may require a long traverse left with some tunnelling!

Central Gully 125m III,4**
I. Clough and J.M. Alexander, 27 January 1959
Starting from the lowest part of the crag, snow slopes are followed to the left of a rocky rib to reach the left-hand of two parallel ice chimneys which cleave the steep central wall. This is climbed for 40m before crossing to the right-hand gully, which leads into the final corniced funnel.

> Central Gully and Central Gully – Right-Hand do not need much ice to provide fun climbing. If there's a thin covering of good ice they can be enjoyable and are about the same grade.

Central Gully – Right-Hand 125m IV,4***
I. MacEacheran and J. Knight
The right-hand chimney gives a fine long pitch. An independent start can be made by climbing the rightward-slanting icefall to the left of North Gully, then traversing left to the foot of the chimney.
Note: It's possible to abseil after climbing the main pitch of either of the previous two routes and then climb the other route. This gives two excellent pitches.

If the cornice is too intimidating it's also possible to descend by abseil back into the corrie.

Wendigo 110m IV,4**
T.W. Patey and J. Brown, 24 February 1963
Start right of the lowest rocks beneath a steep icefall and go steeply up right to a large ledge. Climb mixed ground above to the cornice.

North Gully 110m II*
J.Y. MacDonald and H.W. Turnbull, 24 March 1934
The right-hand and most obvious of the three gullies on this cliff, starts to the left of Number Four Gully. The lower section of the gully almost always holds an ice pitch, but the ice may vary from 3m to 30m. The narrow lower section leads to a wide, easier-angled slope which is followed obliquely rightwards to the cornice. Beware of avalanche danger on the final slopes. A left-fork finish is possible (35m III, *D. Bathgate, J. Knight and A. McKeith, February 1964*) up an ice groove at the back of a steep scoop above the upper snow basin.

Forearm 125m IV,4
D. Cuthbertson, S Clarke, L. Robinson and A.N. Other, March 1999
(no photo topo)
The icy groove in the crest right of North Gully makes a good route when combined with North Gully left fork. Climb the groove, a section of snow then an awkward icy chimney to more snow (50m). A choice of directions lead to the top (75m).

Number Four Gully 150m I
A.E. Maylard, W.W. Naismith and F.C. Squance, April 1895
The easiest winter route on Ben Nevis and the best descent on the North Face. It curls gently round to the right between the cliffs of Creag Coire na Ciste and South Trident Buttress. Its exit is very wide, so it should be possible to find a way through, but not always. An exit far to the right, on the right side of a small rock buttress, sometimes works. There's often a notch in the cornice cut by people descending the gully. This route can't be seen from the CIC hut.

The Trident buttresses

Start	North Face car park, Torlundy
Time	2hr 15min
Crag base altitude	950–1050m
Route lengths	50–260m
Route styles	Mixed rock and ice, snow-ice, and snow patch cascade ice
Avalanches	Number Three and Number Four Gullies often avalanche, and avalanches frequently come down over Central Trident Buttress. Number Five Gully is a notorious avalanche trap, with the runout zone occasionally reaching the lower corrie at 750m.

The area extending from Number Four Gully on the left to Number Five Gully on the right contains the Trident buttresses (South, Central and North), whose crests can be seen cutting the skyline. The area near Lochan Coire na Ciste (NN 162 718) is a useful spot for gearing-up ready for the climbs here and elsewhere, with the buttresses above giving an impression of safety from avalanches. However, large avalanches do sweep over Central Gully from the hidden snow slopes above and the debris has been known to reach the lochan.

Approach
Follow the signed footpath, steeply at first, to the top of the forest, then the well-made path towards the CIC hut (1hr 30min). Cross the stream 150m below the hut and walk up into Coire na Ciste. Go through a band of rocks under Number Five Gully then diagonally left to the lochans. North and Central Trident buttress are above (north-west). South Trident Buttress is a little higher to the west.

Descent
Many of the climbs on South and North Trident Buttress finish by climbing one of the east ridges of Càrn Dearg. From there, descend west into the Red Burn. It's common to abseil down Central Trident Buttress (good anchors above Mega Route X).

The Trident Buttresses

Mega Route X V,6***

1. Number Four Gully I
2. Poseidon Groove IV,4
3. Pinnacle Arete IV,5**
4. Rein ne va Plas V,5
5. Central Gully III
6. Jubilation IV,4*
7. Mega Reve V,5
8. Jubilee Climb II
9. Neptune Gully III
10. Ledge Route II***
11. The Curtain IV,5***

The upper tier of South Trident Buttress

Number Four Gully Buttress 100m II*
J.H.B. Bell, 1 January 1929
(no photo topo)
The broken area to the right of the lower reaches of Number Four Gully and left of South Trident Buttress.

> South Trident Buttress consists of three tiers with steep easy ground in between. The area between the lower and middle tier is known as Middle Ledge. The mixed climbs on the middle tier can be a good choice early in the season when covered in soft snow, since ice is not required for most of the climbs. However, sunshine on the face can strip rime very quickly.

Poseidon Groove 100m IV,5
S. Richardson and I. Small, 3 April 2004
The steep groove splitting the south-facing upper tier. Reach twin grooves in the centre of the wall from the mouth of Number Four Gully. Move into the right-hand groove and climb past two steep sections to a ledge 5m right of a wide vertical crack (35m). Step left and climb the left of two corners, leading to easier ground (50m). Further easier ground leads to the top (15m).

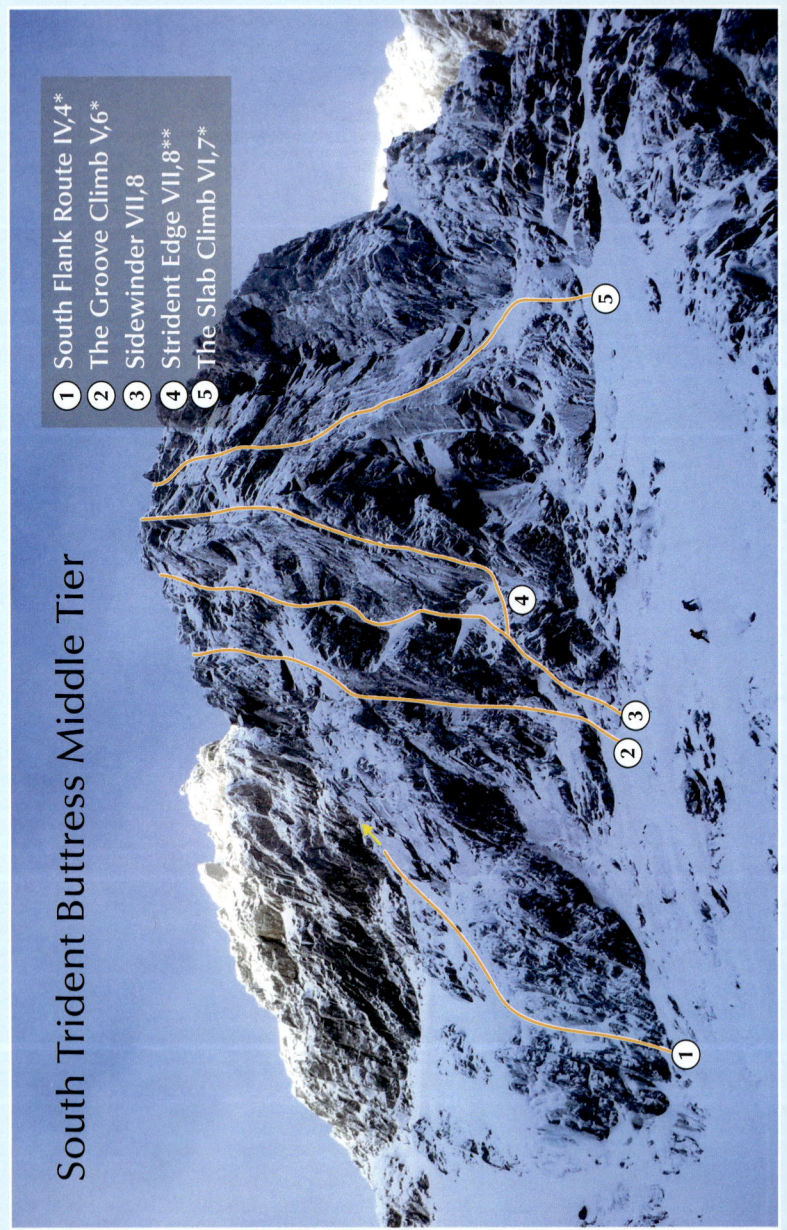

Triton Corners 100m IV,5
C. Cartwright and S. Richardson, 3 April 2006
(no photo topo)
Start 25m right of the previous route. Climb a short bulging offwidth to a stepped corner system leading right. Continue straight up to a good belay under a steep wall (40m). Step left and climb an icy gully and wide snow chute to the plateau (60m).

South Flank Route 150m IV,4*
A. Kimber, N. Hicking and C. Collin, 29 March 1994
To the left of the steep rocks above Middle Ledge of South Trident Buttress on the middle tier, overlooking the approach to Number Four Gully, are some steep ice-smears. Follow the steepest of these, and snow slopes and chimneys above, to the flat section below the upper tier on the crest of South Trident Buttress, whose fine shattered arête is followed to the plateau rim.

> The following six routes climb the middle tier, from which the fine arête of the top tier can be climbed to the plateau, or a descent made down towards Number Four Gully. Route lengths are to the top of middle tier.

The Groove Climb 80m V,6*
J. Main and A. Clarke, 22 December 1992
On the left end of the middle tier, above Middle Ledge, is a deep chimney groove which is climbed to a deep cave (30m). From the cave, an awkward exit is made to a belay (10m). Go left by an icy ramp to the top, from where it's possible to descend left.

Sidewinder 100m VII,8
I. Small and S. Richardson, 8 April 2005
The triple-tiered corner starting 15 metres right of The Groove Climb. Avoid the first chimney by easy ground on the left. Continue up the corner (20m) and the crack and large flake to the top (30m).

Strident Edge 100m VII,8**
E. Brunskill and G. Hughes, 13 January 2005
Sensational but relatively amenable climbing up the arête to the right of Sidewinder. Start as for Sidewinder by easy ground on the left to belay in the corner. Move out right and climb the steep crack just left of the crest, with a possible

belay at 15m (35m). Turn the overhang above by a spike and cracks in the left wall to regain the groove above to the top of the middle tier.

The Slab Climb 90m VI,7*
A. Nisbet and J. Preston, 9 November 2001
Between The Groove Climb and The Clanger is a cracked wall leading to a conspicuous chimney. Gain the cracked wall by steep moves up and right from the Middle Ledge (25m). Climb the cracked wall to the chimney (25m). Climb up the chimney, which is difficult to start, and its continuation (40m).

The Clanger 90m IV,5**
J.R. Marshall, R. Marshall and R.N. Campbell, March 1967
(no photo topo)
Access from the Middle Ledge. Climb the chimney groove at the back of the corner near the right end of the middle tier to a steep cave pitch (35m). Exit the cave by an extremely narrow through-route on the right wall, leading behind a large flake onto the buttress crest. Easier to the top. A route for people of very slight stature and no rucksacks! The chimney groove has been followed all the way, avoiding the tight squeeze, over good steep bulges at VI,7 (*I. Small and D. Hawthorn*).

Pinnacle Arête 100m IV,5**
R.H. Sellars and J. Smith, 1 February 1959
Start from the right end of the snow ledge (Middle Ledge) and climb a series of grooves just right of the crest to a large terrace. The chimney groove above leads to the crest at the top of the middle tier.

> The next two climbs are on the lower tier.

Rien ne va Plus 50m V,5
G. Perroux and J. Blyth, 10 April 1994
An icefall which sometimes forms on the left side of the lower tier of South Trident Buttress. Descend easily leftwards by Middle Ledge or climb one of the routes above.

Under Fire 85m VII,7*
D. MacLeod and M. Tweedley, 6 February 2008
Start below a roofed chimney in the centre of the face. Climb the chimney through the roof (hard) and the corner above. Exit left onto a ledge underneath

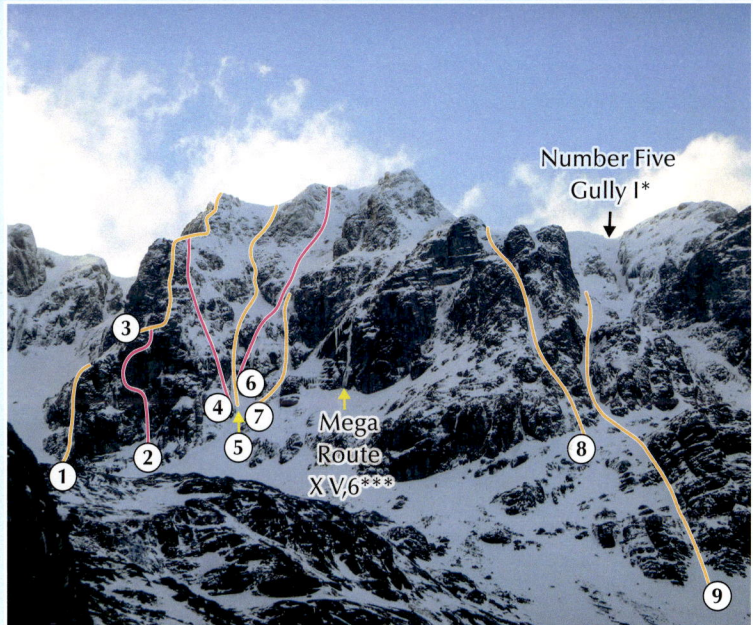

South and Central Trident Buttresses

① Rien ne va Plus V,5
② Under Fire VII,7*
③ Pinnacle Arete IV,5**
④ Joyful Chimneys IV,5
⑤ Central Gully III
⑥ Nasturtium IV,4*
⑦ Jubilation IV,4*
⑧ Neptune Gully III
⑨ Moonlight Gully I/II

an overhanging wall and traverse left for 5m, round to the base of a large slanting corner. Climb the corner and crawl right along a thin ledge to another corner, which leads to the top.

Up to the right of the foot of the lower tier of South Trident Buttress is Central Gully. Large avalanches sweep over Central Gully from the hidden snow slopes above, and the debris has been known to reach the lochan.

Joyful Chimneys 180m IV,5
R. Campbell and J.R. Marshall, February 1971
A discontinuous line of chimneys can be seen on the north-east flank of South Trident Buttress facing the CIC hut. Starts 50 metres left and downhill of Central Gully. These chimneys are either climbed or avoided on their flanks, depending on conditions. The crest of South Trident Buttress at the top of Middle Tier is gained by a series of grooves above the chimneys.

Central Gully 240m III
H. Raeburn and Mr & Mrs C. Inglis-Clark, April 1904
Immediately above (west of) the small lochans (Lochan Coire na Ciste) and right of the steep rocks of South Trident Buttress. This gully can fill up almost completely. Often a steep ice column is found barring the way, or an enormous chockstone. Either pass it by mixed ground up to the left (as on the first ascent) or climb direct (**30m III,4** *L.S. Lovat and K. Bryan, 11 March 1956*). Above, a variety of routes lead to the top, avoiding difficulties as necessary.

Nasturtium 250m IV,4*
D. Cuthbertson and Notts Trent University party, 26 March 2002
Start by following Central Gully to the foot of a curling groove on the right (20m). Climb the groove and belay under a right-facing corner (40m). Climb the corner and belay on a plinth at its top (50m). Climb snow and a 15m icefall to reach another snowfield (40m). Reach the crest of South Trident Buttress up and left and follow it to the top.

Jubilation 240m IV,4*
R. Marshall, J.R. Marshall and J. Stenhouse, December 1963
Follow Jubilee Climb for about 75m. Traverse left into a chimney and climb it on steep ice to a snow bay. Move left into a second chimney and follow this until it eases. A choice of routes lead over easier ground to the top.

Mega Rêve 60m V,5
G. Perroux, J.P. Destercke, C. Deu, P. Gratadour and F. Domanget, 4 April 1994
Climb a narrow chimney on the left of the rightward ramp of Jubilee Climb and well up right of Jubilation. A short, steep icefall is followed by the central of three vertical icefalls.

Jubilee Climb 240m II
G.G. MacPhee, G.C. Williams and D. Henderson, May 1935

THE TRIDENT BUTTRESSES

In the lower part of Central Gully is a rightward-leading branch which is followed on snow and small ice pitches to easy ground and a choice of routes to the top.

Feeding Frenzy 70m VI,7*

N. Gresham and C. Smith, 24 January 1999
(no photo topo)
At the left end of the buttress containing Mega Route X, a free-hanging icicle sometimes forms. This presents a fierce climb, accessed by mixed climbing up a left-slanting ramp and powerful moves to reach the icicle.

Mega Route X 60m V,6***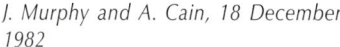

J. Murphy and A. Cain, 18 December 1982
One of the steeper ice climbs on Ben Nevis, this takes the lowest section of Central Trident Buttress, 50 metres right of Jubilee Climb. There's a good belay at 40m on the left below an overhang, and it's common to abseil back down.

Climbing Mega Route X

Heidbanger Direct 75m VIII,8

R. Cross and A. Benson, 23 November 2008
(no photo topo)
Follow the deep lightning crack in the arête to belay in the cave (25m). Follow the offwidth crack out of the cave and trend up and left to the arête (20m). The corner lines past a flake lead to the top (30m).

Left-Hand Ridge 250m IV,4

D.F. Lang and C. Stead, 12 February 1994
(no photo topo)
The ridge left of Neptune Gully. Climb an icefall corner just left of Neptune Gully and follow the crest above, taking the rock tower by a central groove and finishing on a level crest. From here a variety of easier routes take you to the top.

Neptune Gully 260m III

A.J. Bennet and J. Clarkson, February 1956

This S-shaped gully splits the crest of the North Trident (right-hand) Buttress. It has an indefinite entry pitch 10m to the left of the upper section of Moonlight Gully (described below) from the large flat ledge. Climb first on the right and enter the gully higher up, which is followed, turning ice pitches on the left to a large platform overlooking Number Five Gully. Ascend an easy ridge and slopes above to the plateau. In certain conditions all pitches can be taken direct.

Moonlight Gully Buttress

Start	North Face car park, Torlundy
Time	1hr 45min
Crag base altitude	850m
Route lengths	135–460m
Route styles	Mixed rock and ice
Avalanches	Number Five Gully is a notorious avalanche trap, with the runout zone occasionally reaching the lower corrie at 750m.

Moonlight Gully Buttress is at the bottom of Number Five Gully on the left and is split at two-thirds height by a very large (almost flat) ledge. At such a low altitude, the climbs will not be in good condition so often, but they offer alternatives when the weather high up is bad. With no snow-ice some of the routes will be quite hard.

Approach
Follow the signed footpath, steeply at first, to the top of the forest, then the well-made path towards the CIC hut (1hr 30min). Cross the stream 150m below the hut and walk up into Coire na Ciste. Go through a band of rocks under Number Five Gully then up and left to Moonlight Gully Buttress.

Descent
From the top of Moonlight Gully Buttress, traverse left to the lochans in Coire na Ciste.

Moonlight Gully 150m I/II
W. Inglis-Clark and T. Gibson, 3 January 1908
This gully is on the immediate left of Moonlight Gully Buttress and provides a steep and narrow snow climb which ends in the upper area of Number Five Gully.

Diagonal Route 150m III*
D. Hawthorn, C. MacLean and A. Paul, 17 December 1983
Start at the foot of Moonlight Gully. Traverse up right to a broad ledge and continue by the left-hand chimney above to the big ledge. Climb the upper tier by the continuation of the chimney.

Right-Hand Chimney 135m IV,5*
D. Hawthorn, C. MacLean and A. Paul, 17 December 1983
Two chimneys split the front face of the buttress. The right-hand one is better defined. It's climbed directly, and its continuation is followed on the second tier above the big ledge. Sustained, and most people say it's quite hard, probably due to a lack of ice.

Number Five Gully 460m I*
Collie and party, April 1895
Obvious from the CIC hut. Prone to very large avalanches and rarely sufficiently stable to allow an ascent. Lies between the Trident buttresses and Càrn Dearg Buttress, and commences below and well to the right of the main basin of Coire na Ciste. It's a straightforward snow climb once the huge chockstones have been buried in snow.

Above a small pitch the gully narrows, and then opens into a huge funnel. The normal route keeps to the right, to exit near the top of Càrn Dearg NW, depending on the cornice.

Ledge Route 450m II***
SMC party, Easter 1897
The best climb on the mountain at this grade, and a very interesting excursion. Start up Number Five Gully but leave it by a rightward-rising ramp shortly after it becomes a gully proper, about 50m up. The ramp leads out above the top of The Curtain and has an easy-angled 20m rock slab. This can be bare rock, covered in cascade ice or deep snow.

The ramp leads onto a broad, almost horizontal ledge, which fades out to the right. Before the ledge narrows, leave it by a broad, leftward-slanting gully, which comes out onto a sloping snow shelf. Turn right up easier snow to find a large, top-heavy pinnacle. This is a useful landmark and is passed just before rounding the corner to reach the platform at the top of Càrn Dearg Buttress.

An easier but less interesting start reaches this point from Lochan Coire na Ciste, crossing Number Five Gully and slanting easily up to the right to the top-heavy pinnacle.

The route now follows the ridge and is very narrow in places. The ridge leads on up to the summit of Càrn Dearg NW.

In good weather this route gives a more interesting descent than the gullies, especially if it's well covered in snow. The ridge should be followed down to the top of Càrn Dearg Buttress, and then the broad highest shelf (marked by the top-heavy pinnacle at the start) can be followed easily into Number Five Gully. The bottom section of the gully can be descended when there's very good snow cover and low avalanche hazard (stick to the right-hand side looking down), or cross Number Five Gully to where a similar broad shelf leads gradually down from the large ledge at the top of Moonlight Gully Buttress towards Lochan Coire na Ciste.

Càrn Dearg Buttress

Start	North Face car park, Torlundy
Time	1hr 45min
Crag base altitude	800m
Route lengths	100–300m
Route styles	Snow-ice, mixed rock and ice, and cascade ice
Avalanches	Number Five Gully is a notorious avalanche trap, with the runout zone occasionally reaching the lower corrie at 750m.

Càrn Dearg Buttress lies to the right of Number Five Gully. It is the huge rock buttress that's home to many classic rock climbs as well as winter climbs. It is very easily seen on the walk up Allt a' Mhuilinn – in fact it dominates the approach, enticing climbers with its ice smears and steep chimneys and corners.

Winter climbs: Ben Nevis

Approach
Follow the signed footpath, steeply at first, to the top of the forest, then the well-made path towards the CIC hut (1hr 30min). Cross the stream 150m below the hut and walk up into Coire na Ciste. Go through a band of rocks under Number Five Gully, then up and right to Càrn Dearg Buttress

Descent
From the top of Càrn Dearg Buttress, traverse left to find Ledge Route and either ascend or descend this. From the top-heavy tower on Ledge Route it's easy to go down into Number Five Gully and descend this on the right side looking down, or traverse over the top of Moonlight Gully Buttress.

The Curtain Rail 100m IV,4*
D.F. Land, R.T. Richardson and C. Stead, 31 January 1988 (first recorded ascent)
Follows the grooves left of and parallel to The Curtain (see next) and can provide an interesting alternative to that overcrowded climb.

Starting out on the second pitch of The Curtain

The Curtain 110m IV,5***
J. Knight and D. Bathgate, February 1965
The prominent ice climb on the left of the buttress has formed far less often in the last decade than in previous decades. When fully iced, it's a popular climb due to its short approach. Very sustained for a grade IV but easy to abseil off.

Climb the long slab to a belay on the right (45m). Zig-zag up the next pitch to belay on the left wall. Traverse right and climb the final steep ice wall and slab. If you're using 60m ropes it should be possible to climb the second and third pitches in one long pitch.

Descent is made into Number Five Gully by a steep snow slope on the left after the final difficulties.

Route I Direct 210m VI,6***
D. Cuthbertson and J. Sylvester, March 1984
Start at the big right-facing corner at the left end of the foot of the buttress. Climb the corner and then move left across the wall to gain the rib, which leads more easily to the ledge beneath the chimney. This chimney gives the top half of the climb and can be very hard at the top if there's no ice.

Route II Direct 275m VI,7***
G. Smith and I. Sykes, 15 February 1978
A high-quality route of considerable difficulty when in condition. Ice is needed on the slabs of the traverse. Starting in a right-facing corner just right of Route I Direct, climb the corner and traverse left beneath an overhang. Climb up to a large block and climb a groove above it. Traverse right round an arête to a ledge, and climb a bulge above to the traverse ledge.

Climb the first pitch of the chimney of Route I Direct (20m). Then follow an upward diagonal line across the slabs, beneath the overhangs, rightwards to a groove line at the far edge of the buttress. Follow this groove line up the crest to easy ground.

Ring the Alarm 270m VI,5**
M. Duff and J. Tinker, 1 February 1986
(no photo topo)
Start just right of Route II Direct and climb the crack (45m). Follow Route II Direct for 10m and traverse right to a stance on the slab edge (30m). Stay calm whilst traversing the lip of the slab to a groove, which is climbed over an overlap to a stance (45m). Climb ice (The Weep) above to reach Route II (30m), which is followed to the top (120m).

Càrn Dearg Buttress

1. Centurion VIII,8***
2. Sassenach IX,9
3. Shield Direct VII,7***
4. Gemini VI,6***

Centurion 190m VIII,8***

Originally climbed solo using considerable aid over two days (*R. Milward, 1975*). Another ascent (*J. McKenzie and K. Spence, 9 February 1986*) over two days used a bivouac and a rest point at the top of pitch two. The upper section has so far been avoided by finishing up Route II.

Start at the foot of the obvious corner in the centre of the face, climb the left wall to a belay (15m), then go right into the corner, which is climbed to a belay in an overhung bay (35m). Go left to the edge and follow grooves until level with an overhang, then step right and up to a stance (25m). Go back into the corner then left across the wall to beneath an overhung crack. Ascend the arête to a stance (20m) then go up slabby grooves past a block to join Route II (40m).

Sassenach 270m IX,9

A. Turner and T. Stone, 9 March 2009

The summer route – the prominent chimney on the right of the buttress – is followed throughout. Start to the right of the chimney and climb it, with the crux on the overhanging groove and flake of the second pitch. Only a perfect storm will ensure it's snowy and iced in the crux groove.

Shield Direct 290m VII,7***

M. Fowler and A. Saunders, 15 March 1979

Originally the first recorded grade VI on the mountain, this is a soaring line of great difficulty. A long way right of the previous climbs, the front face of Càrn Dearg Buttress turns to form a vertical line of cliffs facing north. Waterfall Gully (described below) is an obvious feature to the right. On the vertical wall is a series of steep chimneys, which give the line of the route.

Start in a steep icy groove (often blank), directly below the chimney line. Follow the groove on cascade ice to a stance at 25m. Climb steeply to a large ledge on the right at the foot of the chimney. Climb the difficult chimney to a cave (30m). Steep ice grooves lead to easier climbing at the top of the chimney flake (75m). Move left past a flake and bulges to trend right by the easiest line to ledges (45m). Climb up right then left to easier ground, followed by an arête to the junction with Ledge Route.

Gemini 300m VI,6***

A. Paul and D. Sanderson, 23 March 1979

A very steep direct start to the left of the first pitch of Waterfall Gully is followed by rightward-sloping ice ramps and steep ice-smears to an enormous detached flake. Climb very steep ice on the wall left of the flake to a ledge and rightward-sloping grooves. Move diagonally up and right on mixed ground to obvious twin

The big smear of cascade ice on Gemini

grooves, either of which can be climbed to a broad ledge, which is followed right. Climb up via iced slabs to easier ground.

Bewilderbeast 130m VI,6**

M. Garthwaite and A. Wainwright, 21 March 1995
(no photo topo)
Starts just above and right of the enormous detached flake on Gemini at the base of a corner. Climb either Gemini or Waterfall Gully to reach this point. Climb an ice-smear on the left of the corner to a steep wall. Go right on thin holds to a small ledge in the corner, then up a chimney to a belay (30m). Climb up the thin corner, over a small roof, and go right to the foot of another corner, which is climbed over a second roof to a small belay on the right (35m). Ascend a very thin groove in the arête on the right of the corner, then go right to another short corner. Belay on the terrace. Go up a thin tongue of ice on the final wall, then move left onto the icefall and direct to finish (45m).

Waterfall Gully 215m IV,4*

D. Pipes, I. Clough, J. Alexander, R. Shaw and A. Flegg, 8 January 1959
The obvious gully immediately right of Càrn Dearg Buttress. After the first steep 45m the angle eases. The snow gully leads to a small cave after 140m, then a rightwards traverse to a shoulder next to the large basin below the summit buttresses. Keep to the left of this area and climb leftwards towards Ledge Route. A direct finish to Waterfall Gully (VI,6**) is possible by continuing straight up where the gully swings right onto the ridge. It consists of pitches – the first on ice up the big corner; the second (crux) a short, stiff pull over the overhang. The crux is escapable.

Staircase Climb 215m IV,5*

D. Haston and J. Stenhouse, February 1987
Starts 15 metres to the right of Waterfall Gully and climbs the higher of two shelves sloping up rightwards. Around the corner a stepped slab is climbed up right to beneath a clean-cut crack in a corner. Climb the crack and a short wall to a platform. The chimney above is climbed to easier ground, and the buttress crest followed towards a pinnacle, which is turned on the left or the right. From the col beyond the pinnacle, take the left-hand of two chimneys and continue up and leftwards towards the top of Càrn Dearg Buttress.

On the steep tier of rocks 100m below the buttress, a number of icefalls may form – the Càrn Dearg Cascades – providing good ice climbing practice at a variety of grades. The big left-hand cascade often gives sustained vertical climbing, and the next right is the best at III or IV if you finish up and left. These first two cascades have good boulders for anchors at the top and an abseil descent is easy. Many lines form further right, and all the cascades are around 55m.

CLIMBS FROM CASTLE COIRE

Castle Coire

Start	North Face car park, Torlundy
Time	1hr 45min
Crag base altitude	800–900m
Route lengths	105–300m
Route styles	Snow-ice, mixed snow, rock and ice, and cascade ice
Avalanches	The Castle gullies often avalanche, with the runout zone occasionally reaching down to Allt a' Mhuilinn. The slopes above The Shroud also avalanche into Castle Coire, and sometimes the runout zone reaches down to the diagonal break used for access.

On the approach up Allt a' Mhuilinn, the first main feature is Castle Ridge with its huge North Face on the right. The area to the left of Castle Ridge is known as Castle Coire and is only seen fully from a point approximately 500 metres downhill of the hut. The main features of the corrie are the North and South Castle gullies, which are separated by The Castle at their top, and join at their foot into a steep rocky icefall/gully descending towards the Halfway Lochan path.

Approach
Follow the signed footpath, steeply at first, to the top of the forest, then the well-made path towards the CIC hut, and cross the stream at 610m above a steeper section of the path, 500 metres before the hut. Walk up the slope to a rightward-leading diagonal break through the band of rocks and follow this into the corrie. Please be aware that many avalanche fatalities have occurred in this area over the years; this approach is exposed to this danger for most of its length.

Another approach is to ascend from the hut to beneath Càrn Dearg Buttress and traverse below it towards the climbs.

Descent
These climbs finish north of Càrn Dearg. Descend north-west towards Lochan Meall an t-Suidhe. High up above and to the right of Waterfall Gully is a large hanging snow corrie. At its bottom lip, an overhung icefall (The Shroud) can sometimes be seen from the approach to the CIC hut. To the right of this icefall is an obvious snow/ice gully – Boomer's Requiem. Descent from the large hanging snow corrie is easiest by Ledge Route, which is gained by ascending the steep slopes on the left side of the corrie to the ridge above. Alternatively, one of the Càrn Dearg summit gullies can be climbed to the top. From there, walk off towards the Red Burn.

Kellett's North Wall Route 200m VII,7
M. Charlton and M. Burrows-Smith, 1 February 1991
(no photo topo)
Starts left of The Shroud below a large flake with a deep chimney to the right. Climb the chimney and exit by a window to continue to a terrace (25m). Climb the corner to the left of an obvious crack to reach another terrace (20m). Go 6m right then move up to a recess, then go right to a steep groove which is climbed to a ledge (30m). Move up left along the ledge and on up a steep turfy groove-line (30m). Exit left into Waterfall Gully, which is followed to the top (95m).

The Past is Close Behind 200m VIII,8
B. Fyffe and I. Small, 18 February 2010
(no photo topo)
A line up the steep wall just left of The Shroud, starting up Harrison's Climb. Climb the easy snow ramp of Harrison's Climb then turn left and climb one short wall to a good ledge (40m). Thin climbing up the wall leads into a technical groove; belay on a ledge on the left (35m). Go back right into the groove then climb the wall and take a rising rightward traverse (15m). Quality climbing follows up the big corner, locking-off on solid chockstones (35m). Bold, slabby climbing leads into an inverted V. Bold, slabby thin ice climbing leads out of the inverted V (30m). Climb more thinly iced slabs and easier ground to Ledge Route (45m) which can be ascended or descended.

The Shroud 200m VI,6**
A. Clarke and J. Main, 2 February 1993
In exceptional conditions an icy drape extends over the cliffs below the hanging corrie left of Harrison's Climb Direct, and can form a free-standing pillar (or

Kellet's North Wall

① Shield Direct VII,7***
② Gemini VI,6***
③ Waterfall Gully IV,4*
④ Staircase Climb IV,5*
⑤ The Shroud VI,6*

hanging icicle). Climb up to belay on the right side of the icefall (50m). Continue to another belay on a narrow ice ledge right of the free-standing pillar (25m). Follow the pillar to the upper ice wall and a belay on ice screws (25m). Continue more easily above (100m) to the hanging snow corrie.

Harrison's Climb Direct 300m IV,4***
K.V. Crocket and C. Gilmore, 7 February 1976
This climb ascends the steep icy chimney underneath The Shroud, then follows the steepening gully on the right to a col. From the col, traverse left to the icefall, and from its right end climb a line up right to gain the edge overlooking Raeburn's Buttress. Continue for several pitches to the upper corrie and a variety of exits. A fine route.

Note: The hanging snow corrie often releases large avalanches, so be wary after strong winds and/or heavy snowfalls.

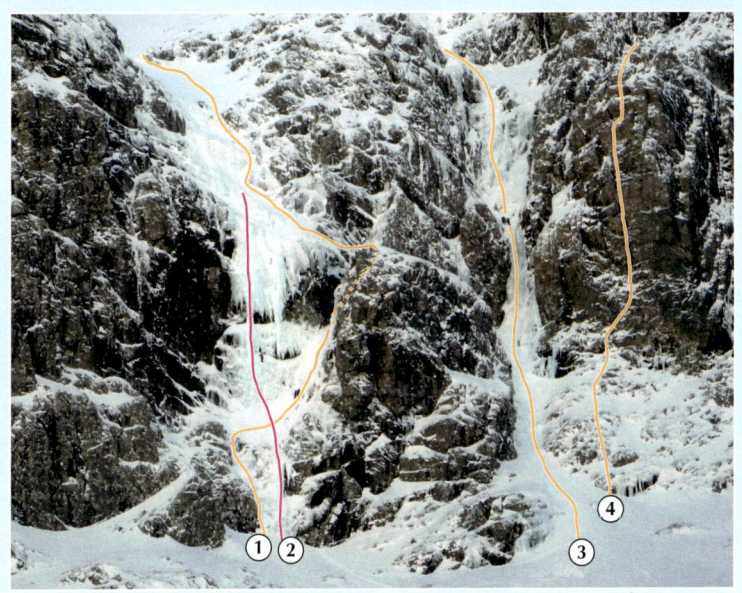

The Shroud and Boomer's Requiem

① Harrison's Climb Direct IV,4***
② The Shroud VI,6***
③ Boomer's Requiem V,5***
④ The Crack VIII,8**

Boomer's Requiem 170m V,5*
C. Higgins and D. MacArthur, February 1973
A deep gully to the right of The Shroud is easily seen from the path up Allt a' Mhuilinn. Climb into the gully and the steep icefall on the back left wall. The corner on the left can be useful. Climb another ice pitch above to the snow beneath the summit gullies, one of which leads to the top.

CARN DEARG SUMMIT GULLIES

These form a logical continuation to some of the previous climbs. They may also be reached by descending into the basin from high up on Ledge Route.

Raeburn's Buttress

① Boomer's Requiem V,5***
② The Crack VIII,8**
③ The Great Corner VIII,8**
④ Compression Crack V,5*

Arch Gully 105m I
I. Clough, P.S. Nicholson and D. Pipes, 8 April 1958
The central gully is marked by a huge block which forms the Arch at about half-height. Straightforward but steep.

Surprise Gully 185m I/II
I. Clough, P.S. Nicholson and D. Pipes, 12 April 1958
The shallow right-hand gully leads by broken rocks to a shoulder, and to the top by an ice groove on the left.

> The following climbs start in Castle Coire and finish to the north of the summit of Carn Dearg.

Raeburn's Buttress/Intermediate Gully 230m V,5**

W.D. Brooker and J.M. Taylor (by the buttress finish), 31 January 1959
Raeburn's Buttress is the tall thin buttress right of Boomer's Requiem. It finishes as a slender tapering arête, to the left of which is the prominent narrow Intermediate Gully.

Start by climbing Boomer's Requiem for about 65m to where an obvious ice line, which is hidden from below, leads up right. This route climbs the ice wall and the snow gully above. There's a cave exit at the top of the gully, which is otherwise straightforward. The crest of Raeburn's Buttress proper is immediately to the right of the foot of the gully. It narrows to a sharp blade at the top, but this may be turned by a corner on the right. Easier slopes lead to the top.

The Crack 250m VIII,8**

C. Cartwright and S. Richardson, 13 February 2000
This very steep route lies on the front face of Raeburn's Buttress, to the right of the entrance gully to Boomer's Requiem, and follows an obvious crack. Mixed ground is climbed to a block belay beneath slabs guarding the entrance to the crack. Go left and up a short wall to a vegetated slab. Move up right and climb overhanging steps to a block just right of the crack (25m).

Climb up the chimney-crack to a ledge on the right (15m). Go back into the crack and up it to a ledge on the left with possible rests en route (25m). Climb down right to a ledge and go along it for 3m, then go up a number of overhanging walls to easier ground (20m). Climb the crest of Raeburn's Buttress for 125m, passing the last rocky blade on the left. A variety of exits towards the plateau exist, depending on the avalanche potential.

The Great Corner 250m VIII,8**

I. Small and S. Richardson, 24 January 2010
The awe-inspiring clean-cut corner on the right flank of Raeburn's Buttress. Start on the girdle traverse terrace, reached by climbing the first two pitches of the Compression Crack icefall. Move left along the terrace to belay below the chimney cutting up into the corner (50m). Climb the chimney to a small exposed ledge at its top (40m). Continue up the imposing corner above and exit into the upper groove. Follow this (sustained) to the top of Raeburn's Buttress (50m). Continue up easier ground to the summit of Càrn Dearg NW.

Compression Crack 250m V,5*

M. Hind and C. Rice, 9 February 1985
It's difficult to find all of this climb in condition, as the first section is climbed on cascade ice and the second on snow-ice. In cold weather, the initial pitches

of cascade ice form readily and are often climbed followed by an abseil on ice-threads.

On the steep wall left of South Castle Gully and below Raeburn's Arête, a series of imposing ice-smears can often be seen. Climb this ice then traverse a long way right to reach snow-ice-filled grooves. Follow the corner above vertically for 15m and a further 20m to easy ground leading to the top.

THE CASTLE

The two Castle gullies can be anything from straightforward snow ascents to awkward chockstone-filled trenches, depending on the amount of snow. They are also very prone to avalanches after strong winds and/or snowfall. Between them lies The Castle, which is not often visited but which gives good climbing.

South Castle Gully 230m I/II*

W. Brunskill, W.W. King and W.W. Naismith, 1 April 1896

The long gully between Raeburn's Buttress and The Castle. Normally an easy snow climb. One small pitch may present difficulties early in the season, at what looks like a chockstone low down in the gully; climb this by a gangway on the left wall. Near the top of the left wall of the gully is an obvious icefall (**Plum Duff 60m V,5** *D. Hawthorn and J. Murphy, February 1984*).

Godspell 215m VII,8

S. Richardson and K. Cordes, 6 March 2005
(no photo topo)

The obvious line of chimneys on the left side of The Castle. Start 50m up The Castle and move left up easy mixed ground to a terrace (50m). Climb the short steep icy gully on the right side of the wall above. Follow the corner above to another terrace (50m). Climb the chimney past a chockstone (15m). Climb the right side of the square-cut recess to a small ledge, and the wall above to a terrace. Another chimney leads past a chockstone to the top of the headwall (45m).

The Castle 220m II/III*

W. Brown, J. MacLay, W.W. Naismith and G. Thomson, April 1896

In summer, an awkward bulging little wall guards the base. Wait until this is all covered in snow; the route then goes straight up. The upper rocks are climbed by means of a gully, slabs, a chimney and a further shallow gully, all in the centre of the buttress, to beneath the final very steep wall. The route now goes up to the

Early morning sunshine and lots of fresh snow on Castle Ridge

right over snow-covered slabs to the top. Great care should be taken on the slabby sections, which are prone to avalanche.

North Castle Gully 230m I/II*
J.H. Bell and R.G. Napier, 4 April 1896
The gully bounding The Castle on the right. Steeper than South Castle Gully, it contains several easy chockstone pitches, often completely covered giving a straightforward snow climb.

Castle Ridge 275m III**
J.N. Collie, W.W. Naismith, G. Thomson and M.W. Traverse, 12 April 1895
A fine outing. The easiest of the Nevis ridges (after Ledge Route) and possible in most conditions. The approach is threatened by avalanches from the Castle gullies and from above The Shroud.

Start 150m below the point where North and South Castle gullies meet. Traverse right onto the blunt crest of the ridge by the easiest line. Ascend via ledges, walls and slabs using the easiest line. A small flattening has a steep section above; traverse right for 10m and climb a groove. This can be tricky but is much easier when banked out with snow. Continue up until the crest is blocked by a band of steep walls.

Climb up behind a big block then a slab, before a traverse up and right to a big block. Above this, a flaky chimney in a very exposed position overlooking the

North Face (crux) leads to a good ledge and belay. Another difficult pitch on the crest leads to an easing in the ridge. Follow a spectacular narrow arête more easily, and the wider ridge to the top.

Note: Teams who are considering descending to the Halfway Lochan (NN 1472) should follow 232° grid for 200 metres from the top of the ridge, then 308° grid. The descent to the Halfway Lochan is over very rough, broken and rocky ground, with one or two small crags in places. A number of accidents have occurred in this area with people falling down the North Face, which is immediately on your right at the top of the ridge. In good weather and with enough time, a fine way to round off this ascent is to go up to the north summit of Càrn Dearg NW (1214m, NN 159 721) and descend Ledge Route. Alternatively, a bearing heading south-west from that summit will lead into the easy Red Burn descent.

North Face of Castle Ridge

Start	North Face car park, Torlundy
Time	1hr 45min
Crag base altitude	700m
Route lengths	190–500m
Route styles	Snow-ice, mixed snow, rock and ice
Avalanches	Generally quite secure apart from spindrift down this enormous face

This face is easily seen on the walk up Allt a' Mhuilinn, but is infrequently climbed. Climbers with an adventurous spirit, a good nose for finding routes and a desire to avoid crowds will be at home here.

Much confusion over the routes and where they go has been caused by the line of Nordwand being misunderstood. The original 1959 route, called simply Nordwand (grade III), starts well to the right of the big cascades falling down the centre of the face. These cascades are Nordwand Direct and Nordwand Superdirect, but they've been mistaken for the original Nordwand since the 1980s. As a result, the lines of Casino Royale and La Petite are uncertain because their starting points have been described in relation to Nordwand. However, the routes as described below make best sense to the author.

NORTH FACE OF CASTLE RIDGE

Approach
Follow the signed footpath, steeply at first, to the top of the forest, then the well-made path towards the CIC hut and cross the stream at about 540m. Walk up rightwards to the foot of the face.

Descent
Descend north-west towards Lochan Meall an t-Suidhe, being careful to stay well back from (west of) the ill-defined edge of the buttress.

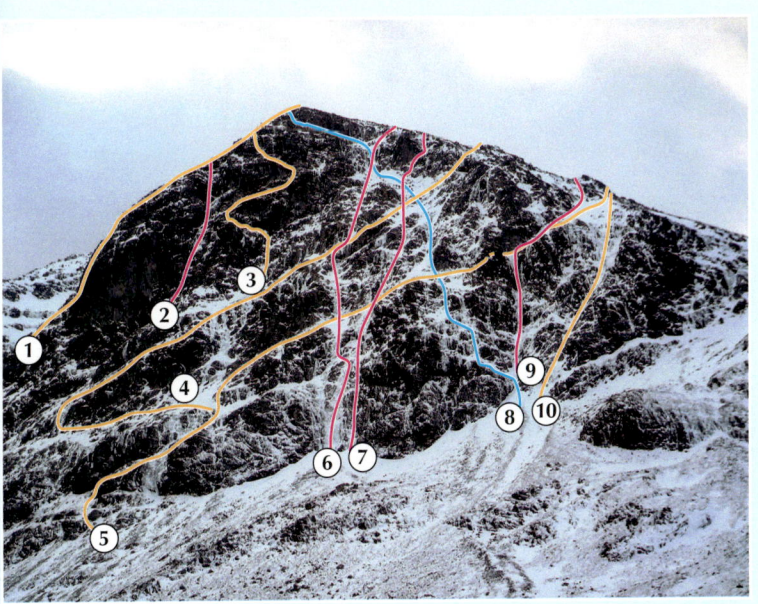

North Face of Castle Ridge

1. Castle Ridge III**
2. Lobby Dancer VI,6***
3. Last Day in Purgatory V,5**
4. The Moat II**
5. The Serpent II
6. Nordwand Direct V,4***
7. Nordwand Superdirect VI,5**
8. Nordwand III
9. Casino Royale V,5
10. La Petite III

The Serpent 300m II
I. Clough, D. Pipes and J. Porter, 12 February 1959
The easiest of the routes on the North Face of Castle Ridge. No technical difficulty, but still serious, with route-finding challenges. Above and to the left of the Lunching Stone (Glen Nevis approach), a small right-slanting gully gives access to a wide shelf which curves up to the right. After 165m this leads into a couloir which slants rightwards, steeply up the face, to come out on the shoulder of Càrn Dearg NW.

The Moat 500m II**
I. Sykes, I. Rae and I. Dewar, 8 February 1972
A great, highly banked snow ledge runs across the face above The Serpent and gives the line of this climb. Follow The Serpent for 70m, then move left to gain the ledge. At the end of the ledge, finish by a steep gully. A fine outing across this huge face.

Lobby Dancer 280m VI,6***
C. Higgins and A. Kimber, 28 February 1977
The left-hand section of the face is dominated by a clean overhanging wall split by a groove. Come in to the foot of the groove from the left by a diagonal ledge, or more directly by ice pitches. Climb the groove for three pitches to a barrier, from where an escape left is made (possibly on aid) to another groove. Go up this groove and on up to Castle Ridge.

Last Day in Purgatory 330m V,5**
C. Higgins and M. Geddes, 8 April 1979
Takes an impressive zig-zag line up ledge systems to the clean face right of Lobby Dancer.

Norwand Direct 400m V,4***
The big line of cascade ice up the centre of the buttress, open to much variation in line. This is a huge face – just about as big as Orion Face, but not quite as serious – with a wonderful outlook. Consecutive ice-screw belays and sustained ice climbing at the start, interspersed with snow patches.

Norwand Superdirect 400m VI,5**
G. Szuca and party, 1989
Climb the narrow ribbon of ice immediately right of Nordwand Direct, and the subsequent icefalls above.

Ben Nevis North Face, Carn Mòr Dearg Arête and Aonach Beag West Face in the distance

Nordwand 425m III
I. Clough, D. Pipes, B. Sarll, F. Jones and J. Porter, 11 February 1959
A fine mixed route, with technical and route-finding challenges similar to those on the Little Brenva Face. Starts fairly well to the right of the centre of the face at a slight bay. A long, vertical snow-filled trench on the screes below the face often shows the way.

Nordwand follows a short gully up the face for 30m and climbs an ice pitch before moving left (or works diagonally left below the ice pitch). It continues to follow the icefalls direct up the centre of the wall, crossing the couloir of The Serpent and continuing by snowfields to the steep summit rocks. An awkward left-rising traverse leads to the top.

Casino Royale 190m V,5
M. Duff, R. Nowack and A. Bond, 29 February 1988
Starts at the same point as Nordwand, at an obvious thin gully just left of La Petite. Climb into a snow bay and an icefall to an open gully. Continue to a thin ice-smear in a corner, which is climbed to a snow terrace on The Serpent. Go rightwards to finish, or up further icefalls above.

La Petite 200m III

D. Pipes and I. Clough, 11 February 1959

The climb starts about 30 metres right of Nordwand and goes up steeply for 40m to gain entry to a couloir. This entry will generally give a 25m ice pitch and then ice-glazed rock. The couloir, which leads obliquely right (not obvious from below), should give two more good ice pitches before finishing on the Càrn Dearg shoulder.

A small buttress well to the right of the face is split by an obvious gully (**Red Gully 120m II** *D. Pipes, I.S. Clough, J. Porter, B. Sarll and F. Jones, 1959*).

The Girdle Traverse 4000m V,4

S.M. Richardson and B. Davison, 21 April 2006
(no photo topo)

A right-to-left girdle traverse from Castle Ridge to North East Buttress. From the top of Castle Ridge, go over The Castle, then descend mixed ground into upper Castle Coire. Cross Ledge Route and the Trident buttresses, descend Number Four Gully, climb North Gully and traverse across Creag Coire na Ciste into Number Three Gully.

Climb Thompson's Route, descend Number Three Gully Buttress, climb Green Gully and descend Hesperides Ledge. Traverse across Comb Gully Buttress, move along the first part of Raeburn's Easy Route and continue left into Glover's Chimney.

Drop down from Tower Gap into Observatory Gully and head off under Indicator Wall and across Observatory Buttress, and enter Point Five Gully above the Rogue Pitch. Exit Point Five via the Left-Hand Finish, and continue across Hadrian's Wall, Observatory Ridge and Zero Gully to finish up Slav Route and reach the crest of North-East Buttress.

GLEN NEVIS

East Ridge of North Buttress, Stob Bàn

MAMORES

Stob Bàn 999m (NN 147 654)

Start	Lower Falls car park (NN 145 683)
Time	2hr
Crag base altitude	750–850m
Route lengths	100–200m
Route styles	Mostly snow gullies and turfy mixed routes
Avalanches	Big cornices form along the summit ridge line, especially north-west of the summit towards the 912m point. Avalanches in South Gully and North Gully are common.

The north-east face of this steep-sided and rocky peak provides good climbing on ridges, buttresses and gullies when in condition. The rock is quartzite and is therefore often well featured with cracks and ledges. Unfortunately, some of the buttresses can be horribly loose before the rocks are held together with snow-ice and frozen in place. North Buttress is more solid, being made up of mica schist and lots of turf. The shapely summit cone is obvious on the skyline as you go up Glen Nevis.

From the path on the walk in, the features are as follows, from left to right: East Wing, South Gully, South (summit) Buttress, North Gully, Central Buttress (this appears as a triangular mass of rock set forward and at a lower level than South Buttress), and a long flat col has North Buttress to its right.

Climbing the North Ridge, descending the East Ridge and continuing around the Devil's Ridge to the summit of Sgùrr a' Mhàim makes a fantastic circuit with very narrow ridge sections at grade I. The East Ridge of North Buttress is an excellent climb and the most popular on Stob Bàn; it's also quite safe to get to and to descend from.

The East Ridge of Stob Bàn with The Devil's Ridge of Sgùrr a' Mhàim behind

Approach
Walk up the path on the east bank of Allt Coire a' Mhusgain. Ascend this path to a point opposite the cliffs (NN 155 660), then descend for a short distance to cross the main stream below the cliffs at 500m above sea level. Approaching the cliffs from this point allows for a good reconnaissance before choosing the correct line of ascent, as the cliffs are more complicated than they look.

Descent
From the summit, two fine airy ridges can be used to descend. The North Ridge is the shortest and descends steeply over two subsidiary summits, point 912 being one of them (grade I). After approximately 2km, bear north-west to avoid steep grass and rocky outcrops before arriving back at the start point.

Alternatively, descend the East Ridge, taking care to avoid the sharply in-cut gullies to your left (north-west). After approximately 1km, a good path leads back in a northerly direction towards the original ascent path.

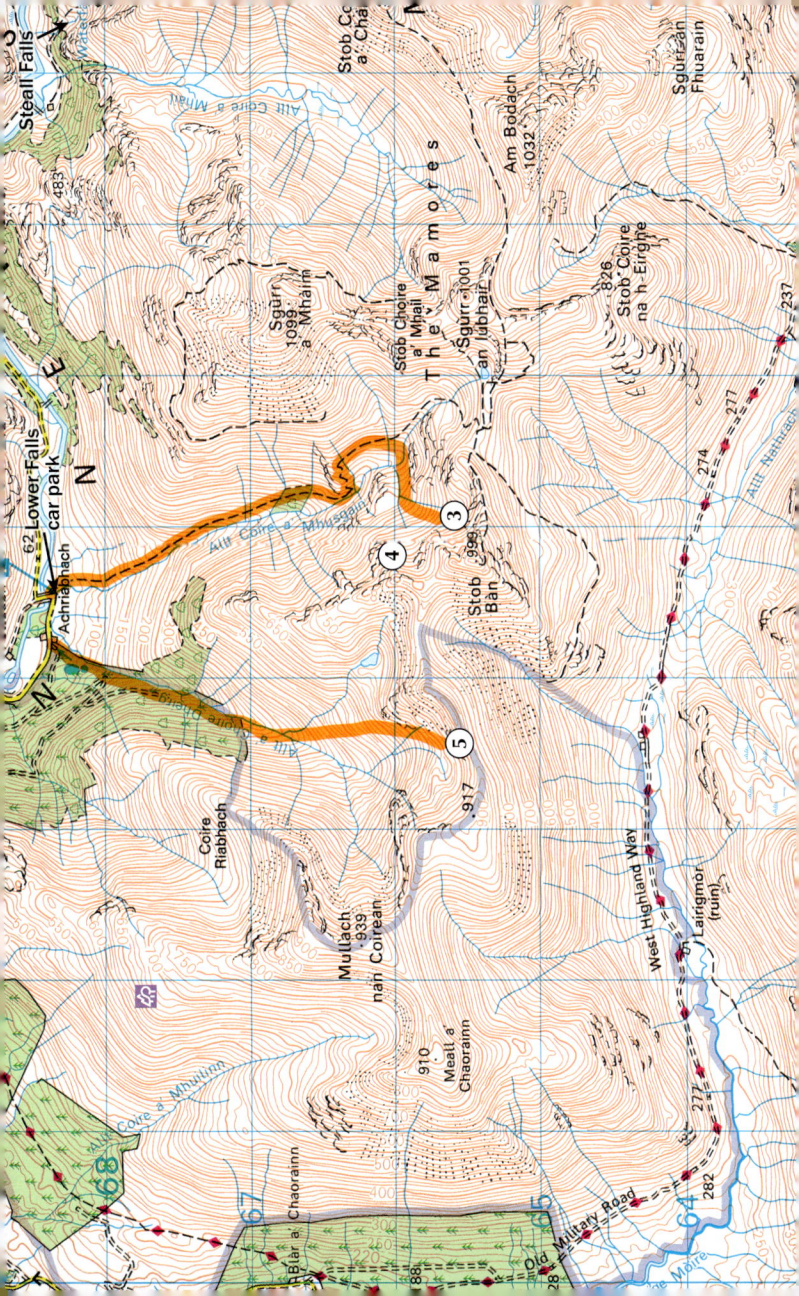

Stob Ban North East Face

- East Wing
- South Buttress
- South Gully I*
- Central Buttress
- alternative approach
- North Buttress – East Ridge
- East Ridge of North Buttress approach

Stob Bàn

(photo: Jamie Hageman)

Central Buttress
South Buttress
East Wing
Eag Blanc II
South Gully I*
Central Gully IV
Triad III*

1. East Wing V,5
2. Summit Groove IV,4*
3. Groove Rider IV,4*
4. Banjo IV,4
5. North Ridge Route IV,4
6. North Gully
7. No Toddy III,4
8. Gendarme Ridge IV,4
9. Skyline Rib IV,4*

Eag Blanc 100m II

V. Chelton and D. McGimpsey, 25 February 2005

The big groove on the left side of the East Wing is mostly grade I, with a couple of grade II steps.

East Wing 180m V,5

D. McGimpsey and A. Nisbet, 26 February 2006

Starting about 15m up South Gully at the highest ramp leading out left, this is a devious but spectacular line near the crest of the very steep East Wing. Reach the crest out to the left, always keeping above steep lower walls (35m). Gain the highest ledge up thick moss, then traverse it leftwards to a vertical column of wedged blocks which is very unstable if not well frozen (25m). Climb the column then a ramp leading up right (40m). The crest leads easily to the top of the buttress (80m).

South Gully 150m I*

The straightforward snow gully.

Summit Groove 140m IV,4*

A. Nisbet and C. Wells, 18 March 2008

Halfway up South Gully, climb a shallow gully leading close to the summit. Would be grade III if well iced.

Groove Rider 160m IV,4*

A. Nisbet and C. Wells, 18 March 2008

Start by traversing out right from South Gully, then climb a small well-defined groove straight up in two pitches. Gain and climb the ridge to the summit (75m).

North Ridge Route 150m IV,4

S. Kennedy and A. Nelson, 29 January 1995

At the foot of South Buttress, near the bottom of South Gully, are two corner lines. Follow the left-hand line (35m) then go right to a belay just before the ridge (15m). Climb the ridge easily to finish close to the summit.

North Gully 150m I

There are three gully lines on the left (north-east) flank of Central Buttress. The right-hand two are close together and all three are the same grade.

Central Gully 150m IV
J. Grieve and C. MacNaughton, 1969
Follow the gully and go back left along an easy ramp to gain the crest of the ridge, which leads easily to the top of the buttress.

Gendarme Ridge 150m IV,4
J. Maclay and Parr, 4 January 1904
On the slender buttress right of Central Gully. Climb up to and past a gendarme 'look-a-like', then steeply to where the angle eases (60m). Finish easily on Central Gully and the ridge above.

Triad 150m III*
D. Hawthorn, R. Lee and D.N. Williams, April 1986
Climbs the right-hand gully. Start between two narrow rock buttresses. Ascend the gully, which gradually steepens and narrows to a chimney. Reach a stance where the right-hand buttress finishes and a ledge runs across the left-hand buttress. Follow a snow ramp on the right, then traverse left along a narrow ledge to the buttress crest. Join the easy leftward-slanting ramp above to join the previous route.

Skyline Rib 120m IV,4*
R.G. Webb and B.A. Mattock, 13 February 1987
Climbs the narrow buttress crest right of Triad (loose). Finish up the ramp of Triad. On loose ground you should normally try not to pull on anything – just push down; but since this route is so loose, try not to push down either!

Bodice Ripper 150m IV,4*
J. Murphy and D.N. Williams, March 1984
(no photo topo)
Climbs the large triangular face on the front of Central Buttress. Start right of centre at the foot of an obvious rightward-slanting gully. Ascend easily to a prominent leftward-slanting ramp. Follow this until it fades, and take a poor stance at the foot of a steep and narrow rightward-slanting slab. Climb the slab with difficulty to its end, and zig-zag up the snow slope above (crux). Continue to the top of the snowfield and ascend the obvious gully. At the top, squeeze up the narrow chimney (Bodice Ripper) leading rightwards. A broad ramp leads left and then by a narrow crest towards the summit.

> **Note:** A short section of arête at the end of all of the routes on Central Buttress links to the main ridge 200 metres north of the summit.

North Buttress – East Ridge 200m II/III**
Brown, Hinxman, Tough and Douglas, Easter 1895

This ridge is best approached from the same direction as all the other routes on Stob Bàn, with a traverse across the corrie floor, and then a hard right (north-west) beneath Central Buttress. Head up towards the route from a flat spot (NN 151 660). Alternatively, make a rising traverse to reach the ridge at a big terrace to miss out the hardest climbing. An excellent exercise in route-finding, with tremendous views down Glen Nevis and a fine arête near the top.

Mullach nan Coirean 850m (NN 135 656)

Start	Lower Falls car park (NN 145 683)
Time	2hr
Crag base altitude	850m
Route lengths	50–80m
Route styles	Mixed climbs with rock and turf
Avalanches	Being north-west-facing, there is often less avalanche risk here

Between Mullach nan Coirean and Stob Bàn, facing north, the base of this granite crag is at 850m and rises to 80m high with a very steep 25m section at the bottom. The routes are mostly snowed-up rock climbing. There are several fine moderate ridges left of the crag as well, up to 200m long and about grade II or III.

Approach
Walk back along the road for 200 metres to Achriabhach (NN 142 684). Find the path through the forest on the west side of Allt a' Choire Dheirg. Follow this to the end of the forest and head south, crossing the stream, to climb the slope diagonally to the crag.

Descent
Descend the snow gully at the west end of the crag back to the base of the crag.

Captain Caveman 70m III,4

M. Brownlow, D. King and M. Pescod, 17 January 2006
(no photo topo)
The obvious line on the left end of the crag, passing several caves.

Not Bad for a Dad 80m VI,7

D. King and A. Turner, 27 November 2005
(no photo topo)
An undercut chimney at the left end of the main section of cliff. Climb into the steep chimney with bold initial moves to an alcove (30m). Continue with tricky moves, exiting the alcove to the top (50m).

Kid Gloves 70m IV,4

M. Brownlow, D. King and M. Pescod, 17 January 2006
(no photo topo)
The right arête of the crag.

Kindergarten Corner 50m VII,8

D. King, M. Brownlow and M. Pescod, 17 January 2006
(no photo topo)
A right-facing corner on the right face of the crag, finishing with a steep move left at the top. Easy finish up the arête of Kid Gloves. This route gives fantastic sustained climbing with good protection apart from the last 6m. The crux moves are getting off the ground and the move left at the top.

GLEN NEVIS

The following routes are outlined as alternatives for a short day if the weather and conditions allow. They are cascade ice climbs – frozen waterfalls – so they freeze rarely and only after a couple of weeks of intensely cold weather.

Five Finger Gully 200m IV,4

M. Tighe, S. McNeish, P. McKellar, G. Hunter and J. McDonald, 31 January 1996
(no photo topo)
This is the first big gully south of the Red Burn. The main branch provides a magnificent ice climb, although rarely in condition. Climb the deep gully over a series of short pitches to the final 35m waterfall. This is climbed on the left by a steep icy groove. It's possible to traverse right below the upper waterfall to a broad rib,

FIVE FINGER GULLY AREA

This quite infamous feature on the south-west side of Ben Nevis has been the scene of many (often fatal) accidents involving climbers trying to descend the 'Mountain Track'. The upper section is in fact a fairly large corrie (Coire Ghaimhnean), and only much lower down does it forms a gully – at The Junction (NN 146 708), around 440m. At this point the main gully cuts into the mountain and another, less-deep gully climbs north-east for 100m, then splits into two narrow defiles known as The Digits. In good icy conditions or on old, firm snow The Digits give good climbs of grade II. They can be quite sheltered, and it's possible to climb up one and down the other.

Access to the foot of the gully is by going over the bridge at the Glen Nevis Youth Hostel (SYHA) and walking along the floor of the glen, aiming for the old graveyard (NN 137 702) which lies within a stand of mature beech trees. It may also be possible to wade over the River Nevis if it's very low. Take a pair of wellies and dry socks! The gully comes down from the mountain above and is marked by a waterfall at its foot at approximately 360m. Entry to the gully is on the north side of this waterfall.

which leads in a fine position to the summit of Càrn Dearg south-west. If Coire Ghaimhnean is gained, an easy gully (I) leads north-east to the Nevis plateau.

Surgeon's Gully 400m V
M. Tighe, P. Coates, A. Finch, M. Jackson and T. Littler, 4 February 1996
(no photo topo)
A considerable undertaking. A drystone wall leads into the foot of this gully, which is a further 550 metres right of Five Finger Gully. On the first ascent, it was climbed as far as the horizontal deer track at 600m in very icy conditions with little snow. Pitch 13 – a 35m ice cascade – was the main feature, along with a difficult overhanging chockstone on the pitch above, which proved to be the crux. Three pitches in the untrodden central branch above the deer track were also climbed before an abseil descent.

Climbing Steall Falls

Steall Waterfall 120m III**
I.G. Rowe, 1 January 1963
(no photo topo)
The large waterfall above Steall Hut (NN 177 683) can provide good sport, if it freezes enough. Abseil descent using the trees on the left side followed by a steep walk down through the wood.

AONACH MÒR,
1221M (NN 193 730) AND
AONACH BEAG,
1234M (NN 196 715)

Aonach Beag West Face and the approach from Steall in Glen Nevis

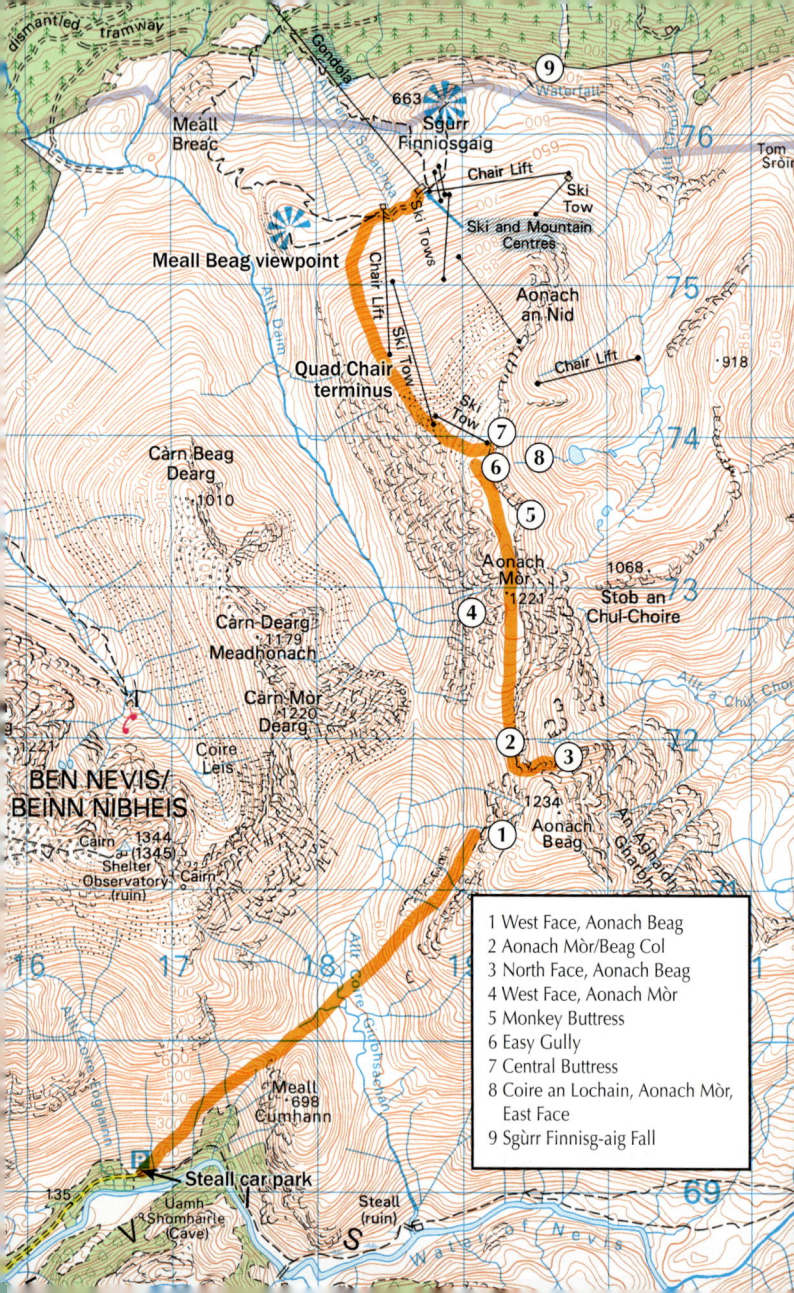

Aonach Mòr East Face – Coire an Lochain

The Nevis Range ski area on Aonach Mòr makes this a popular choice for climbers wanting some help with the approach. Being very high, the climbs are reliable; it has been the case that the only winter climbs on offer are found on Aonach Mòr East Face and Ben Nevis. Check with Nevis Range for times of the early morning climbers' gondola lift (tel 01397 705825). This is often available at 8am, but you do need to be ready to get on with cash in hand at 8am prompt. The gondola only runs for a few minutes to allow climbers and staff to go up.

Climbing on the flanks of these peaks is varied and interesting. The main areas are the East and West faces of Aonach Mòr, and the North and West faces of Aonach Beag.

Aonach Mòr East Face – Coire an Lochain

Start	Nevis Range ski area
Time	40min with the Quad Chair, or 1hr 30min from the gondola
Crag base altitude	1100m
Route lengths	50–150m
Route styles	Turfy mixed climbs and ice climbs
Avalanches	Big cornices normally line the tops of these crags and gullies, demonstrating that a lot of snow is blown over the top of the crags. There's often a steep snow slope beneath the cornice and above the crag as well. Beneath the crags, the slope is steep and continuous to the floor of the corrie at 850m. Avalanches here are common and sometimes the whole corrie has avalanched at once.

These routes come into condition quickly and early in the season due to their altitude. The gullies form snow-ice readily and the turfy buttresses offer good mixed routes, with the rough granite usually offering good protection. It can be possible to climb a couple of routes in a day, as they're short and access is fairly easy.

Despite being easy to access and close to the ski area, this is a serious place to climb. Large cornices form here. The normal approach down Easy Gully involves traversing steep ground; this is best avoided when the avalanche hazard is considerable or high. However, access can be made by

WINTER CLIMBS: BEN NEVIS

abseiling down Central Buttress with much less avalanche risk – check the cornices before trying this, and beware of parties ascending from below. Later in the winter or after heavy snowfall, the routes will bank out.

Some of the climbs may have been completed by RAF parties in the 1960s and not recorded. The routes in this book are described from left to right as the climber faces the corrie. For parties new to the corrie and unsure of the start of routes, it's advised that a first visit is made on a clear day with a viewing from the lochan beneath the cliffs in order to sort out the main features.

Approach
Take the gondola to 650m above sea level. You might also have the option of taking the Quad Chair (chairlift) to 920m, leaving just 270m to be gained. From the gondola it's best to walk up outside the west edge of the ski area by traversing underneath the chairlift first. Walk close to the fence lines and be aware of skiers. From the top of the ski area, find the top of Easy Gully (175m to the south) and abseil through the cornice to make your way along the foot of the crag.

Descent
Walk back down the west edge of the ski area and enjoy a coffee at the café.

The first three climbs are found on Monkey Buttress on the left side of the south defining ridge of Coire an Lochain.

Chimpanzee 60m III
S. Richardson, 1 January 2009
(no photo topo)
The prominent ice line to the left of Monkey Business is climbed with a step right at a bulge.

Monkey Business 70m V,6
S. Richardson and R. Webb, 30 December 2007
(no photo topo)

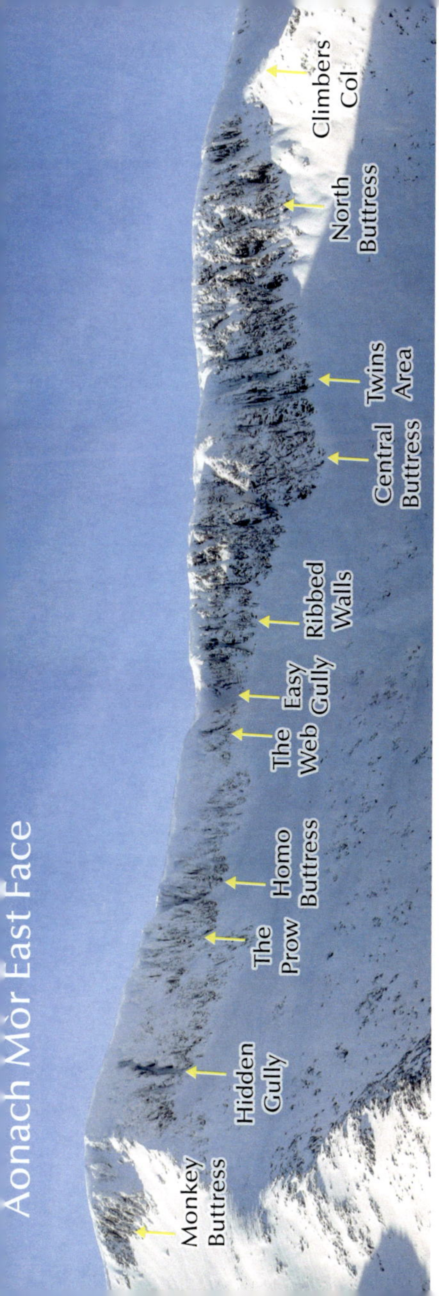

The prominent slim right-facing groove in the upper half of the buttress. Climb easily towards the upper groove (20m). Continue up ice then climb the groove, with a steep exit and short snow slope to the cornice (50m).

Monkey Puzzle 70m III

R. Webb and S. Richardson, 30 December 2007
(no photo topo)
The fault in the right-hand buttress. Easy snow leads to a steepening in the fault which can be avoided on the right or taken direct (III,4).

Hidden Gully 120m II*

R. Webb and C. Rice, 21 January 1989
At the south end of the corrie, some way left of the open descent gully (Easy Gully) but hidden from view until underneath it, is an attractive narrow, twisting couloir.

Ribbon on Edge 120m IV,6

S. Richardson and C. Cartwright, 8 January 1995
The fine arête right of Hidden Gully. Start at the base of Hidden Gully and follow a rightward break to a platform on the buttress front, then a groove on the right with difficulty to a belay (30m). Ascend the turfy wall

Coire an Lochain South Side

1. Ribbon on Edge IV,6
2. Two Queens IV,5*
3. Three Kings IV,5
4. Streamline III*
5. Back Street Boogie VI,6
6. The Wave V,5
7. Stirling Bridge V,7**
8. Homo Robusticus VI,7**

above and then climb the arête, passing two towers on their right side (45m). A further 45m to the top.

Two Queens 70m IV,5*
D. King and M. Pescod, 29 January 2006
Start 5 metres left of Three Kings. Climb a steep groove, then an easier corner leading into a shallow gully. Climb the gully (50m). Climb a short wall and the upper slope (20m).

Three Kings 70m IV,5*
R. Hamilton, S. Kennedy and A. MacDonald, 6 March 2004
The obvious right-leading ramps linked by a steep wall. Reach the corner (20m) and climb it (crux) on the left to a ledge where an exposed move leads back right to the upper ramp. Follow this to a thread belay (50m). Easy ground to the top (20m).

Streamline 90m III*
R. Hamilton and S. Kennedy, 16 February 2004
A wide fault-line left of The Prow (see below) almost forms a gully in its upper reaches. This route takes a rightward-leading ramp at the left side of the fault to below a steep wall (40m). Climb the corner directly under the wall to finish on the left in a spectacular vertical cornice.

> The following five climbs are located on The Prow – a buttress that lies approximately 100 metres left of Easy Gully and just left of a distinctive deep gully.

Back Street Boogie 70m VI,6
M. Pescod and F. MacCallum, 20 December 1999
A short way to the left of The Prow and slightly higher is a small buttress, 5 metres wide. This climb is on the front of that buttress. Go slightly left via a bulge and icy slabs to a right-facing corner, which is climbed to the top of a pillar (30m). Climb turfy cracks above, followed by a snow crest (40m).

The Betrayal 90m IV,4
S. Kennedy and D. Ritchie, 28 March 1990
(no photo topo)
The left-hand of the two parallel grooves on the front of the buttress. Follow the groove over bulges to a small snow bay immediately beneath the prow. Move steeply and awkwardly left to reach easier ground and a cornice finish.

The Prow and Homo Buttress

1. Back Street Boogie VI,6
2. The Wave V,5
3. The Guardian IV,5*
4. Pro Libertate V,6**
5. Stirling Bridge V,7**
6. Ribbon Groove IV,4
7. Gowan Hill V,6
8. Homo Robusticus VI,7**
9. Piranha VII,8**

Aonach Mòr East Face – Coire an Lochain

The Wave 70m V,5
A. Clarke and M. Thompson, 11 January 1995
Follows the prow between The Betrayal and The Guardian, first by grooves, up and then left to a bay (40m). Keep going left to reach the small snow bay on The Betrayal, followed by a wide V-groove above, then a rock wall right of the large cornice (30m).

The Guardian 90m IV,5*
S. Kennedy and D. Ritchie, 28 March 1990
Climb the right-hand of the two parallel grooves and a prominent flake chimney to steep but easier ground.

Stirling Bridge 70m V,7**
S. Kennedy and D. Ritchie, 4 April 1990
An excellent route with a memorable first pitch (steep and strenuous). Follow the prominent right-angled corner near the right edge of the buttress, going right near the top. A short groove above and a block belay on the left leads to easier ground below the cornice.

Ribbon Groove 60m IV,4
A. Forsyth and J. Turner, January 1995
Climbs the left side of the barrel-shaped buttress 20 metres right of Stirling Bridge via a large recess and groove above on the left. Start from the toe of the buttress.

Ribbon Development 60m IV,4**
A. MacDonald and K. Grant, 13 February 2003
(no photo topo)
A variation on Ribbon Groove, starting up the same line into the groove on the left but then moving up and right into a narrowing chimney. Climb the well-protected chimney over a chockstone to easier ground and belay on the left as for Ribbon Groove.

Homo Robusticus 60m VI,7**
M. Garthwaite and A. Clarke, 31 December 1994
The barrel-shaped buttress crest 20 metres right of Stirling Bridge. Climb up to a wide crack, climb it and exit steeply at the top.

Piranha 70m VII,8**

M. Pescod, T. Riley and J. Baird, 19 December 2001

Climbs the right-facing corner right of Homo Robusticus. Climb the icy groove right from the base of the buttress to below the corner. A steep wall leads into the corner, which is climbed with many adze torques until an exit left at the top of the corner can be made onto the front of the buttress to join Homo Robusticus. Finish as for this route.

The Web 100m II/III

C. Grindley and S. Kennedy, 25 November 1989
(no photo topo)

An icy chimney 30 metres left of Easy Gully is climbed. Banks out after heavy snow.

Easy Gully 100m I

The broad snow gully that cuts deep into the plateau and can provide a useful descent route. A large cornice can often be avoided on the right in ascent. Beware of off-piste skiers!

> The area between Easy Gully and Tunnel Vision is known as Ribbed Walls. There are many routes, all at around grade III, which can bank out and be topped by a large impassable cornice, in which case an exit might be made by traversing rightwards.

Barrel Buttress 90m IV,4

S. Kennedy and S. Thirgood, 7 February 1993

Left of Temperance Union Blues is a small recess with a sharp narrow arête on its right and a broad buttress on the left. Climb the buttress directly, starting just to its right and avoiding the steep wall at the top on the left.

Nid Arête 90m IV,5*

S. Kennedy and S. Thirgood, 7 February 1993

A well-protected mixed route which climbs the groove line on the left side of the narrow arête to the right of Barrel Buttress. The groove is climbed direct, taking the furthest corner on the right overlooking the final section of Temperance Union Blues.

Temperance Union Blues 90m III
S. Richards, G. Armstrong, C. Millar and J. Owens, 18 February 1989
Fifty metres to the right of Easy Gully, the cliff is split by a deep cleft at half-height. Climb either of two converging lines to the bottom of the cleft (45m). Ascend the cleft, exiting where it steepens onto a ramp, which is followed to the cornice (45m). Difficult if not sufficiently iced.

> Immediately left of the wide gully of Tunnel Vision, two buttresses are separated by a snowy amphitheatre. On the better-defined right-hand buttress is the fine line of Gondola With the Wind. The main features of the left-hand buttress are two icefalls which form down the left side.

Aquafresh 100m IV,4*
N. Marshall and D. Ritchie, 26 March 1990
Forty metres left of Tunnel Vision. Climb the left-hand icefall, trending left up mixed ground to finish.

White Shark 110m IV,4***
C. Millar and R. Webb, 27 January 1990
The right-hand icefall – a splendid climb. Climb the shallow gully and a steep slabby corner at mid-height to a ledge. Follow the steep ice pitch that forms down the corner to easier ground.

Tinsel Town 110m V,4**
S. Kennedy and P. Mills, 3 February 1991
Follows the groove-line left of Gondola With the Wind. Start 10 metres right of White Shark. Follow a groove system just right of the buttress crest, then a chimney to a stance on the left (40m). Go back right to the main groove and climb steep mixed ground to below the cornice (50m). A long traverse right may be necessary to outflank the huge cornice!

Gondola With the Wind 125m IV,5**
S. Kennedy and S. Thirgood, 30 December 1989
(no photo topo)
A good mixed climb up the right side of the buttress, just left of Tunnel Vision, with an exciting finish. Starts up a short groove 8 metres left of Tunnel Vision, gaining a small amphitheatre and exit on the right (45m). A system of shallow

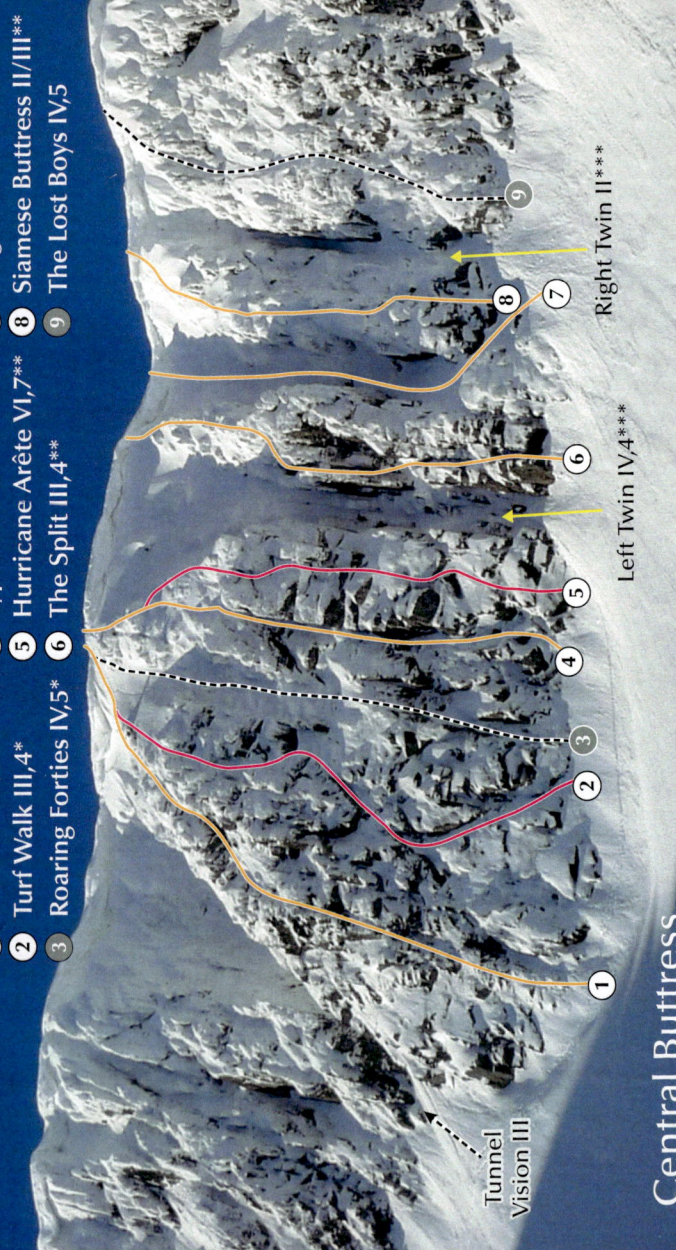

(photo: Blair Fyffe)

grooves close to the buttress edge is followed, then spiral right round the side of the tower to reach a steep corner (35m), which is followed with difficulty to easier ground (45m).

Maneater 90m V,5**
S. Richardson and R. Webb, 14 January 1995
The obvious gully between the buttresses of White Shark and Hammerhead Pillar. Ascend the gully to an overhung cave, then steep thin ice on the left wall to a belay (50m). Climb steeply above the belay to join Tinsel Town and the plateau (40m).

Tunnel Vision 120m III
S. Richardson and R. Everett, 22 January 1989
The wide gully between the Ribbed Walls and Central Buttress. Start at the foot of the gully immediately left of Morwind. An initial narrow section leads to a snow bay with three possible exits. Climb ice-smears up the wall at the back of the bay with interest, in an exposed position, to a steep cornice exit. In full conditions the wall may bank up to a frightening angle and the cornice becomes impassable. The left branch has been climbed (*S. Kennedy and S. Thirgood, 1990*), and it should always be possible to climb the right branch to reach the easy upper section of Morwind.

> Moving right, the area between Tunnel Vision and Left Twin is known as Central Buttress. Some of the finest mixed climbing on the mountain is situated here. The cornice can be massive, but a vague snow arête on the final slopes often provides a possible exit.

Morwind 150m IV,4*** or
R. Everett and S. Richardson, 10 January 1988
A fine mixed climb taking a direct line up a series of grooves on the crest of Central Buttress, starting from the lowest rocks about 30 metres left of Typhoon. A good, technically interesting climb which climbs well as a turfy mixed climb, or with lots of ice in the grooves.

Climb a short gully leading to a shallow chimney line with several

Climbing Morwind

Aonach Mòr East Face – Coire an Lochain

tricky steps on the crest. This leads to a small bay beneath a cave after two pitches. Exit right up mixed ground to easier slopes beneath the cornice (which could be very large late in the season).

Turf Walk 150m III,4*
R.D. Everett and C. Grant, 25 November 1989
Good mixed climbing on the right-slanting fault line that crosses the front side of the buttress on the left. Start 15 metres right of Morwind, following a left-slanting gully to belay in a bay below the fault. Follow the fault to ledges leading right. Step right, then up and left, to belay below steep grooves on the left of the central depression. Follow the groove on the left, stepping left onto the exposed prow and continuing to easier ground above.

Typhoon 130m IV,5***
R. Everett and S. Richardson, 14 January 1989
This excellent climb takes a direct line up the grooves just left of Hurricane Arête. Start 15 metres left of the deep gully of Left Twin. Climb the lower slabby grooves to a belay at the base of a chimney (40m). Climb the chimney and the groove past an overhang (30m). Continue direct on steep ice to exit onto the final slopes (40m). A further 20m leads to the top.

Note: Morwind and Left Twin are often used as abseil descents to the base of climbs in this area. Please respect any parties already climbing up one of these routes and descend elsewhere.

Hurricane Arête 140m VI,7**
S. Richardson and R. Everett, 4 March 1989
The slabby Central Buttress, left of Left Twin, is the highest section of crag in the corrie. On its right-hand side is a steep arête, with several overhangs in its upper section, which forms the left wall of Left Twin. This hard climb takes an intricate line through the overhangs just left of the arête.

Start midway between Typhoon and Left Twin. Climb iced slabs (30m) to a short left-slanting gully. Climb this, then up right along a narrow ramp to a small ledge (20m). Belay below a prominent overhang, just left of a right-facing corner which is capped by another overhang. Pull over the roof directly above the belay onto a steep slab, and follow a left-slanting crack to reach a prominent spike.

Go right below an overhanging wall to a small snow bay (20m) – a short but difficult pitch. Climb grooves on the left to the final overhangs, which are climbed by bridging up left towards easier ground (50m). Another 20m leads to the cornice.

Alien Abduction 120m VII,8
A. Powell and A. Benson, 22 December 1996
The grooves and stepped corner right of Hurricane Arête. Start up Left Twin to a platform on the left. Climb the right edge of Central Buttress to a stance on the right, level with the belay on Hurricane Arête (35m). Go left and climb the right-facing corner and three overhangs. After the third overhang, step left and up to a block belay. Ascend 5m up left, over a slab and onto easier ground (40m). FFA *M. Pescod and D. King, November 2000.*

> Right of Central Buttress are two steep narrow buttresses (Split and Siamese), bordered by three deep gullies. The left side of Split Buttress is characterised by the deep chimney of The Split, containing several jammed blocks which are a good reference point in misty weather.

Left Twin 120m IV,4***
R. Everett and S. Richardson, 22 January 1989
The obvious gully a few metres left of Forgotten Twin and immediately right of Central Buttress. It's climbed direct with some steep moves left on the final hard pitch. The line of ice-filled chimneys on right side of the gully is steeper and harder (**Siamese Twin IV,5****).

The Split 130m III,4**
S. Richardson and R. Everett, 19 February 1989
The left-hand side of the buttress left of Forgotten Twin is split by a deep chimney. Start at the foot of the buttress and climb the introductory chimney to snow slopes to the right of Left Twin (25m). Enter the deep chimney and continue under several large jammed blocks until it's possible to exit to the left some 4m below the final overhang. Continue up the arête to belay (45m). Climb easy snow leftwards to join Left Twin (50m).

Lickety Split 130m IV,5**
G. Mulhemann and S.M. Richardson, 2 December 1989
A fine, varied mixed route. Climb the icefall directly below the gully of Forgotten Twin to a stance below the right-facing corner on the right side of the lower half

AONACH MÒR EAST FACE – COIRE AN LOCHAIN

of Split Buttress (30m). Follow the corner to a stance (20m) and continue up the steep wall above, passing two overhangs to a rock ridge overlooking Left Twin (20m). Go up the ridge to easier ground and the cornice (60m).

Forgotten Twin 120m I/II
R. Everett and S. Richardson, 22 January 1989
The gully between the buttresses of Split and Siamese. A short leftward ramp from the foot of Right Twin leads to an easy gully with a couple of steeper stretches before the cornice exit.

Siamese Buttress 120m II/III**
S. Richardson and R. Everett, 19 February 1989
The well-defined buttress left of Right Twin provides an enjoyable scramble. Harder (grade III) if started up the steep corners on the left.

Right Twin 120m II***
S. Richardson and R. Everett, 22 January 1989
The gully on the right of Siamese Buttress. About 1.5m wide with vertical side walls, it gives an enjoyable traditional climb with steep sections at the bottom and at mid-height. Exit left at the top.

White Bait 100m IV,5
M. 'Ed' Edwards and D. McGimpsey, 5 February 2007
Start about 20 metres right of Right Twin. Climb a short ice groove, go up and right into an icy bay. From its top, gain a narrow ledge on the right and climb through steep walls to a ledge (40m). Continue up, then move right to climb the left side of a large snowy bay (30m). Exit the bay and continue out left, then straight up to the cornice (30m).

> The following three routes start in a large bay about 50 metres left of Grooved Arête.

The Slever 100m III,4
S. Kennedy and D. Ritchie, 2 March 1991
The large icefall on the left margin of the bay is climbed in one long pitch to easier ground. Then move right into a small gully and easily towards the cornice.

Golden Promise 100m VI,7*
B. Davison, S. Kennedy and S. Venables, 23 February 1992
A difficult mixed route which climbs the steep groove line at the top right-hand side of the bay. Climb the easier lower snow gully to a large block belay on the right at the foot of the main difficulties (45m). Climb the steep groove above, pulling over a large bulge at 20m to reach a small cul-de-sac. Exit by a groove on the left and easier grooves above to belay just short of the upper gully of Molar Canal (45m). Climb the gully to the top (10m).

Molar Canal 100m III
C. Jones and S. Kennedy, 25 January 1990
Approximately 35 metres left of Grooved Arête is a gully, deep and wide in the top section. Climb a short icefall and grooves into the gully, which is climbed towards the cornice. This might be impassable direct, in which case a long traverse left is required.

> North Buttress is the final section at the northern side of the corrie. It's separated from Molar Canal by two narrow ribs and is made up of three distinct buttresses, cut by the deep Icicle Gully to the left and the clean groove of Jet Stream on the right.

Grooved Arête 130m V,6**
S. Richardson and R. Everett, 26 November 1988
This superb climb takes the narrow arête immediately left of Icicle Gully. Start at the foot of the gully, gain the arête to the left and follow this, easily at first, then with increasing interest up grooves on its left side before moving back right to belay below a steep tower (45m). Climb a series of steep grooves on the crest of the tower until it's possible to move left to a ledge. Climb the short vertical corner above with difficulty, exiting on the right (35m). Regain the crest and continue more easily to the plateau (50m). Excellent technical climbing.

Icicle Gully 130m III
R. Everett and S. Richardson, 26 November 1988
The gully between Grooved Arête and Force Ten Buttress. Climb the gully line with interest to a belay on the right (50m). Take the wider line to the right of a narrow groove (which is bounded by Grooved Arête to the left). Climb this until it narrows and steepens at an icicle, which leads to a snow bay (50m). Continue up the mixed ground above (30m).

Force Ten Buttress 140m III,4*
R. Everett and S. Richardson, 3 December 1988
This good mixed climb takes the buttress between Icicle Gully and Jet Stream. It's technically hard for the grade, with several short, difficult, well-protected sections, but the rock is very friendly!

Climb mixed ground just left of the crest then move right to a belay at the foot of a short chimney where the buttress steepens (45m). Climb the chimney then step right to climb a short difficult crack (30m). Now climb mixed ground, mainly just to the right of the crest, to join a gully which rises to a col, where the buttress merges into the final slopes (40m).

> In a bay between Force Ten Buttress and North Buttress are two prominent gully lines which form ice easily and, being in the shade, stay in condition throughout the winter.

Solar Wind 110m IV,4*
R.D. Everett and S.M. Richardson, 8 March 1992
Start close beneath Force Ten Buttress and follow the obvious left-hand chimney to a snow patch (45m). Ascend the steep square-cut groove above, exiting left near the top to reach and climb the continuation gully, and belay where Force Ten Buttress merges with the final slopes (40m). Just 25m remain to the cornice.

Jet Stream 100m IV,4***
R. Everett and S. Richardson, 3 December 1988
This is the narrow gully immediately left of North Buttress (and which forms an icicle icefall in its lower part), about 50 metres left of the northerly bounding corrie ridge. Climb the gully over several steep sections to a snow bay (45m). Exit right up a steep, awkward wall to easier ground which leads to below the cornice (45m). Go up to the cornice and over the top (10m). Excellent climbing. When

fully formed, the icefall that forms in the headwall would make an exciting and fitting direct finish.

> To the right of Solar Wind is a chimney that can be used as an alternative start to either of the previous climbs – **Guides Variation 45m IV,4** *S. Allan and D. Etherington, February 1992*.

Foosyerneeps 50m IV,5**
A. Clark and J. Davis, 13 April 1998
The clean pillar at the far right of the corrie, climbed via cracks and corners just right of the prow to finish through a hard V-notch at the top.

Aonach Mòr West Face

Start	Nevis Range ski area
Time	2hr
Crag base altitude	900m
Route lengths	400m
Route styles	Mixed climbing on long, mountaineering, blocky granite ridges, with ice climbing in gullies in between
Avalanches	Facing west means this is often a more secure venue than most. However, big open slopes need to be crossed and there's ample chance of cross-loading in the many gullies that line the face.

The West Face of Aonach Mòr presents several granite ridges of moderate angle at 400m high. The steepest of these are directly below the summit cairn and, being in a slightly recessed bay, they are hidden from many viewpoints. The climbs provide excellent mountaineering routes in a wild and remote setting. To locate the buttresses, follow Allt Daim until opposite the distinctive Pinnacle Ridge descending from the summit of Càrn Dearg Meadhonach.

Approach

Take the gondola to 650m above sea level. Follow the path to the Meall Beag viewpoint and descend south to Allt Daim (descending 100m through steep ground). Walk up the east bank of Allt Daim to NN 186 729 (stream junction) and go uphill (east). Finding the start of the climbs is not easy! The bottom of the gully between Golden Oldie and Western Rib on the West Face is at NN 18962 72971.

Descent

The routes finish on or close to the summit, from which a walk of 1km north gets you back to the ski area. Do not underestimate the difficulty of this walk in poor visibility; it's a stern test of navigation skills while trying to avoid the cornices that overhang the East Face.

Following the floor of the glen alongside Allt Daim to the main climbing area beneath the summit, parties will pass below a number of shallow gully lines or iced slabs. On closer inspection these gullies and slabs can provide very good cascade ice climbing. After the initial steep pitches the ground eases, and it may be possible to abseil and climb another route or alternatively continue more easily to a ridge above. These gullies and slabs were climbed on in the 1978/79 winters by Joint Service Mountain Training parties, but never recorded. Further up the glen (1hr) the buttresses become more massive and well-defined as follows.

Golden Oldie 400m II***

A. Kimber, 21 December 1979

Follow the leftmost buttress, which becomes better defined and narrower higher up, with deep gullies to the left and right. From below it appears as a square blocky buttress.

Western Rib 400m II/III**

S. Richardson, 17 December 1988

From below, the second buttress from the left appears as a flying buttress joining the third, broader buttress (Daim Buttress), although it is in fact separated by a deep gully. A delightful long route with sustained interest, never very hard. The **left-hand start** is popular, by an independent rib which then joins the main buttress at a small col.

Aonach Mòr West Face

1. Golden Oldie II***
2. Western Rib Left Hand Start II/III**
3. Western Rib II/III**
4. Spare Rib Gully III**
5. Daim Buttress II/III
6. Solitaire II

Spare Rib Gully 400m III**

C. Bailey, M. Cooper and R. Hudson, 25 January 1993 (first recorded ascent)
Climb the lowest gully between Western Rib and Daim Buttress in three pitches to easier ground (100m). Carry on up the easy gully or move left onto Western Rib, or right onto Daim Buttress and follow either to the summit.

Daim Buttress 400m II/III

R. Everett, N. Barratt and S. Richardson, 25 February 1989
This is the third buttress from the left, characterised by a prominent slab just above half-height. Start directly below the slab at the foot of the buttress. The first 200m gives enjoyable mixed climbing up snow and rocky corners to ledges at the foot of the slab. Move left and climb cracks on the left edge of the slab to a platform (50m). Take the cracks and corners up the buttress above (50m). Scrambling leads to the top.

Solitaire 400m II

R.D. Everett and S.M. Richardson, 1 January 1990
The right-hand ridge, starting just left of a deep gully. Slightly easier than the other routes hereabouts. A good scramble in the summer (Difficult!).

SGÙRR FINNISG-AIG – ALLT NA H-AIRE WATERFALL

This stream descends from the Aonach Mòr gondola restaurant area in a north-easterly direction and provides good cascade ice climbing up to grade IV,4 after a prolonged heavy freeze down to sea level. It can be seen from the A82 just south of Spean Bridge. The main fall was probably first climbed by Loch Eil Centre and JSMTC staff in the 1970s and never recorded. Access is from the Nevis Range car park by bike or on foot on forest tracks to NN 196 769, then up steeply south to the waterfall. It's possible to climb on the fall and descend from the side banks back into the forest – or continue up and catch a gondola down, thus saving on knee cartilage!

Sgùrr Finnisg-aig Fall 200m IV,4*

(no photo topo)
The main line of the stream with several steps and the last 50m pitch being the crux. Left of the main fall is a diagonal descent line, and left of this two thin ice lines sometimes form. The left-hand one, which is 150 metres left of the main fall, has been climbed – **Incidental Fall IV,4** *S. Dring and J. Lyall, 1 February 1996.*

Sally Hudson climbing cascade ice on Sgùrr Finnisg-aig Fall

Taking the left fork at the base of Sgùrr Finnisg-aig Fall and going left and right by the easiest line gives **Saints Slip II/III** *D.W.M. Whalley, S. Coleby and party, 22 December 1996.*

Aonach Beag North Face

Start	Nevis Range ski area
Time	1hr 15min to the Aonach Mòr/Beag col with the Quad chairlift; or 2hr from the gondola
Crag base altitude	1050m
Route lengths	120–460m
Route styles	Ice climbing of the highest quality
Avalanches	Cornices and avalanches are less of a problem on this crag due to its northerly aspect and exposure to the wind blowing across it, but the approach from the Aonach Mòr/Beag col is often prone to avalanche.

Very steep and impressive snow patch cascade-style ice climbs form here, with sufficient thaw-freeze cycles allowing water from the snow to drip down the rocks to form the ice. If Mega Route X and Gemini on Ben Nevis are formed, the big ice climbs here will be good as well.

The climbs are described from right to left as if descending from the Aonach Mòr/Beag col. After 100 metres a wide icefall is seen on the right; this splits below a steep rock headwall, forming a 'Y' shape. Whiteout (II) takes the right branch, Stand and Deliver climbs the prominent central section of the icefall hanging down the wall, and Blackout takes the narrow ice chimney 15 metres to the right. The routes are difficult to protect, and a selection of rock protection and ice gear is recommended for the harder climbs.

Approach
Take the gondola to 650m above sea level. There might also be the option of taking the Quad Chair to 920m, which leaves just 270m to be gained to the top of the ski area. From the top of the ski area walk 1km south to the summit of Aonach Mòr and follow gentle slopes down to the Aonach Mòr/Beag col. Descend north-east into the corrie to reach the climbs.

Descent
Descend back to the Aonach Mòr/Beag col and retrace your steps back over Aonach Mòr to the ski area.

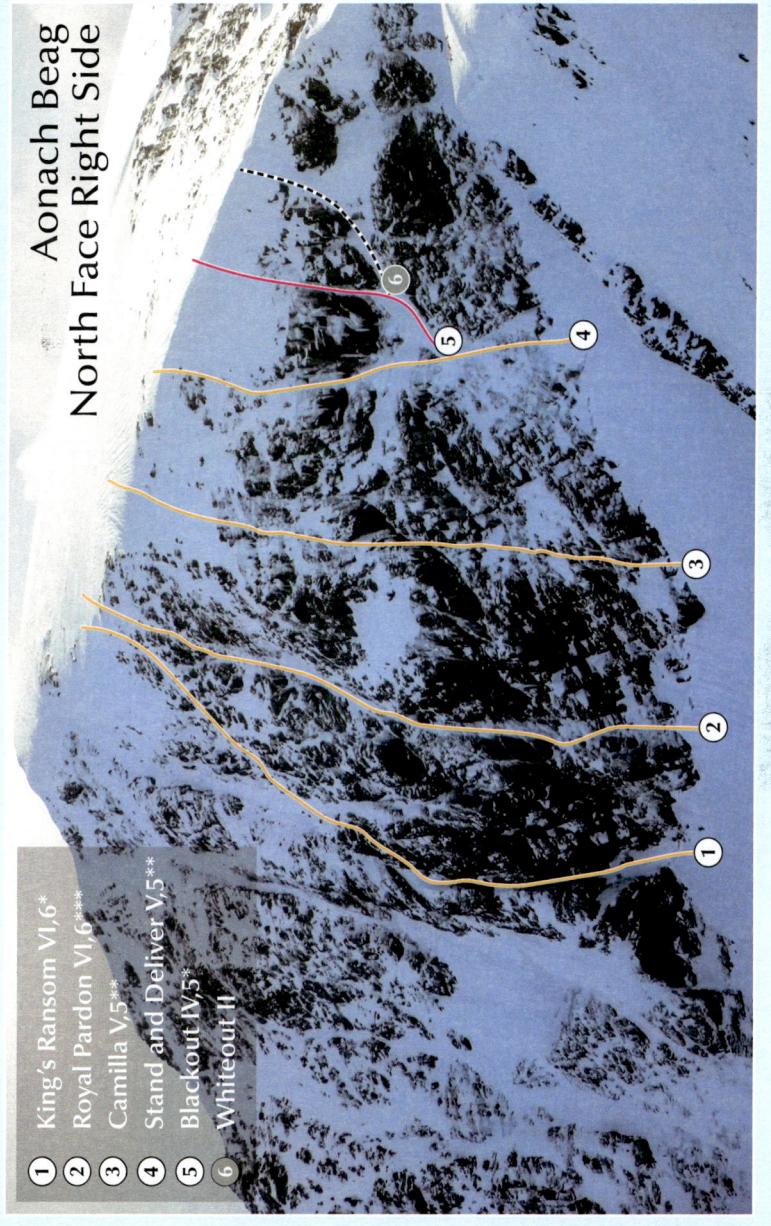

Royal Pardon VI,6***

Aonach Beag North Face Left Side

① Mayfly III*
② The Black Prince II
③ Queen's View III

Blackout 120m IV,5*
J. Dunn and R.G. Webb, 21 February 1987
Follow the wide prominent icefall for 50m to a snowfield. Go right via a short icefall to another snow slope. Climb the chimney in the steep buttress above in one long hard pitch on its left wall.

Stand And Deliver 120m V,5**
C. Cartwright and R. Clothier, 16 April 1989
The imposing icefall directly above the initial gully of Whiteout. A long and sustained ice pitch.

Camilla 230m V,5**
R.D. Everett and S.M. Richardson, 31 January 1993
A serious ice route which climbs the twin icicles that hang down the overhanging right side of the face at mid-height. Start at the foot of the buttress, 25 metres right of the prominent icefall taken by Royal Pardon. Climb snow and steep ice to the crest of the buttress (40m). Go up the snow slope above and a shallow icy gully to below the twin icicles (50m); belay on the right. Climb the right-hand icicle and easier ground to the crest of the buttress (50m). Continue up ice on the left and a snowfield to the top (90m).

Royal Pardon 220m VI,6***
R. Webb and S. Richardson, 18 February 1987
About 50 metres right of King's Ransom is a prominent thin ice-smear running down the centre of the buttress. Similar to Smith's Route on Gardyloo Buttress, but with steeper and thinner ice. Climb a series of icefalls for 55m to belay at the bottom right-hand side of the smear. Climb the vertical (for 2m) smear (40m); poor belay on the right, or a better one slightly higher (10m). A short pitch up ice leads to a broad snow couloir (20m). Follow the couloir for 50m, then go left up two good steep ice pitches to the summit plateau.

King's Ransom 250m VI,6*
S. Richardson and R. Webb, 14 February 1987
A fine and varied route with difficult mixed climbing in places. Start about 40 metres left of Royal Pardon. The very left side of the buttress is split by a narrow gully; follow the gully for two pitches until it fades, passing a large chockstone (possibly behind) and climbing a free-standing ice pillar en route (90m). Belay on a spike below the steep wall on the left side of the buttress. An escape left is possible from here, avoiding the difficulties of the upper pillar.

Follow a ramp on the right until it fades, then the steep wall (hard) above to a second ramp, which is followed delicately to the buttress crest. Another 120m of climbing follows a fine snow arête and easier mixed ground to the plateau.

Stob Coire Bhealaich and An Aghaidh Gharbh both offer remote and very quiet venues for adventurous climbers in search of solitude. Many routes have been recorded here; they are not included in this guide but may be worth exploring.

Winter Climbs: Ben Nevis

> The following climbs have a very different character, being less well-defined, long mountaineering climbs.

Queen's View 250m III

P. Moores and A. Nelson, 8 February 1995
Gain the snowfield in the centre of the face between Mayfly and King's Ransom via a runnel. Leave the snowfield by a narrow gully which leads directly to the highest part of the face above.

The Black Prince 300m II

A. Nisbet, 6 April 2000
Start up a slabby buttress left of Queen's View into a snow basin, then follow the easiest line up a wide ridge to the final few metres of the North-East Ridge.

Mayfly 210m III*

K. Schwartz, 9 May 1979
There's a large triangular face between the Aonach Mòr/Beag col and the North-East Ridge of Aonach Beag. The face has a steep buttress nearest the col, an easier gully area in the centre, and a lower rocky section. Just left of the centre (NN 197 718), an initially wide gully, marked on its lower right by a rock rib, leads to above the pinnacles of the North-East Ridge. This climb takes the gully.

After 90m an 18m-high and equally wide icefall is reached and climbed on its right side. Continue by a much narrower gully above, which leads via an awkward ice bulge to the easier upper section. Finish up North-East Ridge to the summit.

North-East Ridge 460m III,4*

J. Maclay, W.W. Naismith and G. Thomson, April 1895
The original climb on Aonach Beag, this long ridge descends well into the corrie below the mountain. The lower section of the ridge is not particularly difficult, but the middle part of the climb is quite narrow, with several pinnacles at half-height, which may be hard in icy conditions. The pinnacles are turned on the right, and after regaining the crest an overhung nose is passed on the left. (The pinnacles may be climbed direct at a much harder grade.) A knife-edge snow ridge leads to the broader and easier upper section, finishing about 50 metres to the north-west of the summit.

Aonach Beag West Face

Start	Steall car park, Glen Nevis (NN 167 691)
Time	2hr 30min to Raw Egg Buttress
Crag base altitude	1000m
Route lengths	70–180m
Route styles	Turfy mixed climbing with a few ice climbs
Avalanches	Facing west and being exposed to the usual winds, this is often a secure place to climb.

In clear weather the main features of this face are easily seen from the top of North-East Buttress or the end of Carn Mòr Dearg Arête on Ben Nevis, and climbers in that area could help themselves by spying out the lines. It's common to walk in from Steall in Glen Nevis, but it's equally possible to reach the climbs from the Aonach Beag/Mòr col, which itself is reached over Aonach Mòr from the Nevis Range ski area using the gondola and chairlift.

Approach
Head up grass slopes out of the car park, north then north-east, heading for the col to the north of Meall Cumhann. There's a slight path. Go through the col and continue in the same direction, descending slightly to cross Allt Coire Giubhsachan. Climb steep slopes on the other side of the corrie to the crag.

Descent
North to the Aonach Mòr/Beag col and then south-west down into the corrie; or south-west and south down the steep slopes which then lead west back to the corrie.

From left to right, on approaching from the Aonach Mòr/Beag Col, the first feature is a broad gully bounded on its right by Broken Axe Buttress, which has another deep easy gully on its right. Right of this gully is a lot of broken ground, which forms several icefalls. Right again is the most prominent buttress, Raw Egg Buttress (approx. NN 191 711), some 700 metres south-west of the col. The climbs are described from left to right.

Twinkle 150m IV,5**

R. Everett and S. Richardson, 20 February 1988

An excellent mixed route that follows the crest of Broken Axe Buttress directly. Technically quite hard for the grade, but well protected and with several escapes possible to easier ground. Climb a chimney groove to the left of the steep wall left of Axeless, then move right to belay above the wall (30m). Climb the open groove above to a small ledge, step right and climb the continuation groove to a small col junction with Axeless (40m). Step right to a steep corner. Climb this and the overhanging chimney above, then continue direct to join the final easy arête (50m). Follow Axeless to the top.

Axeless 150m III*

R. Webb and R. Everett, 16 January 1988
(no photo topo)

This climb takes an indirect but interesting line up Broken Axe Buttress. Start at a steep wall at the foot of the buttress in a small snow bay. Climb a groove on the right to a ledge overlooking the gully. Step right onto steep ice and climb up to snow, which leads back left to the crest of the buttress at a col. Move left to avoid the steep step above, then trend back right to gain a fine ridge which leads to the top.

Aonacrack 150m IV,5**

J. Ashbridge and S.M. Richardson, 21 March 1993

A good mixed climb which climbs the prominent crack on the right side of the buttress. Start close to the small snowy bay right of Axeless. Follow a ramp awkwardly to the base of the crack (15m). Climb the crack and a steep bulge to a ledge below a huge perched block. Follow a crack on the left side of the block to a belay on the top (25m). Continue in the crack and a steep bulging groove to a ledge (40m). Follow the broken ridge easily to the snow arête of Twinkle (40m), which is followed for another 30m.

> About 400 metres further right across the face (south) is Raw Egg Buttress. Between Broken Axe Buttress and Raw Egg Buttress is very steep broken ground that sometimes forms cascade ice climbs such as Beyond the Call of Duty (III,4).

Raw Egg Buttress

Ruadh Eigg Chimney V,6*

(photo: Jamie Hageman)

1. Eggsclamation II
2. Aonach Wall V,6*
3. Raw Egg Buttress IV,4*
4. Top Gun VI,6**
5. Salmonella VII,8**

Eggsclamation 150m II
S.Richardson and R.Everett, 5 April 1987
Immediately left of Raw Egg Buttress is an icy couloir. Follow this over short steps until the main line trends left (Poached Egg, II). Climb a short wall to gain the steeper direct continuation to the top of the buttress.

Aonach Wall 150m V,6*
R. Everett and S. Richardson, 27 March 1988
This climb takes a direct line just to the right of the left arête of Raw Egg Buttress, taking in enjoyable technical climbing of steadily increasing difficulty. Start to the left of Raw Egg Buttress below the steep tower with the prominent perched block. Climb up and avoid the tower on the right to belay by the notch – as for Raw Egg Buttress (55m).

Climb directly up via a short corner to gain snow below a longer corner which leads to the crest of the arête (40m). Easy snow leads to the base of the headwall (20m). Climb a groove and wide crack straight above to a ledge (20m). Move right to gain the obvious V-groove, which provides the only line up the final wall. Climb this with difficulty to the top (15m).

Raw Egg Buttress 180m IV,4**
R. Everett and S. Richardson, 5 April 1987
A good, well-protected mixed climb, with several short difficult steps, which takes a line up the front face trending from left to right. Start to the left of the lowest rocks on the left side of the crag. Climb an icy groove to below an overhanging corner, and then traverse right below a steep wall until it's possible to climb it (30m).

Now trend up and left over mixed ground to belay next to a notch in the ridge on the left, formed by a tower with a prominent perched block (50m). Follow the icy groove line above for two long pitches, always trending right, over several steep steps and corners (85m). The last pitch takes a steep corner to the left of a steep wall and has a difficult exit (15m).

Top Gun 160m VI,6**
S. Richardson and A. Mullin, 23 February 1999
Start 30m right of Raw Egg Buttress, 5m up and right of the foot of the lowest rocks. Follow a left-slanting chimney ramp to its top, then up to the barrier wall of Raw Egg Buttress (40m). Climb a short icefall in the wall and go up right via chimneys to a good ledge (Salmonella first pitch finishes here) (40m). Above are three parallel right-trending grooves. Climb the middle groove to a ledge below the right of the headwall. Go left to a belay below a steep corner (50m). The corner

Aonach Beag West Face behind the Carn Mòr Dearg Arête

above with obvious flakes on its left wall is climbed to a ledge (20m). A further 10m up the corner to the top.

Salmonella 125m VII,8**
R. Everett and S. Richardson, 23 March 1991
A very hard mixed climb. Start about 30m up and right of the previous climb, below a prominent right-facing corner which cuts the lower tier and is gained

by moderate mixed ground. Climb the overhanging corner for 20m, then continue more easily to a ledge and easy ground (35m). Possible escape down to the right.

Scramble up to the obvious V-groove (15m). Climb the groove past a ledge, then continue up a chimney to belay below the prominent overhanging offwidth (40m). Climb the offwidth to a ledge (10m), then gain an alcove and pull over an overhang to easier ground (25m).

> Well up and right (40m) of the previous route is an impressive rock wall which has a couple of good summer climbs on it. The right edge of this wall is defined by a deep gully which steepens into a narrow chimney, capped by three giant chockstones (Ruadh Eigg Chimney).

Blackbeard 70m VII,8
S.M. Richardson and I. Small, 4 January 2008
(no photo topo)
Spectacular steep mixed climbing up the right arête of the steep wall, just left of Ruadh Eigg Chimney. Start directly below the arête. Climb the first of two corners to a narrow ledge, step right and climb the cracked right edge to a good ledge on the right (25m). Pull through the overhang on the right then trend left up a steep wall to regain the arête. Steep cracks on the edge of the buttress reach a left-trending ramp to the top (45m).

Ruadh Eigg Chimney 60m V,6*
R. Everett, G. Muhlemann and S. Richardson, 28 March 1992
Follow snowy steps to the foot of the chimney, then go up over the chockstones and ice on the left wall.

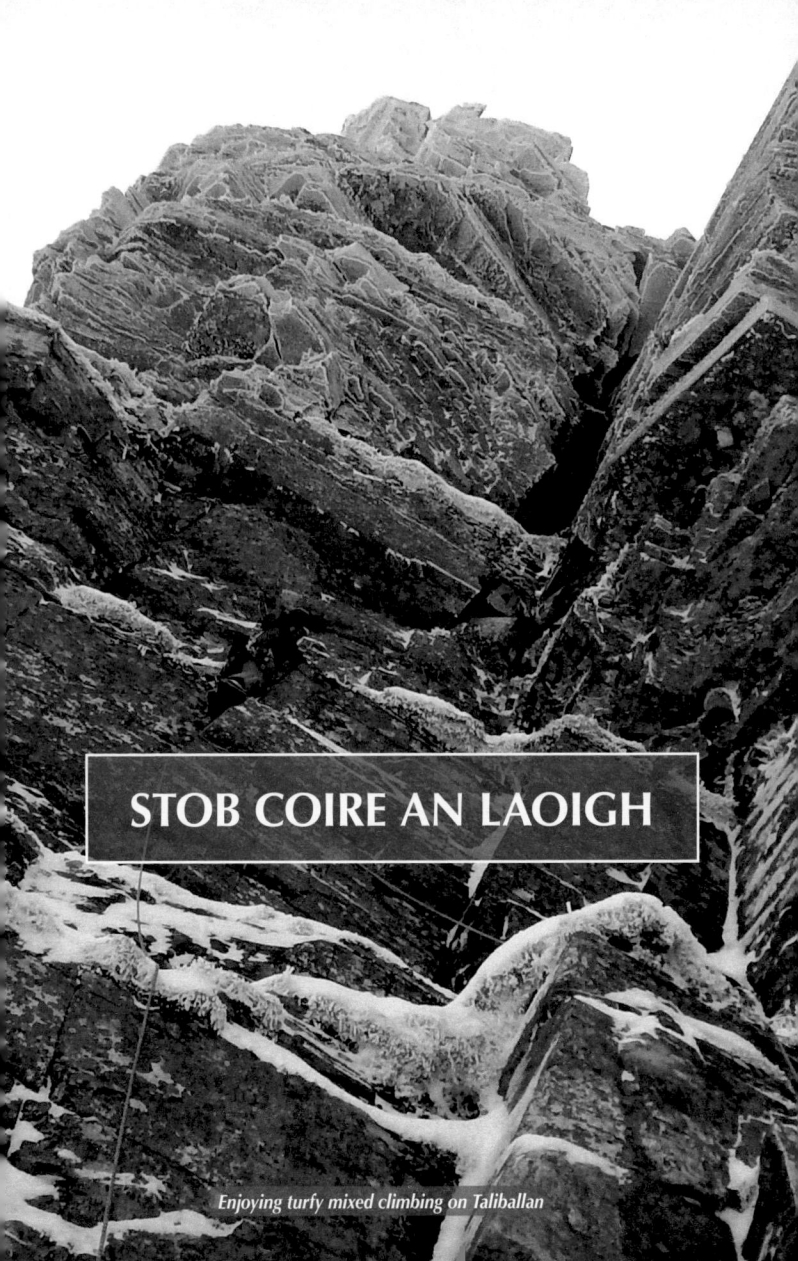

STOB COIRE AN LAOIGH

Enjoying turfy mixed climbing on Taliballan

Stob Coire an Laoigh 1116m (NN 239 725)

Start	NN 253 794, close to the track junction
Time	3hr with the cycle, or 3hr 20min walking
Crag base altitude	950m
Route lengths	50–120m
Route styles	Turfy mixed climbing
Avalanches	Rarely too much of a problem

Developed relatively recently, this crag in the Grey Corries offers steep mixed climbs on well-featured and turfy quartzite. In fact, most of the routes look impossibly steep until the helpful nature of the rock is discovered.

Approach
Drive to the end of the public road at Coirechoille and up the track to park at a junction (NN 252 794) about three miles from Spean Bridge. A long walk in can be helped by cycling along forest tracks to the dam at the edge of the forest (NN 240 765). Walk up the east bank of Allt Choimhlidh high above the stream to the stream junction at NN 242 755.

Cross the east stream (impossible in spate) and ascend the slope between the streams, then bear right to a shoulder from where the crag can easily be seen and approached.

Descent
Walk down and around either end of the crag.

End Game 50m II
D. McGimpsey and A. Nisbet, 24 December 2000
The short blocky ridge starting on the left.

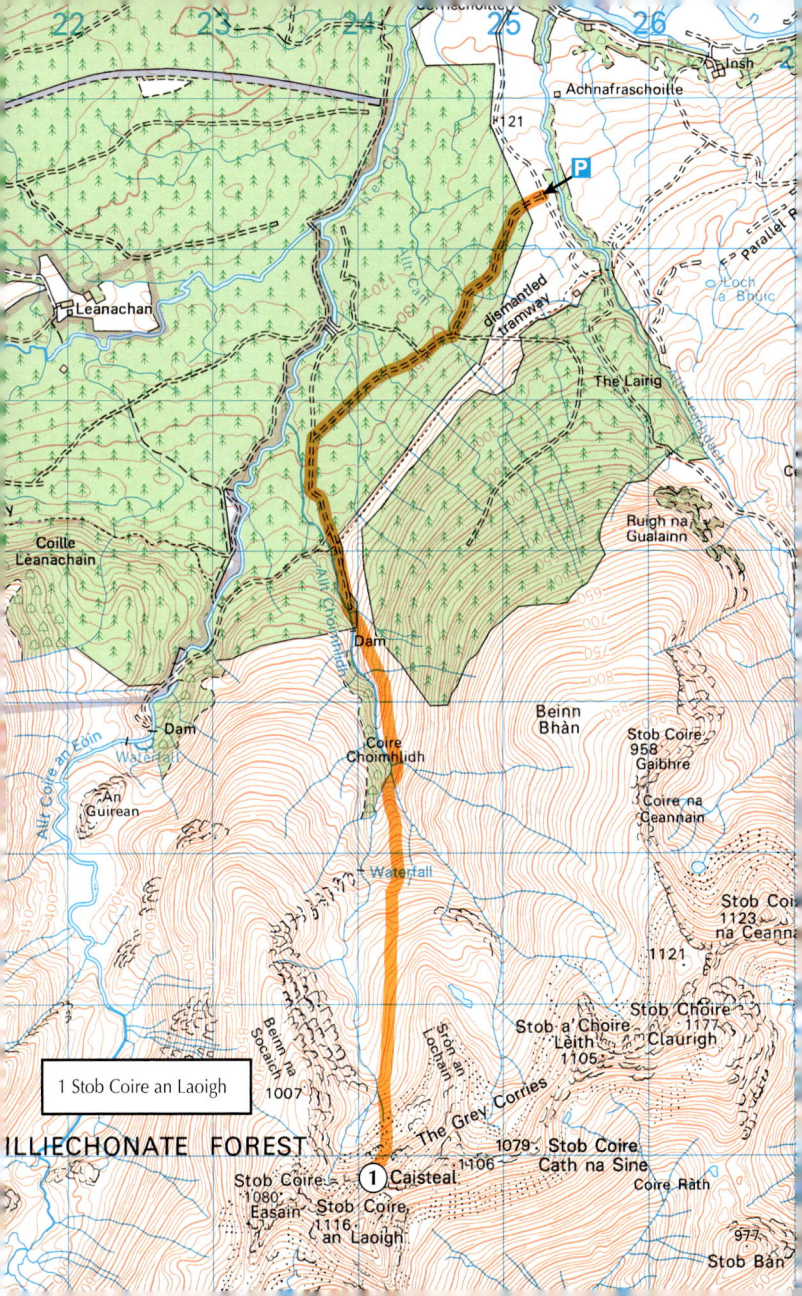

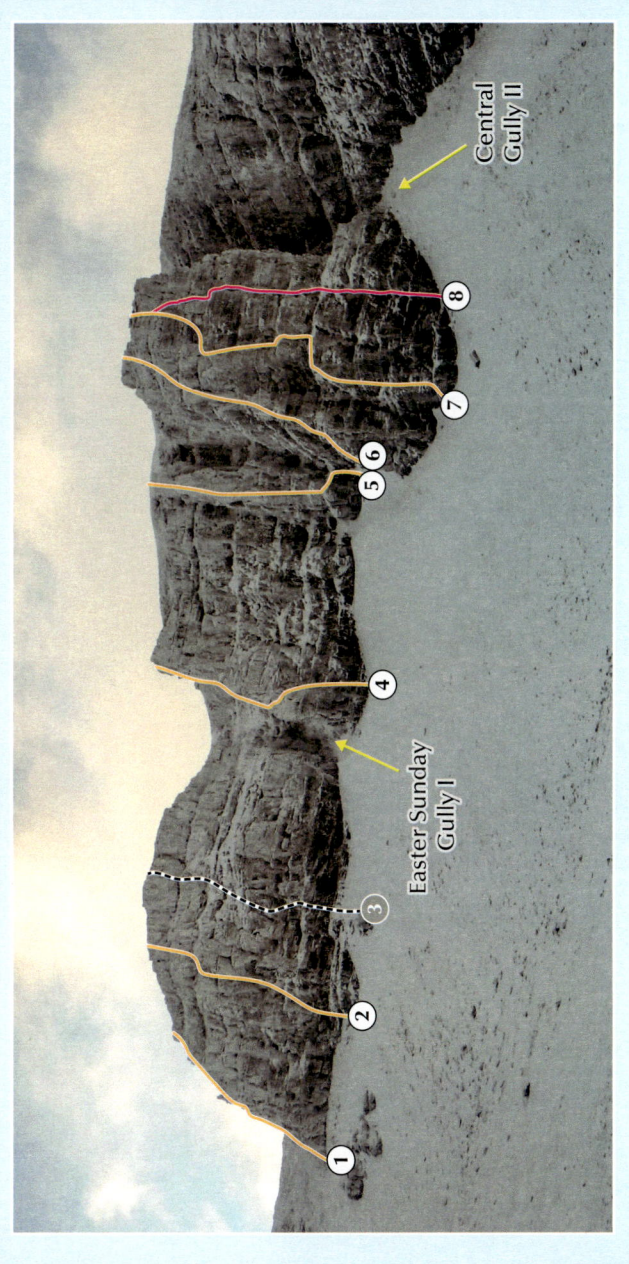

Stob Coire nan Laoigh Left Side

① End Game II
② White Widow V,6**
③ Arachnaphobe V,5
④ Loupy Louie IV,5*
⑤ Slim Jim V,6*
⑥ New Labour V,6*
⑦ Centrepoint VI,7***
⑧ Blue Rinse VI,7***

White Widow 55m V,6**
D. McGimpsey and A. Nisbet, 21 December 2002
Climb a short clean-cut and undercut corner directly under a groove at 15m. Climb the steep but helpful groove (15m). Go left and back right before finishing up steep walls.

Tarantula 55m V,6*
D. McGimpsey and A. Nisbet, 2 January 2003
(no photo topo)
Start at a corner about 10 metres left of Arachnaphobe, at the left end of ledges leading out from that route. Climb the corner to a ledge and traverse left to a crack in the right side of an arête. Climb the helpful crack to a huge smooth block (30m). Go round the block on the right and finish up the less-distinct arête.

Easter Sunday Gully 80m I
S. Richardson and J Ashbridge, March 1993
The snow gully right of the leftmost buttress.

Loopy Louie 60m IV,5*
D. McGimpsey and A. Nisbet, 8 February 2002
The arête to the right of Easter Sunday Gully. Start right of the arête, climb an awkward wall and move left to a col behind a small pinnacle. Continue up the short wall and the crest above (30m). Follow the crest, moving left into grooves to avoid steep walls. With little snow at the base there might be an overhanging wall blocking access, in which case approach the col from the left of the arête.

Tit Gully 60m V,5
D. McGimpsey and A. Nisbet, 18 February 2002
(no photo topo)
Climb the steep ice gully on the left of Slim Jim, moving onto the right at about half-height.

Slim Jim 80m V,6*
B. Davison, D. McGimpsey and A. Nisbet, 17 February 2001
The narrow pillar left of the central buttress, approached by a 10m traverse from the gully to its right. Climb just right of the crest to an easing in the angle. Traverse left and go up a chimney on the left of the crest (30m). Climb the chimney and steep ground above to a col behind a pinnacle (not obvious from below). A short awkward wall leads to the top (40m).

Stob Coire an Laoigh

Tat Gully 70m IV,4*
V. Chelton and D. McGimpsey, 13 February 2002
(no photo topo)
The gully right of Slim Jim, climbed over a steep section and up a groove on the right to an awkward belay (30m). Head for the upper right-hand groove by short leftward traverses and steep grooves (40m).

New Labour 70m V,6*
D. McGimpsey and A. Nisbet, 16 February 2002
This climbs the left edge of the central buttress. Start round to the left and climb diagonally right to a ledge just left of the edge (15m). Walls and shallow grooves follow a line just left of the edge (35m). Move round to the front face and easily to the top (20m).

Centrepoint 90m VI,7***
D. McGimpsey and A. Nisbet, 24 December 2000
Central Buttress is the most prominent feature of the crag, and this superb route takes the front face. Start at the left of the lowest rocks. Climb diagonally right across a low ledge then straight up over blocks and a short wall. Move left on turf and up to the top of lower tier, then walk 10m right to below the leftmost groove in the upper tier (40m).

Climb the groove and traverse left to a ledge. Climb a short wall and groove then step left and go up to a wider crack with chockstones. Traverse right, make a long step to a turf ledge and belay on a higher ledge (25m). Trend rightwards up a wall then climb a crack to the right of a roof and the top (25m).

Blue Rinse 80m VI,7***
D. McGimpsey and A. Nisbet, 18 February 2002
On the right side of the front face of the central buttress, this route climbs the big roofed corner. Sensational climbing that requires very well-frozen turf. Start to the right of the buttress and climb a big corner leading directly to the base of the corner in the upper buttress (25m). Climb this over a roof and swing left at the second roof (30m). Climb blocks and trend left to finish as for Centrepoint.

Central Gully 120m II
B. Davison, D. McGimpsey and A. Nisbet, 17 February 2001
The biggest gully of the crag, to the right of the central buttress. Usually contains a short ice pitch but can vary from grade I to IV.

Cobra Corner 80m VI,6**
B. Davison and A. Nisbet, 13 December 2002
The huge roofed corner to the right of Central Gully is slow to freeze and is another line that's more amenable than it looks. The gully is climbed over two steps (20m) followed by the corner, then a right-trending line to a turf ledge and groove to another steep corner (30m). The corner and its continuation lead to an escape on a ledge to the left.

Jammy Dodger 85m VI,6**
D. McGimpsey and A. Nisbet, 3 February 2002
Mostly climbed on ice on the first ascent, this route takes the right wall of the huge roofed gully of Cobra Corner. Start as for Cobra Corner up the gully until level with the large slab on the right (20m). Make a serious traverse on turf rightwards, then steep moves up to a ledge 5m from the arête (20m). Climb a short crack and move right to the arête; continue around the arête and climb a steep groove until an easier traverse left can be made to an alcove (40m). A final bulge on the right leads to the top (5m).

Some Like it Hot 70m VII,7***
M. 'Ed' Edwards, D. McGimpsey and A. Nisbet, 13 February 2007
Steep and sustained, starting about halfway along the wall, below and just right of a right-facing corner 20m up. Climb over a short wall into a V-groove, go left and step back right onto a 'diving board' above the roof of the V-groove. A steep wall leads to the corner (25m). Climb the corner.

White Heat 65m VI,7*
M. 'Ed' Edwards, J. Edwards-Lihocka and A. Nisbet, 20 March 2007
(no photo topo)
The left-facing corner and its sensational right arête. Start as for Some Like it Hot and climb into its roofed groove, but pull out right onto blocks. A shallow groove on the right leads to below the corner (15m). Climb the corner to stand on a block below overhangs. Step out right, move up to a small platform on the arête, and climb blocks and cracks mostly just left of the arête to a ledge below a roof (30m). Move right into the finishing groove of Serve Chilled. Go up this for 10m but move left and finish up the rib on the left (20m).

Serve Chilled 70m VII,6**
D. McGimpsey and A. Nisbet, 6 February 2002
A very serious ice route that takes the groove just left of the rib between the roofed gully of Jammy Dodger and the chimney of Taliballan. Climb a short chimney and traverse right into the groove. Climb the groove, trending slightly

left, then a vertical sheet to an excellent belay in a niche (40m). Continue up the groove through a slot then left and up another groove leading slightly rightwards to the top.

Full Frontal 60m VII,8*

T. Stone and V. Scott, 22 November 2008
(no photo topo)
The rib left of Taliballan and the overhanging offwidth at the top. Steep and exposed. Halfway along the wall left of Taliballan, climb a corner to a ledge. Climb another short corner above then move left up cracks to a block on the arête. Go up from this left then back right to beneath a left-facing groove (25m). Climb the left-facing groove, and traverse the wall beneath a roof to a second left-facing groove which leads to a turf ledge. Climb a bulging groove on the right, a steep wall and a slab to blocks above with sustained interest to a large ledge. A steep corner leads to the overhanging offwidth which is exited on the right (45m).

Taliballan 70m V,6*** or

D. McGimpsey and A. Nisbet, 27 December 2001
A superb mixed route and a modern classic, climbing the bottomless chimney blocked by a large roof. The turf needs to be well frozen and there can be variable quantities of ice, which changes the nature of the climbing but does not change the quality or difficulty.

Climb towards the chimney to a vertical wall, traverse left 5m and climb a cracked ramp back into the chimney (20m). A steep turf bulge starts the chimney, which is climbed to the big roof (20m). Cracks in the right wall lead around the roof to a good stance (10m). Continue to a chockstone below a steeper groove, traverse left and go up and right over blocks into the less-steep groove to finish (20m).

APPENDIX A
Route summary table by area

This is the order in which the routes appear in this guide.

Route name	Area	Route length (metres)	Overall grade	Technical grade	Main style	Sub-style(s)	Rating	Page
BEN NEVIS								13
Coire Leis								24
Final Buttress	Little Brenva Face	55	III	-	Ice	Cascade		26
Moonwalk	Little Brenva Face	270	IV	3	Ice	Snow-ice	**	26
Cresta	Little Brenva Face	275	III	-	Ice	Snow-ice	**	26
Slalom	Little Brenva Face	275	III	-	Ice	Snow-ice	**	26
Super G	Little Brenva Face	270	VI	6	Ice	Snow patch cascade	**	27
Isandhlwana	Little Brenva Face	280	V	5	Mixed	Ice	**	27
Route Major	Little Brenva Face	300	IV	3	Ice	Snow-ice	***	27
North East Buttress	Little Brenva Face	400	IV	5	Mixed	Ice, rock	***	27
Observatory Gully								31
Newbigging's Route	North East Buttress First Platform	180	IV	4	Mixed	Ice	**	33
Raeburn's Arête	North East Buttress First Platform	230	IV	5	Mixed	Ice	***	33

WINTER CLIMBS: BEN NEVIS

Route name	Area	Route length (metres)	Overall grade	Technical grade	Main style	Sub-style(s)	Rating	Page
Green Hollow Route	North East Buttress First Platform	200	IV	4	Ice	Snow-ice	**	33
Slingsby's Chimney	North East Buttress First Platform	125	III	-	Mixed	General		33
Right-Hand Wall Route	Minus Face	140	IV	5	Ice	Snow-ice		35
Platforms Rib	Minus Face	150	IV	4	Ice	Snow-ice	*	35
Minus Three Gully	Minus Face	160	IV	5	Ice	Snow-ice	**	36
Left-Hand Route	Minus Face	270	VI	6	Ice	Thin face	**	36
Central Route	Minus Face	270	VI	7	Mixed	Ice, rock		37
Right-Hand Route	Minus Face	270	VI	6	Ice	Thin face	*	37
Subtraction	Minus Face	270	VIII	8	Mixed	Ice	*	37
Minus Two Gully	Minus Face	270	V	5	Ice	Snow-ice	***	37
Minus One Direct	Minus Face	290	VIII	8	Mixed	Ice, rock	***	37
Minus One Gully	Minus Face	290	VI	5	Ice	Snow-ice	***	38
Astronomy	Orion Face	300	VI	5	Ice	Thin face	***	40
The Black Hole	Orion Face	350	VI	6	Ice	Thin face	**	41
Urban Spaceman	Orion Face	350	VII	6	Mixed	Ice	***	41
Orion Direct	Orion Face	420	V	5	Ice	Snow-ice-	***	41
Astral Highway	Orion Face	240	V	5	Ice	Snow-ice	***	42
Journey into Space	Orion Face	240	VII	6	Ice	Thin face	**	43

Appendix A – Route summary table by area

Route name	Area	Route length (metres)	Overall grade	Technical grade	Main style	Sub-style(s)	Rating	Page
Long Climb Finish	Orion Face	240	VI	5	Ice	Thin face	***	43
Slav Route	Orion Face	420	V	5	Ice	Thin face	***	44
Zero Gully	Orion Face	300	V	4	Ice	Snow-ice	**	44
East Face to Observatory Ridge	Orion Face	170	IV	5	Ice	Snow-ice	*	44
Observatory Ridge	Orion Face	500	V	4	Mixed	Rock, ice	***	45
Abacus	Point Five Gully	110	IV	4	Ice	Snow-ice	*	46
Antonine Wall to Observatory Ridge	Point Five Gully	150	V	5	Ice	Snow-ice	*	46
Vade Mecum to Observatory Ridge	Point Five Gully	180	V	5	Ice	Snow patch cascade	***	48
Hadrian's Wall Direct	Point Five Gully	320	V	5	Ice	Snow-ice	***	48
Sickle	Point Five Gully	300	V	5	Ice	Snow-ice	***	48
Galactic Hitchhiker	Point Five Gully	300	VI	5	Ice	Thin face	***	49
Nemesis	Point Five Gully	290	VI	5	Ice	Thin face	*	50
Pointless	Point Five Gully	300	VII	6	Mixed	Ice	*	50
Interstellar Overdrive	Point Five Gully	300	VI	5	Ice	Thin face	*	50
Point Five Gully	Point Five Gully	325	V	5	Ice	Snow-ice	***	50

Winter climbs: Ben Nevis

Route name	Area	Route length (metres)	Overall grade	Technical grade	Main style	Sub-style(s)	Rating	Page
Point Blank	Point Five Gully	340	VII	6	Ice, mixed	Snow-ice, general	***	52
Left Edge Route	Point Five Gully	360	V	5	Ice	Thin face	**	53
Matchpoint	Point Five Gully	360	VI	5	Ice	Thin face	*	54
Rubicon Wall	Point Five Gully	360	VI	5	Ice	Thin face	**	54
Observatory Buttress	Point Five Gully	360	V	5	Ice	Snow-ice	***	54
North-West Face to Girdle Traverse ledge	Point Five Gully	100	IV	4	Ice	Snow-ice	*	54
Good Friday Climb	Indicator Wall	150	III	-	Ice	Snow-ice	**	55
Indicator Wall	Indicator Wall	160	V	4	Ice	Snow-ice	***	56
Riders on the Storm	Indicator Wall	165	VI	5	Ice	Thin face	***	57
Ship of Fools	Indicator Wall	170	VIII	7	Ice	Thin face	**	58
Albatross	Indicator Wall	160	VI	5	Ice	Thin face	***	58
Rime of the Ancient Mariner	Indicator Wall	160	VII	7	Mixed	Ice	**	58
Stormy Petrel	Indicator Wall	160	VII	6	Ice	Thin face	***	59
Psychedelic Wall	Indicator Wall	165	VI	5	Ice	Thin face	***	59
Satanic Verses	Indicator Wall	130	V	5	Ice	Thin face	***	59
Shot in the Dark	Indicator Wall	120	V	5	Ice	Thin face	***	59
Gardyloo Gully	Indicator Wall	170	II/III	-	Snow or ice	Snow-ice	**	60

Appendix A – Route summary table by area

Route name	Area	Route length (metres)	Overall grade	Technical grade	Main style	Sub-style(s)	Rating	Page
Kellett's Route	Gardyloo Buttress	120	VI	6	Ice	Snow-ice	***	61
Smith's Route	Gardyloo Buttress	130	V	5	Ice	Snow-ice	***	63
The Great Glen	Gardyloo Buttress	130	VI	5	Ice	Snow-ice	*	63
Tower Gully	Gardyloo Buttress	120	I	-	Snow	-		64
Tower Scoop	Tower Ridge East Side	75	III	-	Ice	Snow-ice	***	66
Tower Cleft	Tower Ridge East Side	75	III	-	Ice	Snow-ice	*	66
Clefthanger	Tower Ridge East Side	90	VI	6	Mixed	Rock, ice	**	66
Faith Healer	Tower Ridge East Side	170	VIII	7	Mixed	Ice, turf	*	66
The Edge of Beyond	Tower Ridge East Side	200	VI	6	Mixed	Rock, ice	**	67
The Brass Monkey	Tower Ridge East Side	135	VII	8	Mixed	Rock, ice		69
The Great Chimney	Tower Ridge East Side	65	V	6	Mixed	Rock, ice	***	69
Tower Ridge	Tower Ridge	500 ascent; 1000 climbing	IV	3	Mixed	Rock, ice	***	71
Douglas Gap East Gully	Douglas Boulder	70	I	-	Snow	-	**	73
Direct Route	Douglas Boulder	215	IV	4	Mixed	Rock, ice	*	75
Turf War	Douglas Boulder	250	V	6	Mixed	Rock, turf	**	75
Left-Hand Chimney	Douglas Boulder	215	V	6	Mixed	Rock		76
North-West Face Route	Douglas Boulder	215	V	5	Mixed	Ice, rock		76

Winter climbs: Ben Nevis

Route name	Area	Route length (metres)	Overall grade	Technical grade	Main style	Sub-style(s)	Rating	Page
Right-Hand Chimney	Douglas Boulder	215	VI	7	Mixed	Rock, ice		76
Gutless to South West Ridge	Douglas Boulder	150	IV	5	Mixed	Rock, turf	*	76
Cutlass to South West Ridge	Douglas Boulder	145	VI	7	Mixed	Rock or ice	**	76
Jacknife to South West Ridge	Douglas Boulder	90	IV	6	Mixed	Rock		77
South West Ridge	Douglas Boulder	180	III	4	Mixed	Rock	*	77
Douglas Gap West Gully	Douglas Boulder	180	I	-	Snow	-	**	77
Coire na Ciste								79
Fawlty Towers	Tower Ridge West Side	155	II/III	-	Ice	Snow-ice		80
1934 Route	Tower Ridge West Side	200	II/III	-	Ice	Snow-ice	**	80
Vanishing Gully	Tower Ridge West Side	200	V	5	Ice	Snow-ice	***	81
Pirate	Tower Ridge West Side	200	IV	4	Mixed	Rock, ice		82
Fish Eye Chimney	Tower Ridge West Side	150	V	5	Mixed	Rock, ice		83
1931 Route	Tower Ridge West Side	125	IV	4	Mixed	Ice		83
The Italian Climb	Tower Ridge West Side	180	III	-	Ice	Snow-ice	*	83
Italian Climb – Right-Hand	Tower Ridge West Side	180	IV	4	Ice	Snow-ice	***	83

Appendix A – Route summary table by area

Route name	Area	Route length (metres)	Overall grade	Technical grade	Main style	Sub-style(s)	Rating	Page
The Chute	Tower Ridge West Side	230	V	4	Ice	Snow patch cascade	**	83
Garadh Gully	Tower Ridge West Side	95	II/III	-	Ice or snow	Cascade		84
Broad Gully	Pinnacle Buttress	230	II	-	Snow	-		86
Fatal Error	Pinnacle Buttress	230	IV	4	Mixed	Ice	**	86
Stringfellow	Pinnacle Buttress	240	VI	6	Mixed	Ice, rock	**	86
Pinnacle Buttress Direct	Pinnacle Buttress	200	V	5	Mixed	Ice	**	86
Glover's Chimney	Pinnacle Buttress	200	III	4	Mixed	Ice	**	87
The Gutter	Goodeve's Buttress and the Cascades	275	IV	4	Ice	Snow-ice	**	88
The White Line	Goodeve's Buttress and the Cascades	275	IV	3	Ice	Snow-ice	***	89
Goodytwoshoes	Goodeve's Buttress and the Cascades	140	V	6	Mixed	Ice	*	89
Beam Me Up Scotty	Goodeve's Buttress and the Cascades	155	III	-	Ice	Snow-ice	*	90
Upper Cascades	Goodeve's Buttress and the Cascades	125	V	6	Ice	Snow patch cascade	**	90
Adieu and Farewell	Goodeve's Buttress and the Cascades	100	V	5	Ice	Snow patch cascade		90

WINTER CLIMBS: BEN NEVIS

Route name	Area	Route length (metres)	Overall grade	Technical grade	Main style	Sub-style(s)	Rating	Page
La Panthere Rose	Goodeve's Buttress and the Cascades	50	VI	6	Ice	Snow patch cascade	*	90
Expert's Choice	Goodeve's Buttress and the Cascades	150	III	4	Ice	Snow-ice	*	90
Raeburn's Easy Route	Goodeve's Buttress and the Cascades	250	II/III	–	Ice, snow	Snow-ice		90
The Cascade	Goodeve's Buttress and the Cascades	50	V	5	Ice	Cascade	**	91
Five-Finger Discount	Goodeve's Buttress and the Cascades	135	IV	4	Ice	Snow-ice	**	91
Burrito's Groove	Goodeve's Buttress and the Cascades	135	IV	5	Ice	Snow-ice	**	91
JP is Back	Goodeve's Buttress and the Cascades	120	III	4	Ice	Snow-ice		91
Number Two Gully Buttress	Goodeve's Buttress and the Cascades	120	II/III	–	Ice	Snow-ice	**	93
Number Two Gully	Goodeve's Buttress and the Cascades	120	II	–	Snow or ice	Snow-ice	***	93
Comb Gully Buttress	The Comb	150	IV	4	Ice	Snow-ice	**	94
Clough's Chimney	The Comb	150	VI	5	Mixed	Rock or ice	*	94
Roaring Forties	The Comb	150	V	5	Mixed	Ice	**	94

Appendix A – Route summary table by area

Route name	Area	Route length (metres)	Overall grade	Technical grade	Main style	Sub-style(s)	Rating	Page
Comb Gully	The Comb	160	IV	4	Ice	Snow-ice	**	94
The Comb – Left Flank	The Comb	160	IV	4	Ice	Snow-ice	*	94
Hesperides Ledge	The Comb	200	III	-	Mixed	Ice	*	95
The Good Groove	The Comb	200	VII	7	Mixed	Rock, ice	**	95
Tower Face of The Comb	The Comb	250	VI	6	Mixed	Ice	***	96
Bell's Chimney: Variation	The Comb	250	V	5	Mixed	Ice		97
Don't Die of Ignorance	The Comb	200	XI	11	Mixed	Rock		97
Anubis	The Comb	200	XII	-	Mixed	Rock		97
Pigott's Route	The Comb	245	V	6	Mixed	Ice	*	98
Mercury	The Comb	180	V	5	Ice	Snow-ice	**	99
Green Gully	The Comb	180	IV	4	Ice	Snow-ice	***	99
Tramp	Number Three Gully Buttress	180	IV	4	Mixed	Ice	*	100
Diana	Number Three Gully Buttress	195	V	5	Ice	Thin face	*	100
Vulture	Number Three Gully Buttress	180	V	5	Ice	Thin face	**	100

WINTER CLIMBS: BEN NEVIS

Route name	Area	Route length (metres)	Overall grade	Technical grade	Main style	Sub-style(s)	Rating	Page
Quickstep	Number Three Gully Buttress	180	V	5	Ice	Thin face	**	101
Number Three Gully Buttress	Number Three Gully Buttress	200	III	-	Ice, mixed	Snow-ice, rock	***	101
Two-Step Corner	Number Three Gully Buttress	180	V	5	Ice	Snow-ice	***	102
Chinook	Number Three Gully Buttress	65	IV	5	Mixed	Ice or rock		102
The Survivor	Number Three Gully Buttress	180	VII	3	Mixed	Rock		102
The Knuckleduster	Number Three Gully Buttress	180	VIII	9	Mixed	Rock	***	102
Sioux Wall	Number Three Gully Buttress	150	VII	8	Mixed	Rock	***	103
The Banshee	Number Three Gully Buttress	150	V	5	Mixed	Ice		103
Thompson's Route	Number Three Gully Buttress	130	IV	4	Mixed or ice	Snow-ice, ice	***	103
Gremlins	Number Three Gully Buttress	120	VI	5	Ice	Thin face	*	103
Gargoyle Wall	Number Three Gully Buttress	120	VI	5	Mixed	Rock or ice	**	105
Hobgoblin	Number Three Gully Buttress	120	VI	7	Mixed	Rock	***	105

Appendix A – Route summary table by area

Route name	Area	Route length (metres)	Overall grade	Technical grade	Main style	Sub-style(s)	Rating	Page
Babylon	Number Three Gully Buttress	115	VII	7	Mixed	Rock	**	105
Winter Chimney	Number Three Gully Buttress	60	IV	5	Ice	Snow-ice	*	105
Number Three Gully	Number Three Gully Buttress	150	I	-	Snow	-	***	106
The Secret	Creag Coire na Ciste	70	VIII	8	Mixed	Rock	***	107
Cornucopia	Creag Coire na Ciste	100	VII	8	Mixed	Rock	*	107
Darth Vader	Creag Coire na Ciste	100	VII	7	Mixed	Rock	***	108
Avenging Angel Direct	Creag Coire na Ciste	110	VIII	8	Mixed	Rock	***	108
Cold Play	Creag Coire na Ciste	110	VIII	8	Mixed	Rock		109
South Sea Bubble	Creag Coire na Ciste	110	VII	7	Mixed	Ice		109
South Gully	Creag Coire na Ciste	125	III	-	Ice	Snow-ice	*	109
The Sorcerer	Creag Coire na Ciste	140	VII	8	Mixed	Rock		109
Lost the Place	Creag Coire na Ciste	140	V	5	Mixed	Ice or rock	**	111
Une Journée Ordinaire dans un Enfer Quotidien	Creag Coire na Ciste	105	VI	6	Ice	Snow patch cascade	**	111
Central Gully	Creag Coire na Ciste	125	III	4	Ice	Snow-ice	**	111
Central Gully – Right-Hand	Creag Coire na Ciste	125	IV	4	Ice	Snow-ice	***	111

WINTER CLIMBS: BEN NEVIS

Route name	Area	Route length (metres)	Overall grade	Technical grade	Main style	Sub-style(s)	Rating	Page
Wendigo	Creag Coire na Ciste	110	IV	4	Ice	Snow-ice	**	112
North Gully	Creag Coire na Ciste	110	II	-	Ice	Snow-ice	*	112
Forearm	Creag Coire na Ciste	125	IV	4	Ice	Snow-ice		112
Number Four Gully	Creag Coire na Ciste	150	I	-	Snow	-		112
Number Four Gully Buttress	Trident buttresses	100	II	-	Ice	Snow-ice	*	115
Poseidon Groove	Trident buttresses	100	IV	5	Mixed	Rock		115
Triton Corners	Trident buttresses	100	IV	5	Mixed	Rock		117
South Flank Route	Trident buttresses	150	IV	4	Mixed	Ice	*	117
The Groove Climb	Trident buttresses	80	V	5	Mixed	Rock	*	117
Sidewinder	Trident buttresses	100	VII	3	Mixed	Rock		117
Strident Edge	Trident buttresses	100	VII	3	Mixed	Rock	**	117
The Slab Climb	Trident buttresses	90	VI	7	Mixed	Turf, rock	*	118
The Clanger	Trident buttresses	90	IV	5	Mixed	Ice, turf, rock	**	118
Pinnacle Arête	Trident buttresses	100	IV	5	Mixed	Ice	**	118
Rien ne va Plus	Trident buttresses	50	V	5	Ice	Snow patch cascade		118
Under Fire	Trident buttresses	85	VII	7	Mixed	Rock	*	118
Joyful Chimneys	Trident buttresses	180	IV	5	Ice	Snow-ice		120

Appendix A – Route summary table by area

Route name	Area	Route length (metres)	Overall grade	Technical grade	Main style	Sub-style(s)	Rating	Page
Central Gully	Trident buttresses	240	III	-	Ice	Snow-ice		120
Nasturtium	Trident buttresses	250	IV	4	Ice	Snow-ice	*	120
Jubilation	Trident buttresses	240	IV	4	Ice	Snow-ice	*	120
Mega Rêve	Trident buttresses	60	V	5	Mixed	Ice		120
Jubilee Climb	Trident buttresses	240	II	-	Ice	Snow-ice		120
Feeding Frenzy	Trident buttresses	70	VI	7	Ice	Snow patch cascade	*	121
Mega Route X	Trident buttresses	60	V	6	Ice	Snow patch cascade	***	121
Heidbanger Direct	Trident buttresses	75	VIII	8	Mixed	Rock		121
Left-Hand Ridge	Trident buttresses	250	IV	4	Mixed	Ice		121
Neptune Gully	Trident buttresses	260	III	-	Ice	Snow-ice		122
Moonlight Gully	Moonlight Gully Buttress	150	I/II	-	Snow	-		124
Diagonal Route	Moonlight Gully Buttress	150	III	-	Mixed	Ice	*	124
Right-Hand Chimney	Moonlight Gully Buttress	135	IV	5	Mixed	Ice	*	124
Number Five Gully	Moonlight Gully Buttress	460	I	-	Snow	-	*	124
Ledge Route	Moonlight Gully Buttress	450	II	-	Snow, mixed	Rock	***	124
The Curtain Rail	Càrn Dearg Buttress	100	IV	4	Ice	Snow-ice	*	126

Winter climbs: Ben Nevis

Route name	Area	Route length (metres)	Overall grade	Technical grade	Main style	Sub-style(s)	Rating	Page
The Curtain	Càrn Dearg Buttress	110	IV	5	Ice	Snow-ice	***	127
Route I Direct	Càrn Dearg Buttress	210	VI	6	Mixed	Rock, ice	***	127
Route II Direct	Càrn Dearg Buttress	275	VI	7	Mixed	Rock, ice	***	127
Ring the Alarm	Càrn Dearg Buttress	270	VI	5	Mixed	Ice	**	127
Centurion	Càrn Dearg Buttress	190	VIII	8	Mixed	Rock	***	129
Sassenach	Càrn Dearg Buttress	270	IX	9	Mixed	Rock		129
Shield Direct	Càrn Dearg Buttress	290	VII	7	Ice, mixed	Cascade, general	***	129
Gemini	Càrn Dearg Buttress	300	VI	6	Ice, mixed	Cascade, general	***	129
Bewilderbeast	Càrn Dearg Buttress	130	VI	6	Ice	Snow-ice	**	131
Waterfall Gully	Càrn Dearg Buttress	215	IV	4	Ice	Snow-ice	*	131
Staircase Climb	Càrn Dearg Buttress	215	IV	5	Mixed	Rock, ice	*	131
Castle Coire								132
Kellett's North Wall Route	Castle Coire	200	VII	7	Mixed	Rock, turf		133
The Past is Close Behind	Castle Coire	200	VIII	8	Mixed	Rock, ice		133
The Shroud	Castle Coire	200	VI	6	Ice	Snow patch cascade	**	133

Appendix A – Route summary table by area

Route name	Area	Route length (metres)	Overall grade	Technical grade	Main style	Sub-style(s)	Rating	Page
Harrison's Climb Direct	Castle Coire	300	IV	4	Ice	Snow-ice	***	134
Boomer's Requiem	Castle Coire	170	V	5	Ice	Snow-ice	***	135
Arch Gully	Castle Coire	105	I	-	Snow	-		136
Surprise Gully	Castle Coire	185	I/II	-	Mixed	General		136
Raeburn's Buttress/ Intermediate Gully	Castle Coire	230	V	5	Ice	Snow-ice	**	137
The Crack	Castle Coire	250	VIII	8	Mixed	Rock	**	137
The Great Corner	Castle Coire	250	VIII	8	Mixed	Rock	**	137
Compression Crack	Castle Coire	250	V	5	Ice	Snow-ice, Cascade	*	137
South Castle Gully	Castle Coire	230	I/II	-	Snow	-	*	138
Godspell	Castle Coire	215	VII	8	Mixed	Ice, rock		138
The Castle	Castle Coire	220	II/III	-	Ice	Snow-ice	*	138
North Castle Gully	Castle Coire	230	I/II	-	Snow	-	*	139
Castle Ridge	Castle Coire	275	III	-	Mixed	Rock	**	139
The Serpent	North Face of Castle Ridge	300	II	-	Snow	-		142
The Moat	North Face of Castle Ridge	500	II	-	Snow	-	**	142
Lobby Dancer	North Face of Castle Ridge	280	VI	6	Mixed	Ice	***	142

WINTER CLIMBS: BEN NEVIS

Route name	Area	Route length (metres)	Overall grade	Technical grade	Main style	Sub-style(s)	Rating	Page
Last Day in Purgatory	North Face of Castle Ridge	330	V	5	Mixed	Ice	**	142
Norwand Direct	North Face of Castle Ridge	400	V	4	Ice	Cascade	***	142
Norwand Superdirect	North Face of Castle Ridge	400	VI	5	Ice	Cascade	**	142
Norwand	North Face of Castle Ridge	425	III	-	Ice	Snow-ice		143
Casino Royale	North Face of Castle Ridge	190	V	5	Ice	Snow-ice		143
La Petite	North Face of Castle Ridge	200	III	-	Ice	Snow-ice		144
The Girdle Traverse	North Face of Castle Ridge	4000	V	4	Mixed	Ice		144
GLEN NEVIS								145
Mamores								146
Eag Blanc	Stob Bàn	100	II	-	Ice	Snow-ice		152
East Wing	Stob Bàn	180	V	5	Mixed	Turf		152
South Gully	Stob Bàn	150	I	-	Snow	-	*	152
Summit Groove	Stob Bàn	140	IV	4	Mixed	General	*	152
Groove Rider	Stob Bàn	160	IV	4	Mixed	General	*	152

Appendix A – Route summary table by area

Route name	Area	Route length (metres)	Overall grade	Technical grade	Main style	Sub-style(s)	Rating	Page
North Ridge Route	Stob Bàn	150	IV	4	Mixed	General		152
North Gully	Stob Bàn	150	I	-	Snow	-		152
Central Gully	Stob Bàn	150	IV	-	Mixed	Ice		154
Gendarme Ridge	Stob Bàn	150	IV	4	Mixed	Rock		154
Triad	Stob Bàn	150	III	-	Mixed	Ice	*	154
Skyline Rib	Stob Bàn	120	IV	4	Mixed	Rock	*	154
Bodice Ripper	Stob Bàn	150	IV	4	Mixed	Ice	*	154
North Buttress – East Ridge	Stob Bàn	200	II/III	-	Mixed	General	**	155
Captain Caveman	Mullach nan Coirean	70	III	4	Mixed	Turf		156
Not Bad for a Dad	Mullach nan Coirean	80	VI	7	Mixed	Rock		156
Kid Gloves	Mullach nan Coirean	70	IV	4	Mixed	Turf		156
Kindergarten Corner	Mullach nan Coirean	50	VII	8	Mixed	Rock		156
Five Finger Gully	Five Finger Gully	200	IV	4	Ice	Cascade		156
Surgeon's Gully	Five Finger Gully	400	V	-	Ice	Cascade		157
Steall Waterfall	Five Finger Gully	120	III	-	Ice	Cascade	**	158
AONACH MÒR AND AONACH BEAG								159
Chimpanzee	Aonach Mòr East Face – Coire an Lochain	60	III	-	Ice	Snow-ice		162

WINTER CLIMBS: BEN NEVIS

Route name	Area	Route length (metres)	Overall grade	Technical grade	Main style	Sub-style(s)	Rating	Page
Monkey Business	Aonach Mòr East Face – Coire an Lochain	70	V	6	Mixed	General		162
Monkey Puzzle	Aonach Mòr East Face – Coire an Lochain	70	III	-	Mixed	General		163
Hidden Gully	Aonach Mòr East Face – Coire an Lochain	120	II	-	Snow	-	*	163
Ribbon on Edge	Aonach Mòr East Face – Coire an Lochain	120	IV	6	Mixed	Turf		163
Two Queens	Aonach Mòr East Face – Coire an Lochain	70	IV	5	Mixed	General	*	165
Three Kings	Aonach Mòr East Face – Coire an Lochain	70	IV	5	Mixed	General	*	165
Streamline	Aonach Mòr East Face – Coire an Lochain	90	III	-	Ice	Snow-ice	*	165
Back Stree Boogie	Aonach Mòr East Face – Coire an Lochain	70	VI	6	Mixed	Turf		165
The Betrayal	Aonach Mòr East Face – Coire an Lochain	90	IV	4	Mixed	Ice		165
The Wave	Aonach Mòr East Face – Coire an Lochain	70	V	5	Mixed	Ice		167
The Guardian	Aonach Mòr East Face – Coire an Lochain	90	IV	5	Mixed	Ice	*	167

APPENDIX A – ROUTE SUMMARY TABLE BY AREA

Route name	Area	Route length (metres)	Overall grade	Technical grade	Main style	Sub-style(s)	Rating	Page
Stirling Bridge	Aonach Mòr East Face – Coire an Lochain	70	V	7	Mixed	Rock	**	167
Ribbon Groove	Aonach Mòr East Face – Coire an Lochain	60	IV	4	Mixed	Ice		167
Ribbon Development	Aonach Mòr East Face – Coire an Lochain	60	IV	4	Mixed	Ice	**	167
Homo Robusticus	Aonach Mòr East Face – Coire an Lochain	60	VI	7	Mixed	Rock	**	167
Piranha	Aonach Mòr East Face – Coire an Lochain	70	VII	8	Mixed	Rock	**	169
The Web	Aonach Mòr East Face – Coire an Lochain	100	II/III	-	Ice	Snow-ice		169
Easy Gully	Aonach Mòr East Face – Coire an Lochain	100	I	-	Snow	-		169
Barrel Buttress	Aonach Mòr East Face – Coire an Lochain	90	IV	4	Mixed	Ice		169
Nid Arête	Aonach Mòr East Face – Coire an Lochain	90	IV	5	Mixed	General	*	169
Temperance Union Blues	Aonach Mòr East Face – Coire an Lochain	90	III	-	Ice	Snow-ice		171
Aquafresh	Aonach Mòr East Face – Coire an Lochain	100	IV	4	Ice	Snow-ice	*	171

WINTER CLIMBS: BEN NEVIS

Route name	Area	Route length (metres)	Overall grade	Technical grade	Main style	Sub-style(s)	Rating	Page
White Shark	Aonach Mòr East Face – Coire an Lochain	110	IV	4	Ice	Snow-ice	***	171
Tinsel Town	Aonach Mòr East Face – Coire an Lochain	110	V	4	Mixed	Ice	**	171
Gondola With the Wind	Aonach Mòr East Face – Coire an Lochain	125	IV	5	Mixed	Ice	**	171
Maneater	Aonach Mòr East Face – Coire an Lochain	90	V	5	Mixed	Ice	**	173
Tunnel Vision	Aonach Mòr East Face – Coire an Lochain	120	III	-	Ice	Snow-ice		173
Morwind	Aonach Mòr East Face – Coire an Lochain	150	IV	4	Mixed	Ice or turf	***	173
Turf Walk	Aonach Mòr East Face – Coire an Lochain	150	III	4	Mixed	Turf	*	175
Typhoon	Aonach Mòr East Face – Coire an Lochain	130	IV	5	Mixed	Ice	***	175
Hurricane Arête	Aonach Mòr East Face – Coire an Lochain	140	VI	7	Mixed	Ice	**	175
Alien Abduction	Aonach Mòr East Face – Coire an Lochain	120	VII	8	Mixed	Ice, rock		176
Left Twin	Aonach Mòr East Face – Coire an Lochain	120	IV	4	Ice	Snow-ice	***	176

Appendix A – Route summary table by area

Route name	Area	Route length (metres)	Overall grade	Technical grade	Main style	Sub-style(s)	Rating	Page
The Split	Aonach Mòr East Face – Coire an Lochain	130	III	4	Mixed	Ice	**	176
Lickety Split	Aonach Mòr East Face – Coire an Lochain	130	IV	5	Mixed	Ice	**	176
Forgotten Twin	Aonach Mòr East Face – Coire an Lochain	120	I/II	-	Snow	-		177
Siamese Buttress	Aonach Mòr East Face – Coire an Lochain	120	II/III	-	Mixed	General	**	177
Right Twin	Aonach Mòr East Face – Coire an Lochain	120	II	-	Mixed	Ice	***	177
White Bait	Aonach Mòr East Face – Coire an Lochain	100	IV	5	Mixed	Ice		177
The Slever	Aonach Mòr East Face – Coire an Lochain	100	III	4	Ice	Snow-ice		177
Golden Promise	Aonach Mòr East Face – Coire an Lochain	100	VI	7	Mixed	General	*	179
Molar Canal	Aonach Mòr East Face – Coire an Lochain	100	III	-	Ice	Snow-ice		179
Grooved Arête	Aonach Mòr East Face – Coire an Lochain	130	V	6	Mixed	Rock	**	179
Icicle Gully	Aonach Mòr East Face – Coire an Lochain	130	III	-	Ice	Snow-ice		180

WINTER CLIMBS: BEN NEVIS

Route name	Area	Route length (metres)	Overall grade	Technical grade	Main style	Sub-style(s)	Rating	Page
Force Ten Buttress	Aonach Mòr East Face – Coire an Lochain	140	III	4	Mixed	General	*	180
Solar Wind	Aonach Mòr East Face – Coire an Lochain	110	IV	4	Ice	Snow-ice	*	180
Jet Stream	Aonach Mòr East Face – Coire an Lochain	100	IV	4	Ice	Snow-ice	***	180
Foosyerneeps	Aonach Mòr East Face – Coire an Lochain	50	IV	5	Mixed	Ice	**	181
Golden Oldie	Aonach Mòr West Face	400	II	-	Mixed	General	***	183
Western Rib	Aonach Mòr West Face	400	II/III	-	Mixed	General	**	183
Spare Rib Gully	Aonach Mòr West Face	400	III	-	Ice	Cascade	**	185
Daim Buttress	Aonach Mòr West Face	400	II/III	-	Mixed	General		185
Solitaire	Aonach Mòr West Face	400	II	-	Mixed	General		185
Sgùrr Finnisg-aig Fall	Sgùrr Finnisg-aig	200	IV	4	Ice	Cascade	*	185
Blackout	Aonach Beag North Face	120	IV	5	Ice, mixed	Snow-ice, general	*	190
Stand and Deliver	Aonach Beag North Face	120	V	5	Ice	Snow patch cascade	**	190
Camilla	Aonach Beag North Face	230	V	5	Ice	Snow patch cascade	**	191

Appendix A – Route summary table by area

Route name	Area	Route length (metres)	Overall grade	Technical grade	Main style	Sub-style(s)	Rating	Page
Royal Pardon	Aonach Beag North Face	220	VI	6	Ice	Snow patch cascade	***	191
King's Ransom	Aonach Beag North Face	250	VI	6	Ice, mixed	Snow-ice, general	*	191
Queen's View	Aonach Beag North Face	250	III	-	Ice	Snow-ice		192
The Black Prince	Aonach Beag North Face	300	II	-	Ice	Snow-ice		192
Mayfly	Aonach Beag North Face	210	III	-	Ice	Snow-ice	*	192
North-East Ridge	Aonach Beag North Face	460	III	4	Mixed	Rock, turf	*	192
Twinkle	Aonach Beag West Face	150	IV	5	Mixed	Rock, ice	**	195
Axeless	Aonach Beag West Face	150	III	-	Mixed	Rock, ice	*	195
Aonacrack	Aonach Beag West Face	150	IV	5	Mixed	General	**	195
Eggsclamation	Aonach Beag West Face	150	II	-	Ice	Snow-ice		197
Aonach Wall	Aonach Beag West Face	150	V	6	Mixed	Rock	*	197
Raw Egg Buttress	Aonach Beag West Face	180	IV	4	Mixed	Ice	**	197
Top Gun	Aonach Beag West Face	160	VI	6	Mixed	Ice	**	197
Salmonella	Aonach Beag West Face	125	VII	8	Mixed	Rock	**	198
Blackbeard	Aonach Beag West Face	70	VII	8	Mixed	Rock		200
Ruadh Eigg Chimney	Aonach Beag West Face	60	V	6	Mixed	Ice, rock	*	200

WINTER CLIMBS: BEN NEVIS

Route name	Area	Route length (metres)	Overall grade	Technical grade	Main style	Sub-style(s)	Rating	Page
STOB COIRE AN LAOIGH								201
End Game	Stob Coire an Laoigh	50	II	-	Mixed	Turf		202
White Widow	Stob Coire an Laoigh	55	V	6	Mixed	Turf	**	206
Tarantula	Stob Coire an Laoigh	55	V	6	Mixed	Turf	*	206
Easter Sunday Gully	Stob Coire an Laoigh	80	I	-	Snow	-		206
Loopy Louie	Stob Coire an Laoigh	60	IV	5	Mixed	Turf	*	206
Tit Gully	Stob Coire an Laoigh	60	V	5	Ice	Snow-ice		206
Slim Jim	Stob Coire an Laoigh	80	V	6	Mixed	Turf	*	206
Tat Gully	Stob Coire an Laoigh	70	IV	4	Mixed	Ice	*	207
New Labour	Stob Coire an Laoigh	70	V	6	Mixed	Turf	*	207
Centrepoint	Stob Coire an Laoigh	90	VI	7	Mixed	Turf	***	207
Blue Rinse	Stob Coire an Laoigh	80	VI	7	Mixed	Turf	***	207
Central Gully	Stob Coire an Laoigh	120	II	-	Ice	Snow-ice		207
Cobra Corner	Stob Coire an Laoigh	80	VI	6	Mixed	Turf	**	209
Jammy Dodger	Stob Coire an Laoigh	85	VI	6	Mixed	Ice	**	209
Some Like it Hot	Stob Coire an Laoigh	70	VII	7	Mixed	Turf	***	209
White Heat	Stob Coire an Laoigh	65	VI	7	Mixed	Turf	*	209
Serve Chilled	Stob Coire an Laoigh	70	VII	6	Ice	Snow-ice	**	209
Full Frontal	Stob Coire an Laoigh	60	VII	8	Mixed	Turf	*	210
Taliballan	Stob Coire an Laoigh	70	V	6	Mixed	Turf or ice	***	210

APPENDIX B
Route summary table by style

Appendix B – Route summary table by style

Route name	Area	Route length (metres)	Overall grade	Technical grade	Main style	Sub-style(s)	Rating	Page
Moonwalk	Little Brenva Face	270	IV	3	Ice	Snow-ice	**	26
Cresta	Little Brenva Face	275	III	-	Ice	Snow-ice	**	26
Slalom	Little Brenva Face	275	III	-	Ice	Snow-ice	**	26
Route Major	Little Brenva Face	300	IV	3	Ice	Snow-ice	***	27
Green Hollow Route	North East Buttress First Platform	200	IV	4	Ice	Snow-ice	**	33
Right-Hand Wall Route	Minus Face	140	IV	5	Ice	Snow-ice		35
Platforms Rib	Minus Face	150	IV	4	Ice	Snow-ice	*	35
Minus Three Gully	Minus Face	160	IV	5	Ice	Snow-ice	**	36
Minus Two Gully	Minus Face	270	V	5	Ice	Snow-ice	***	37
Minus One Gully	Minus Face	290	VI	6	Ice	Snow-ice	***	38
Orion Direct	Orion Face	420	V	5	Ice	Snow-ice	***	41
Astral Highway	Orion Face	240	V	5	Ice	Snow-ice	***	42
Zero Gully	Orion Face	300	V	4	Ice	Snow-ice	**	44

WINTER CLIMBS: BEN NEVIS

Route name	Area	Route length (metres)	Overall grade	Technical grade	Main style	Sub-style(s)	Rating	Page
East Face to Observatory Ridge	Orion Face	170	IV	5	Ice	Snow-ice	*	44
Abacus	Point Five Gully	110	IV	4	Ice	Snow-ice	*	46
Antonine Wall to Observatory Ridge	Point Five Gully	150	V	5	Ice	Snow-ice	*	46
Hadrian's Wall Direct	Point Five Gully	320	V	5	Ice	Snow-ice	***	48
Sickle	Point Five Gully	300	V	5	Ice	Snow-ice	***	48
Point Five Gully	Point Five Gully	325	V	5	Ice	Snow-ice	***	50
Observatory Buttress	Point Five Gully	360	V	5	Ice	Snow-ice	***	54
North-West Face to Girdle Traverse ledge	Point Five Gully	100	IV	4	Ice	Snow-ice	*	54
Good Friday Climb	Indicator Wall	150	III	-	Ice	Snow-ice	**	55
Indicator Wall	Indicator Wall	160	V	4	Ice	Snow-ice	***	56
Kellett's Route	Gardyloo Buttress	120	VI	6	Ice	Snow-ice	***	61
Smith's Route	Gardyloo Buttress	130	V	5	Ice	Snow-ice	***	63
The Great Glen	Gardyloo Buttress	130	VI	5	Ice	Snow-ice	*	63
Tower Scoop	Tower Ridge East Side	75	III	-	Ice	Snow-ice	***	66

APPENDIX B – ROUTE SUMMARY TABLE BY STYLE

Route name	Area	Route length (metres)	Overall grade	Technical grade	Main style	Sub-style(s)	Rating	Page
Tower Cleft	Tower Ridge East Side	75	III	-	Ice	Snow-ice	*	66
Fawlty Towers	Tower Ridge West Side	155	II/III	-	Ice	Snow-ice		80
1934 Route	Tower Ridge West Side	200	II/III	-	Ice	Snow-ice	**	80
Vanishing Gully	Tower Ridge West Side	200	V	5	Ice	Snow-ice	***	81
The Italian Climb	Tower Ridge West Side	180	III	-	Ice	Snow-ice	*	83
Italian Climb – Right-Hand	Tower Ridge West Side	180	IV	4	Ice	Snow-ice	***	83
The Gutter	Goodeve's Buttress and the Cascades	275	IV	4	Ice	Snow-ice	**	88
The White Line	Goodeve's Buttress and the Cascades	275	IV	3	Ice	Snow-ice	***	89
Beam Me Up Scotty	Goodeve's Buttress and the Cascades	155	III	-	Ice	Snow-ice	*	90
Expert's Choice	Goodeve's Buttress and the Cascades	150	III	4	Ice	Snow-ice	*	90
Five-Finger Discount	Goodeve's Buttress and the Cascades	135	IV	4	Ice	Snow-ice	**	91
Burrito's Groove	Goodeve's Buttress and the Cascades	135	IV	5	Ice	Snow-ice	**	91

Winter climbs: Ben Nevis

Route name	Area	Route length (metres)	Overall grade	Technical grade	Main style	Sub-style(s)	Rating	Page
JP is Back	Goodeve's Buttress and the Cascades	120	III	4	Ice	Snow-ice		91
Number Two Gully Buttress	Goodeve's Buttress and the Cascades	120	II/III	-	Ice	Snow-ice	**	93
Comb Gully Buttress	The Comb	150	IV	4	Ice	Snow-ice	**	94
Comb Gully	The Comb	160	IV	4	Ice	Snow-ice	**	94
The Comb – Left Flank	The Comb	160	IV	4	Ice	Snow-ice	*	94
Mercury	The Comb	180	V	5	Ice	Snow-ice	**	99
Green Gully	The Comb	180	IV	4	Ice	Snow-ice	***	99
Two-Step Corner	Number Three Gully Buttress	180	V	5	Ice	Snow-ice	***	102
Winter Chimney	Number Three Gully Buttress	60	IV	5	Ice	Snow-ice	*	105
South Gully	Creag Coire na Ciste	125	III	-	Ice	Snow-ice	*	109
Central Gully	Creag Coire na Ciste	125	III	4	Ice	Snow-ice	**	111
Central Gully – Right-Hand	Creag Coire na Ciste	125	IV	4	Ice	Snow-ice	***	111
Wendigo	Creag Coire na Ciste	110	IV	4	Ice	Snow-ice	**	112

Appendix B – Route summary table by style

Route name	Area	Route length (metres)	Overall grade	Technical grade	Main style	Sub-style(s)	Rating	Page
North Gully	Creag Coire na Ciste	110	II	-	Ice	Snow-ice	*	112
Forearm	Creag Coire na Ciste	125	IV	4	Ice	Snow-ice		112
Number Four Gully Buttress	Trident buttresses	100	II	-	Ice	Snow-ice	*	115
Joyful Chimneys	Trident buttresses	180	IV	5	Ice	Snow-ice		120
Central Gully	Trident buttresses	240	III	-	Ice	Snow-ice		120
Nasturtium	Trident buttresses	250	IV	4	Ice	Snow-ice	*	120
Jubilation	Trident buttresses	240	IV	4	Ice	Snow-ice	*	120
Jubilee Climb	Trident buttresses	240	II	-	Ice	Snow-ice		120
Neptune Gully	Trident buttresses	260	III	-	Ice	Snow-ice		122
The Curtain Rail	Càrn Dearg Buttress	100	IV	4	Ice	Snow-ice	*	126
The Curtain	Càrn Dearg Buttress	110	IV	5	Ice	Snow-ice	***	127
Bewilderbeast	Càrn Dearg Buttress	130	VI	6	Ice	Snow-ice	**	131
Waterfall Gully	Càrn Dearg Buttress	215	IV	4	Ice	Snow-ice	*	131
Harrison's Climb Direct	Castle Coire	300	IV	4	Ice	Snow-ice	***	134
Boomer's Requiem	Castle Coire	170	V	5	Ice	Snow-ice	***	135
Raeburn's Buttress/ Intermediate Gully	Castle Coire	230	V	5	Ice	Snow-ice	**	137

WINTER CLIMBS: BEN NEVIS

Route name	Area	Route length (metres)	Overall grade	Technical grade	Main style	Sub-style(s)	Rating	Page
The Castle	Castle Coire	220	II/III	-	Ice	Snow-ice	*	138
Norwand	North Face of Castle Ridge	425	III	-	Ice	Snow-ice		143
Casino Royale	North Face of Castle Ridge	190	V	5	Ice	Snow-ice		143
La Petite	North Face of Castle Ridge	200	III	-	Ice	Snow-ice		144
Eag Blanc	Stob Bàn	100	II	-	Ice	Snow-ice		152
Chimpanzee	Aonach Mòr East Face – Coire an Lochain	60	III	-	Ice	Snow-ice		162
Streamline	Aonach Mòr East Face – Coire an Lochain	90	III	-	Ice	Snow-ice	*	165
The Web	Aonach Mòr East Face – Coire an Lochain	100	II/III	-	Ice	Snow-ice		169
Temperance Union Blues	Aonach Mòr East Face – Coire an Lochain	90	III	-	Ice	Snow-ice		171
Aquafresh	Aonach Mòr East Face – Coire an Lochain	100	IV	4	Ice	Snow-ice	*	171
White Shark	Aonach Mòr East Face – Coire an Lochain	110	IV	4	Ice	Snow-ice	***	171

Appendix B – Route summary table by style

Route name	Area	Route length (metres)	Overall grade	Technical grade	Main style	Sub-style(s)	Rating	Page
Tunnel Vision	Aonach Mòr East Face – Coire an Lochain	120	III	-	Ice	Snow-ice		173
Left Twin	Aonach Mòr East Face – Coire an Lochain	120	IV	4	Ice	Snow-ice	***	176
The Slever	Aonach Mòr East Face – Coire an Lochain	100	III	4	Ice	Snow-ice		177
Molar Canal	Aonach Mòr East Face – Coire an Lochain	100	III	-	Ice	Snow-ice		179
Icicle Gully	Aonach Mòr East Face – Coire an Lochain	130	III	-	Ice	Snow-ice		180
Solar Wind	Aonach Mòr East Face – Coire an Lochain	110	IV	4	Ice	Snow-ice	*	180
Jet Stream	Aonach Mòr East Face – Coire an Lochain	100	IV	4	Ice	Snow-ice	***	180
Queen's View	Aonach Beag North Face	250	III	-	Ice	Snow-ice		192
The Black Prince	Aonach Beag North Face	300	II	-	Ice	Snow-ice		192
Mayfly	Aonach Beag North Face	210	III	-	Ice	Snow-ice	*	192
Eggsclamation	Aonach Beag West Face	150	II	-	Ice	Snow-ice		197
Tit Gully	Stob Coire an Laoigh	60	V	5	Ice	Snow-ice		206
Central Gully	Stob Coire an Laoigh	120	II	-	Ice	Snow-ice		207

Winter climbs: Ben Nevis

Route name	Area	Route length (metres)	Overall grade	Technical grade	Main style	Sub-style(s)	Rating	Page
Serve Chilled	Stob Coire an Laoigh	70	VII	6	Ice	Snow-ice	**	209
Final Buttress	Little Brenva Face	55	III	-	Ice	Cascade		26
The Cascade	Goodeve's Buttress and the Cascades	50	V	5	Ice	Cascade	**	91
Compression Crack	Castle Coire	250	V	5	Ice	Snow-ice, Cascade	*	137
Norwand Direct	North Face of Castle Ridge	400	V	4	Ice	Cascade	***	142
Norwand Superdirect	North Face of Castle Ridge	400	VI	5	Ice	Cascade	**	142
Five Finger Gully	Five Finger Gully	200	IV	4	Ice	Cascade		156
Surgeon's Gully	Five Finger Gully	400	V	-	Ice	Cascade		157
Steall Waterfall	Five Finger Gully	120	III	-	Ice	Cascade	**	158
Spare Rib Gully	Aonach Mòr West Face	400	III	-	Ice	Cascade	**	185
Sgùrr Finnisg-aig Fall	Sgùrr Finnisg-aig	200	IV	4	Ice	Cascade	*	185
Super G	Little Brenva Face	270	VI	6	Ice	Snow patch cascade	**	27

Appendix B – Route summary table by style

Route name	Area	Route length (metres)	Overall grade	Technical grade	Main style	Sub-style(s)	Rating	Page
Vade Mecum to Observatory Ridge	Point Five Gully	180	V	5	Ice	Snow patch cascade	***	48
The Chute	Tower Ridge West Side	230	V	4	Ice	Snow patch cascade	**	83
Upper Cascades	Goodeve's Buttress and the Cascades	125	V	6	Ice	Snow patch cascade	**	90
Adieu and Farewell	Goodeve's Buttress and the Cascades	100	V	5	Ice	Snow patch cascade		90
La Panthere Rose	Goodeve's Buttress and the Cascades	50	VI	6	Ice	Snow patch cascade	*	90
Une Journée Ordinaire dans un Enfer Quotidien	Creag Coire na Ciste	105	VI	6	Ice	Snow patch cascade	**	111
Rien ne va Plus	Trident buttresses	50	V	5	Ice	Snow patch cascade		118

Winter climbs: Ben Nevis

Route name	Area	Route length (metres)	Overall grade	Technical grade	Main style	Sub-style(s)	Rating	Page
Feeding Frenzy	Trident buttresses	70	VI	7	Ice	Snow patch cascade	*	121
Mega Route X	Trident buttresses	60	V	6	Ice	Snow patch cascade	***	121
The Shroud	Castle Coire	200	VI	6	Ice	Snow patch cascade	**	133
Stand and Deliver	Aonach Beag North Face	120	V	5	Ice	Snow patch cascade	**	190
Camilla	Aonach Beag North Face	230	V	5	Ice	Snow patch cascade	**	191
Royal Pardon	Aonach Beag North Face	220	VI	6	Ice	Snow patch cascade	***	191
Left-Hand Route	Minus Face	270	VI	6	Ice	Thin face	**	36
Right-Hand Route	Minus Face	270	VI	6	Ice	Thin face	*	37
Astronomy	Orion Face	300	VI	5	Ice	Thin face	***	40
The Black Hole	Orion Face	350	VI	6	Ice	Thin face	**	41

Appendix B – Route summary table by style

Route name	Area	Route length (metres)	Overall grade	Technical grade	Main style	Sub-style(s)	Rating	Page
Journey into Space	Orion Face	240	VII	6	Ice	Thin face	**	43
Long Climb Finish	Orion Face	240	VI	5	Ice	Thin face	***	43
Slav Route	Orion Face	420	V	5	Ice	Thin face	***	44
Galactic Hitchhiker	Point Five Gully	300	VI	5	Ice	Thin face	***	49
Nemesis	Point Five Gully	290	VI	5	Ice	Thin face	*	50
Interstellar Overdrive	Point Five Gully	300	VI	5	Ice	Thin face	*	50
Left Edge Route	Point Five Gully	360	V	5	Ice	Thin face	**	53
Matchpoint	Point Five Gully	360	VI	5	Ice	Thin face	*	54
Rubicon Wall	Point Five Gully	360	VI	5	Ice	Thin face	**	54
Riders on the Storm	Indicator Wall	165	VI	5	Ice	Thin face	***	57
Ship of Fools	Indicator Wall	170	VIII	7	Ice	Thin face	**	58
Albatross	Indicator Wall	160	VI	5	Ice	Thin face	***	58
Stormy Petrel	Indicator Wall	160	VII	6	Ice	Thin face	***	59
Psychedelic Wall	Indicator Wall	165	VI	5	Ice	Thin face	***	59
Satanic Verses	Indicator Wall	130	V	5	Ice	Thin face	***	59
Shot in the Dark	Indicator Wall	120	V	5	Ice	Thin face	***	59
Diana	Number Three Gully Buttress	195	V	5	Ice	Thin face	*	100

WINTER CLIMBS: BEN NEVIS

Route name	Area	Route length (metres)	Overall grade	Technical grade	Main style	Sub-style(s)	Rating	Page
Vulture	Number Three Gully Buttress	180	V	5	Ice	Thin face	**	100
Quickstep	Number Three Gully Buttress	180	V	5	Ice	Thin face	**	101
Gremlins	Number Three Gully Buttress	120	VI	6	Ice	Thin face	*	103
Point Blank	Point Five Gully	340	VII	6	Ice, mixed	Snow-ice, general	***	52
Blackout	Aonach Beag North Face	120	IV	5	Ice, mixed	Snow-ice, general	*	190
King's Ransom	Aonach Beag North Face	250	VI	6	Ice, mixed	Snow-ice, general	*	191
Shield Direct	Càrn Dearg Buttress	290	VII	7	Ice, mixed	Cascade, general	***	129
Gemini	Càrn Dearg Buttress	300	VI	6	Ice, mixed	Cascade, general	***	129
Number Three Gully Buttress	Number Three Gully Buttress	200	III	-	Ice, mixed	Snow-ice, rock	***	101
Raeburn's Easy Route	Goodeve's Buttress and the Cascades	250	II/III	-	Ice, snow	Snow-ice		90
Garadh Gully	Tower Ridge West Side	95	II/III	-	Ice or snow	Cascade		84

Appendix B – Route summary table by style

Route name	Area	Route length (metres)	Overall grade	Technical grade	Main style	Sub-style(s)	Rating	Page
Slingsby's Chimney	North East Buttress First Platform	125	III	-				33
Surprise Gully	Castle Coire	185	I/II	-	Mixed	General		136
Summit Groove	Stob Bàn	140	IV	4	Mixed	General	*	152
Groove Rider	Stob Bàn	160	IV	4	Mixed	General	*	152
North Ridge Route	Stob Bàn	150	IV	4	Mixed	General		152
North Buttress – East Ridge	Stob Bàn	200	II/III	-	Mixed	General	**	155
Monkey Business	Aonach Mòr East Face – Coire an Lochain	70	V	6	Mixed	General		162
Monkey Puzzle	Aonach Mòr East Face – Coire an Lochain	70	III	-	Mixed	General		163
Two Queens	Aonach Mòr East Face – Coire an Lochain	70	IV	5	Mixed	General	*	165
Three Kings	Aonach Mòr East Face – Coire an Lochain	70	IV	5	Mixed	General	*	165
Nid Arête	Aonach Mòr East Face – Coire an Lochain	90	IV	5	Mixed	General	*	169
Siamese Buttress	Aonach Mòr East Face – Coire an Lochain	120	II/III	-	Mixed	General	**	177

WINTER CLIMBS: BEN NEVIS

Route name	Area	Route length (metres)	Overall grade	Technical grade	Main style	Sub-style(s)	Rating	Page
Golden Promise	Aonach Mòr East Face – Coire an Lochain	100	VI	7	Mixed	General	*	179
Force Ten Buttress	Aonach Mòr East Face – Coire an Lochain	140	III	4	Mixed	General	*	180
Golden Oldie	Aonach Mòr West Face	400	II	-	Mixed	General	***	183
Western Rib	Aonach Mòr West Face	400	II/III	-	Mixed	General	**	183
Daim Buttress	Aonach Mòr West Face	400	II/III	-	Mixed	General		185
Solitaire	Aonach Mòr West Face	400	II	-	Mixed	General		185
Aonacrack	Aonach Beag West Face	150	IV	5	Mixed	General	**	195
Isandhlwana	Little Brenva Face	280	V	5	Mixed	Ice	**	27
Newbigging's Route	North East Buttress First Platform	180	IV	4	Mixed	Ice	**	33
Raeburn's Arête	North East Buttress First Platform	230	IV	5	Mixed	Ice	***	33
Subtraction	Minus Face	270	VIII	8	Mixed	Ice	*	37
Urban Spaceman	Orion Face	350	VII	6	Mixed	Ice	***	41
Pointless	Point Five Gully	300	VII	6	Mixed	Ice	*	50
Rime of the Ancient Mariner	Indicator Wall	160	VII	7	Mixed	Ice	**	58

Appendix B – Route summary table by style

Route name	Area	Route length (metres)	Overall grade	Technical grade	Main style	Sub-style(s)	Rating	Page
1931 Route	Tower Ridge West Side	125	IV	4	Mixed	Ice		83
Fatal Error	Pinnacle Buttress	230	IV	4	Mixed	Ice	**	86
Pinnacle Buttress Direct	Pinnacle Buttress	200	V	5	Mixed	Ice	**	86
Clover's Chimney	Pinnacle Buttress	200	III	4	Mixed	Ice	**	87
Goodytwoshoes	Goodeve's Buttress and the Cascades	140	V	6	Mixed	Ice	*	89
Roaring Forties	The Comb	150	V	5	Mixed	Ice	**	94
Hesperides Ledge	The Comb	200	III	-	Mixed	Ice	*	95
Tower Face of The Comb	The Comb	250	VI	6	Mixed	Ice	***	96
Bell's Chimney: Variation	The Comb	250	V	5	Mixed	Ice		97
Pigott's Route	The Comb	245	V	6	Mixed	Ice	*	98
Tramp	Number Three Gully Buttress	180	IV	4	Mixed	Ice	*	100
The Banshee	Number Three Gully Buttress	150	V	5	Mixed	Ice		103
South Sea Bubble	Creag Coire na Ciste	110	VII	7	Mixed	Ice		109
South Flank Route	Trident buttresses	150	IV	4	Mixed	Ice	*	117

Winter climbs: Ben Nevis

Route name	Area	Route length (metres)	Overall grade	Technical grade	Main style	Sub-style(s)	Rating	Page
Pinnacle Arête	Trident buttresses	100	IV	5	Mixed	Ice	**	118
Mega Rêve	Trident buttresses	60	V	5	Mixed	Ice		120
Left-Hand Ridge	Trident buttresses	250	IV	4	Mixed	Ice		121
Diagonal Route	Moonlight Gully Buttress	150	III	-	Mixed	Ice	*	124
Right-Hand Chimney	Moonlight Gully Buttress	135	IV	5	Mixed	Ice	*	124
Ring the Alarm	Càrn Dearg Buttress	270	VI	5	Mixed	Ice	**	127
Lobby Dancer	North Face of Castle Ridge	280	VI	6	Mixed	Ice	***	142
Last Day in Purgatory	North Face of Castle Ridge	330	V	5	Mixed	Ice	**	142
The Girdle Traverse	North Face of Castle Ridge	4000	V	4	Mixed	Ice		144
Central Gully	Stob Bàn	150	IV	-	Mixed	Ice		154
Triad	Stob Bàn	150	III	-	Mixed	Ice	*	154
Bodice Ripper	Stob Bàn	150	IV	4	Mixed	Ice	*	154
The Betrayal	Aonach Mòr East Face – Coire an Lochain	90	IV	4	Mixed	Ice		165
The Wave	Aonach Mòr East Face – Coire an Lochain	70	V	5	Mixed	Ice		167

Appendix B – Route summary table by style

Route name	Area	Route length (metres)	Overall grade	Technical grade	Main style	Sub-style(s)	Rating	Page
The Guardian	Aonach Mòr East Face – Coire an Lochain	90	IV	5	Mixed	Ice	*	167
Ribbon Groove	Aonach Mòr East Face – Coire an Lochain	60	IV	4	Mixed	Ice		167
Ribbon Development	Aonach Mòr East Face – Coire an Lochain	60	IV	4	Mixed	Ice	**	167
Barrel Buttress	Aonach Mòr East Face – Coire an Lochain	90	IV	4	Mixed	Ice		169
Tinsel Town	Aonach Mòr East Face – Coire an Lochain	110	V	4	Mixed	Ice	**	171
Gondola With the Wind	Aonach Mòr East Face – Coire an Lochain	125	IV	5	Mixed	Ice	**	171
Maneater	Aonach Mòr East Face – Coire an Lochain	90	V	5	Mixed	Ice	**	173
Typhoon	Aonach Mòr East Face – Coire an Lochain	130	IV	5	Mixed	Ice	***	175
Hurricane Arête	Aonach Mòr East Face – Coire an Lochain	140	VI	7	Mixed	Ice	**	175
The Split	Aonach Mòr East Face – Coire an Lochain	130	III	4	Mixed	Ice	**	176

Winter climbs: Ben Nevis

Route name	Area	Route length (metres)	Overall grade	Technical grade	Main style	Sub-style(s)	Rating	Page
Lickety Split	Aonach Mòr East Face – Coire an Lochain	130	IV	5	Mixed	Ice	**	176
Right Twin	Aonach Mòr East Face – Coire an Lochain	120	II	-	Mixed	Ice	***	177
White Bait	Aonach Mòr East Face – Coire an Lochain	100	IV	5	Mixed	Ice		177
Foosyerneeps	Aonach Mòr East Face – Coire an Lochain	50	IV	5	Mixed	Ice	**	181
Raw Egg Buttress	Aonach Beag West Face	180	IV	4	Mixed	Ice	**	197
Top Gun	Aonach Beag West Face	160	VI	6	Mixed	Ice	**	197
Tat Gully	Stob Coire an Laoigh	70	IV	4	Mixed	Ice	*	207
Jammy Dodger	Stob Coire an Laoigh	85	VI	6	Mixed	Ice	**	209
North East Buttress	Little Brenva Face	400	IV	5	Mixed	Ice, rock	***	27
Central Route	Minus Face	270	VI	7	Mixed	Ice, rock		37
Minus One Direct	Minus Face	290	VIII	8	Mixed	Ice, rock	***	37
North-West Face Route	Douglas Boulder	215	V	5	Mixed	Ice, rock		76
Stringfellow	Pinnacle Buttress	240	VI	6	Mixed	Ice, rock	**	86
Chinook	Number Three Gully Buttress	65	IV	5	Mixed	Ice or rock		102

Appendix B – Route summary table by style

Route name	Area	Route length (metres)	Overall grade	Technical grade	Main style	Sub-style(s)	Rating	Page
Lost the Place	Creag Coire na Ciste	140	V	5	Mixed	Ice or rock	**	111
Godspell	Castle Coire	215	VII	8	Mixed	Ice, rock		138
Alien Abduction	Aonach Mòr East Face – Coire an Lochain	120	VII	3	Mixed	Ice, rock		176
Ruadh Eigg Chimney	Aonach Beag West Face	60	V	6	Mixed	Ice, rock	*	200
Faith Healer	Tower Ridge East Side	170	VIII	7	Mixed	Ice, turf	*	66
Morwind	Aonach Mòr East Face – Coire an Lochain	150	IV	4	Mixed	Ice or turf	***	173
The Clanger	Trident buttresses	90	IV	5	Mixed	Ice, turf, rock	**	118
Gendarme Ridge	Stob Bàn	150	IV	4	Mixed	Rock		154
Skyline Rib	Stob Bàn	120	IV	4	Mixed	Rock	*	154
Not Bad for a Dad	Mullach nan Coirean	80	VI	7	Mixed	Rock		156
Kindergarten Corner	Mullach nan Coirean	50	VII	8	Mixed	Rock		156
Stirling Bridge	Aonach Mòr East Face – Coire an Lochain	70	V	7	Mixed	Rock	**	167
Homo Robusticus	Aonach Mòr East Face – Coire an Lochain	60	VI	7	Mixed	Rock	**	167

WINTER CLIMBS: BEN NEVIS

Route name	Area	Route length (metres)	Overall grade	Technical grade	Main style	Sub-style(s)	Rating	Page
Piranha	Aonach Mòr East Face – Coire an Lochain	70	VII	8	Mixed	Rock	**	169
Grooved Arête	Aonach Mòr East Face – Coire an Lochain	130	V	6	Mixed	Rock	**	179
Aonach Wall	Aonach Beag West Face	150	V	6	Mixed	Rock	*	197
Salmonella	Aonach Beag West Face	125	VII	8	Mixed	Rock	**	198
Blackbeard	Aonach Beag West Face	70	VII	8	Mixed	Rock		200
Left-Hand Chimney	Douglas Boulder	215	V	6	Mixed	Rock		76
Jacknife to South West Ridge	Douglas Boulder	90	IV	6	Mixed	Rock		77
South West Ridge	Douglas Boulder	180	III	4	Mixed	Rock	*	77
Don't Die of Ignorance	The Comb	200	XI	11	Mixed	Rock		97
Anubis	The Comb	200	XII	-	Mixed	Rock		97
The Survivor	Number Three Gully Buttress	180	VII	8	Mixed	Rock		102
The Knuckleduster	Number Three Gully Buttress	180	VIII	9	Mixed	Rock	***	102
Sioux Wall	Number Three Gully Buttress	150	VII	8	Mixed	Rock	***	103

Appendix B – Route summary table by style

Route name	Area	Route length (metres)	Overall grade	Technical grade	Main style	Sub-style(s)	Rating	Page
Hobgoblin	Number Three Gully Buttress	120	VI	7	Mixed	Rock	***	105
Babylon	Number Three Gully Buttress	115	VII	7	Mixed	Rock	**	105
The Secret	Creag Coire na Ciste	70	VIII	8	Mixed	Rock	***	107
Cornucopia	Creag Coire na Ciste	100	VII	8	Mixed	Rock	*	107
Darth Vader	Creag Coire na Ciste	100	VII	7	Mixed	Rock	***	108
Avenging Angel Direct	Creag Coire na Ciste	110	VIII	8	Mixed	Rock	***	108
Cold Play	Creag Coire na Ciste	110	VIII	8	Mixed	Rock		109
The Sorcerer	Creag Coire na Ciste	140	VII	8	Mixed	Rock		109
Poseidon Groove	Trident buttresses	100	IV	5	Mixed	Rock		115
Triton Corners	Trident buttresses	100	IV	5	Mixed	Rock		117
The Groove Climb	Trident buttresses	80	V	6	Mixed	Rock	*	117
Sidewinder	Trident buttresses	100	VII	8	Mixed	Rock		117
Strident Edge	Trident buttresses	100	VII	8	Mixed	Rock	**	117
Under Fire	Trident buttresses	85	VII	7	Mixed	Rock	*	118
Heidbanger Direct	Trident buttresses	75	VIII	8	Mixed	Rock		121
Centurion	Càrn Dearg Buttress	190	VIII	8	Mixed	Rock	***	129

WINTER CLIMBS: BEN NEVIS

Route name	Area	Route length (metres)	Overall grade	Technical grade	Main style	Sub-style(s)	Rating	Page
Sassenach	Càrn Dearg Buttress	270	IX	9	Mixed	Rock		129
The Crack	Castle Coire	250	VIII	8	Mixed	Rock	**	137
The Great Corner	Castle Coire	250	VIII	8	Mixed	Rock	**	137
Castle Ridge	Castle Coire	275	III	-	Mixed	Rock	**	139
Observatory Ridge	Orion Face	500	V	4	Mixed	Rock, ice	***	45
Clefthanger	Tower Ridge East Side	90	VI	6	Mixed	Rock, ice	**	66
The Edge of Beyond	Tower Ridge East Side	200	VI	6	Mixed	Rock, ice	**	67
The Brass Monkey	Tower Ridge East Side	135	VII	8	Mixed	Rock, ice		69
The Great Chimney	Tower Ridge East Side	65	V	6	Mixed	Rock, ice	***	69
Tower Ridge	Tower Ridge	500 ascent; 1000 climbing	IV	3	Mixed	Rock, ice	***	71
Direct Route	Douglas Boulder	215	IV	4	Mixed	Rock, ice	*	75
Right-Hand Chimney	Douglas Boulder	215	VI	7	Mixed	Rock, ice		76
Cutlass to South West Ridge	Douglas Boulder	145	VI	7	Mixed	Rock or ice	**	76
Pirate	Tower Ridge West Side	200	IV	4	Mixed	Rock, ice		82
Fish Eye Chimney	Tower Ridge West Side	150	V	5	Mixed	Rock, ice		83

Appendix B – Route summary table by style

Route name	Area	Route length (metres)	Overall grade	Technical grade	Main style	Sub-style(s)	Rating	Page
Clough's Chimney	The Comb	150	VI	6	Mixed	Rock or ice	*	94
The Good Groove	The Comb	200	VII	7	Mixed	Rock, ice	**	95
Gargoyle Wall	Number Three Gully Buttress	120	VI	6	Mixed	Rock or ice	**	105
Route I Direct	Càrn Dearg Buttress	210	VI	6	Mixed	Rock, ice	***	127
Route II Direct	Càrn Dearg Buttress	275	VI	7	Mixed	Rock, ice	***	127
Staircase Climb	Càrn Dearg Buttress	215	IV	5	Mixed	Rock, ice	*	131
The Past is Close Behind	Castle Coire	200	VIII	8	Mixed	Rock, ice		133
Twinkle	Aonach Beag West Face	150	IV	5	Mixed	Rock, ice	**	195
Axeless	Aonach Beag West Face	150	III	-	Mixed	Rock, ice	*	195
Turf War	Douglas Boulder	250	V	6	Mixed	Rock, turf	**	75
Gutless to South West Ridge	Douglas Boulder	150	IV	5	Mixed	Rock, turf	*	76
Kellett's North Wall Route	Castle Coire	200	VII	7	Mixed	Rock, turf		133
North-East Ridge	Aonach Beag North Face	460	III	4	Mixed	Rock, turf	*	192
East Wing	Stob Bàn	180	V	5	Mixed	Turf		152
Captain Caveman	Mullach nan Coirean	70	III	4	Mixed	Turf		156

Winter climbs: Ben Nevis

Route name	Area	Route length (metres)	Overall grade	Technical grade	Main style	Sub-style(s)	Rating	Page
Kid Gloves	Mullach nan Coirean	70	IV	4	Mixed	Turf		156
Ribbon on Edge	Aonach Mòr East Face – Coire an Lochain	120	IV	6	Mixed	Turf		163
Back Stree Boogie	Aonach Mòr East Face – Coire an Lochain	70	VI	6	Mixed	Turf		165
Turf Walk	Aonach Mòr East Face – Coire an Lochain	150	III	4	Mixed	Turf	*	175
End Game	Stob Coire an Laoigh	50	II	-	Mixed	Turf		202
White Widow	Stob Coire an Laoigh	55	V	6	Mixed	Turf	**	206
Tarantula	Stob Coire an Laoigh	55	V	6	Mixed	Turf	*	206
Loopy Louie	Stob Coire an Laoigh	60	IV	5	Mixed	Turf	*	206
Slim Jim	Stob Coire an Laoigh	80	V	6	Mixed	Turf	*	206
New Labour	Stob Coire an Laoigh	70	V	6	Mixed	Turf	*	207
Centrepoint	Stob Coire an Laoigh	90	VI	7	Mixed	Turf	***	207
Blue Rinse	Stob Coire an Laoigh	80	VI	7	Mixed	Turf	***	207
Cobra Corner	Stob Coire an Laoigh	80	VI	6	Mixed	Turf	**	209
Some Like it Hot	Stob Coire an Laoigh	70	VII	7	Mixed	Turf	***	209
White Heat	Stob Coire an Laoigh	65	VI	7	Mixed	Turf	*	209
Full Frontal	Stob Coire an Laoigh	60	VII	8	Mixed	Turf	*	210

Appendix B – Route summary table by style

Route name	Area	Route length (metres)	Overall grade	Technical grade	Main style	Sub-style(s)	Rating	Page
Taliballan	Stob Coire an Laoigh	70	V	6	Mixed	Turf or ice	***	210
The Slab Climb	Trident buttresses	90	VI	7	Mixed	Turf, rock	*	118
Thompson's Route	Number Three Gully Buttress	130	IV	4	Mixed or ice	Ice, snow-ice	***	103
Tower Gully	Gardyloo Buttress	120	I	-	Snow	-		64
Douglas Gap East Gully	Douglas Boulder	70	I	-	Snow	-	**	73
Douglas Gap West Gully	Douglas Boulder	180	I	-	Snow	-	**	77
Broad Gully	Pinnacle Buttress	230	II	-	Snow	-		86
Number Three Gully	Number Three Gully Buttress	150	I	-	Snow	-	***	106
Number Four Gully	Creag Coire na Ciste	150	I	-	Snow	-		112
Moonlight Gully	Moonlight Gully Buttress	150	I/II	-	Snow	-		124
Number Five Gully	Moonlight Gully Buttress	460	I	-	Snow	-	*	124
Arch Gully	Castle Coire	105	I	-	Snow	-		136
South Castle Gully	Castle Coire	230	I/II	-	Snow	-	*	138
North Castle Gully	Castle Coire	230	I/II	-	Snow	-	*	139

Route name	Area	Route length (metres)	Overall grade	Technical grade	Main style	Sub-style(s)	Rating	Page
The Serpent	North Face of Castle Ridge	300	II	-	Snow	-		142
The Moat	North Face of Castle Ridge	500	II	-	Snow	-	**	142
South Gully	Stob Bàn	150	I	-	Snow	-	*	152
North Gully	Stob Bàn	150	I	-	Snow	-		152
Hidden Gully	Aonach Mòr East Face – Coire an Lochain	120	II	-	Snow	-	*	163
Easy Gully	Aonach Mòr East Face – Coire an Lochain	100	I	-	Snow	-		169
Forgotten Twin	Aonach Mòr East Face – Coire an Lochain	120	I/II	-	Snow	-		177
Easter Sunday Gully	Stob Coire an Laoigh	80	I	-	Snow	-		206
Ledge Route	Moonlight Gully Buttress	450	II	-	Snow, mixed	Rock	***	124
Gardyloo Gully	Indicator Wall	170	II/III	-	Snow or ice	Snow-ice	**	60
Number Two Gully	Goodeve's Buttress and the Cascades	120	II	-	Snow or ice	Snow-ice	***	93

NOTES

LISTING OF CICERONE UK GUIDES

BRITISH ISLES CHALLENGES, COLLECTIONS AND ACTIVITIES

Cycling Land's End to John o' Groats
Great Walks on the England Coast Path
The Big Rounds
The Book of the Bivvy
The Book of the Bothy
The Mountains of England & Wales:
  Vol 1 Wales
  Vol 2 England
The National Trails
Walking The End to End Trail

SCOTLAND

Ben Nevis and Glen Coe
Cycle Touring in Northern Scotland
Cycling in the Hebrides
Great Mountain Days in Scotland
Mountain Biking in Southern and Central Scotland
Mountain Biking in West and North West Scotland
Not the West Highland Way Scotland
Scotland's Mountain Ridges
Scottish Wild Country Backpacking
Skye's Cuillin Ridge Traverse
The Borders Abbeys Way
The Great Glen Way
The Great Glen Way Map Booklet
The Hebridean Way
The Hebrides
The Isle of Mull
The Isle of Skye
The Skye Trail
The Southern Upland Way
The Speyside Way
The Speyside Way Map Booklet
The West Highland Way
The West Highland Way Map Booklet
Walking Ben Lawers, Rannoch and Atholl
Walking in the Cairngorms
Walking in the Pentland Hills
Walking in the Scottish Borders
Walking in the Southern Uplands
Walking in Torridon, Fisherfield, Fannichs and An Teallach
Walking Loch Lomond and the Trossachs
Walking on Arran
Walking on Harris and Lewis
Walking on Jura, Islay and Colonsay
Walking on Rum and the Small Isles
Walking on the Orkney and Shetland Isles
Walking on Uist and Barra
Walking the Cape Wrath Trail
Walking the Corbetts
  Vol 1 South of the Great Glen
  Vol 2 North of the Great Glen
Walking the Galloway Hills
Walking the Munros
  Vol 1 – Southern, Central and Western Highlands
  Vol 2 – Northern Highlands and the Cairngorms
Winter Climbs Ben Nevis and Glen Coe

NORTHERN ENGLAND ROUTES

Cycling the Reivers Route
Cycling the Way of the Roses
Hadrian's Cycleway
Hadrian's Wall Path
Hadrian's Wall Path Map Booklet
The C2C Cycle Route
The Coast to Coast Map Booklet
The Coast to Coast Walk
The Pennine Way
The Pennine Way Map Booklet
Walking the Dales Way
Walking the Dales Way Map Booklet

NORTH-EAST ENGLAND, YORKSHIRE DALES AND PENNINES

Cycling in the Yorkshire Dales
Great Mountain Days in the Pennines
Mountain Biking in the Yorkshire Dales
St Oswald's Way and St Cuthbert's Way
The Cleveland Way and the Yorkshire Wolds Way
The Cleveland Way Map Booklet
The North York Moors
The Reivers Way
Trail and Fell Running in the Yorkshire Dales
Walking in County Durham
Walking in Northumberland
Walking in the North Pennines
Walking in the Yorkshire Dales: North and East
Walking in the Yorkshire Dales: South and West

NORTH-WEST ENGLAND AND THE ISLE OF MAN

Cycling the Pennine Bridleway
Isle of Man Coastal Path
The Lancashire Cycleway
The Lune Valley and Howgills
Walking in Cumbria's Eden Valley
Walking in Lancashire
Walking in the Forest of Bowland and Pendle
Walking on the Isle of Man
Walking on the West Pennine Moors
Walks in Silverdale and Arnside

LAKE DISTRICT

Cycling in the Lake District
Great Mountain Days in the Lake District
Joss Naylor's Lakes, Meres and Waters of the Lake District
Lake District Winter Climbs
Lake District: High Level and Fell Walks
Lake District: Low Level and Lake Walks
Mountain Biking in the Lake District
Outdoor Adventures with Children – Lake District
Scrambles in the Lake District – North
Scrambles in the Lake District – South
Trail and Fell Running in the Lake District
Walking The Cumbria Way
Walking the Lake District Fells –
  Borrowdale
  Buttermere
  Coniston
  Keswick
  Langdale
  Mardale and the Far East
  Patterdale
  Wasdale
Walking the Tour of the Lake District

DERBYSHIRE, PEAK DISTRICT AND MIDLANDS

Cycling in the Peak District
Dark Peak Walks
Scrambles in the Dark Peak
Walking in Derbyshire
Walking in the Peak District – White Peak East
Walking in the Peak District – White Peak West

SOUTHERN ENGLAND

20 Classic Sportive Rides in South East England
20 Classic Sportive Rides in South West England
Cycling in the Cotswolds
Mountain Biking on the North Downs
Mountain Biking on the South Downs
Suffolk Coast and Heath Walks
The Cotswold Way
The Cotswold Way Map Booklet
The Kennet and Avon Canal
The Lea Valley Walk
The North Downs Way
The North Downs Way Map Booklet
The Peddars Way and Norfolk Coast Path
The Pilgrims' Way
The Ridgeway National Trail
The Ridgeway Map Booklet
The South Downs Way
The South Downs Way Map Booklet
The Thames Path
The Thames Path Map Booklet
The Two Moors Way
The Two Moors Way Map Booklet
Walking Hampshire's Test Way
Walking in Cornwall
Walking in Essex
Walking in Kent
Walking in London
Walking in Norfolk
Walking in the Chilterns
Walking in the Cotswolds
Walking in the Isles of Scilly
Walking in the New Forest
Walking in the North Wessex Downs
Walking on Dartmoor
Walking on Guernsey
Walking on Jersey
Walking on the Isle of Wight
Walking the Jurassic Coast
Walking the South West Coast Path
Walking the South West Coast Path Map Booklets
Vol 1: Minehead to St Ives
Vol 2: St Ives to Plymouth
Vol 3: Plymouth to Poole
Walks in the South Downs National Park

WALES AND WELSH BORDERS

Cycle Touring in Wales
Cycling Lon Las Cymru
Glyndwr's Way
Great Mountain Days in Snowdonia
Hillwalking in Shropshire
Hillwalking in Wales – Vols 1&2
Mountain Walking in Snowdonia
Offa's Dyke Path
Offa's Dyke Path Map Booklet
Ridges of Snowdonia
Scrambles in Snowdonia
Snowdonia: 30 Low-level and Easy Walks – North
Snowdonia: 30 Low-level and Easy Walks – South
The Cambrian Way
The Ceredigion and Snowdonia Coast Paths
The Pembrokeshire Coast Path
The Pembrokeshire Coast Path Map Booklet
The Severn Way
The Snowdonia Way
The Wye Valley Walk
Walking in Carmarthenshire
Walking in Pembrokeshire
Walking in the Brecon Beacons
Walking in the Forest of Dean
Walking in the Wye Valley
Walking on Gower
Walking the Shropshire Way
Walking the Wales Coast Path

MOUNTAIN LITERATURE

8000 metres
A Walk in the Clouds
Abode of the Gods
Fifty Years of Adventure
The Pennine Way – the Path, the People, the Journey
Unjustifiable Risk?

TECHNIQUES

Fastpacking
Geocaching in the UK
Map and Compass
Outdoor Photography
Polar Exploration
The Mountain Hut Book

MINI GUIDES

Alpine Flowers
Navigation
Pocket First Aid and Wilderness Medicine
Snow

For full information on all our guides, books and eBooks, visit our website:
www.cicerone.co.uk

CICERONE

Trust Cicerone to guide your next adventure, wherever it may be around the world...

Discover guides for hiking, mountain walking, backpacking, trekking, trail running, cycling and mountain biking, ski touring, climbing and scrambling in Britain, Europe and worldwide.

Connect with Cicerone online and find inspiration.

- buy books and ebooks
- articles, advice and trip reports
- podcasts and live events
- GPX files and updates
- regular newsletter

cicerone.co.uk